Crossing the Line

New World Studies

J. Michael Dash, Editor

Frank Moya Pons and
Sandra Pouchet Paquet,
Associate Editors

Crossing the Line

Early Creole Novels and Anglophone Caribbean Culture in the Age of Emancipation

Candace Ward

University of Virginia Press
Charlottesville and London

University of Virginia Press
© 2017 by the Rector and Visitors of the University of Virginia
All rights reserved
Printed in the United States of America on acid-free paper

First published 2017

9 8 7 6 5 4 3 2 1

Library of Congress Cataloging-in-Publication Data

Names: Ward, Candace, author.
Title: Crossing the line : early creole novels and anglophone Caribbean culture in the age of emancipation / Candace Ward.
Description: Charlottesville : University of Virginia Press, 2017. | Series: New World studies | Includes bibliographical references and index.
Identifiers: LCCN 2017001104 | ISBN 9780813940007 (cloth : alk. paper) | ISBN 9780813940014 (pbk. : alk. paper) | ISBN 9780813940021 (e-book)
Subjects: LCSH: Caribbean fiction (English)—19th century—History and criticism. | West Indian fiction (English)—19th century—History and criticism. | Creoles—Caribbean Area—History—18th century. | Colonies in literature. | Plantation life in literature. | Caribbean Area—In literature. | West Indies—In literature.
Classification: LCC PR9205.4 .W37 2017 | DDC 823/.7099729—dc23
LC record available at https://lccn.loc.gov/2017001104

Cover art: "The Torrid Zone. Or, Blessings of Jamaica," A[braham] J[ames], ca. 1803. (Courtesy of The Lewis Walpole Library, Yale University)

For Matthew

In memory of my father,
Bob Ward,
June 13, 1933–December 12, 2015

Contents

	List of Illustrations	ix
	Acknowledgments	xi
	Introduction: Why Creole? Why the Novel?	1
1.	Hortus Creolensis: Cultivating the Creole Novel	27
2.	"A Permanent Revolution": Time, History, and Constructions of Africa in Cynric Williams's *Hamel, the Obeah Man*	57
3.	"Lost Subjects": The Specter of Idleness and the Work of *Marly; or, A Planter's Life in Jamaica*	80
4.	Recentering the Caribbean: Revolution and the Creole Cosmopolis in *Warner Arundell*	112
	Conclusion: The Unfinished Business of Early Creole (Historical) Novels	141
	Notes	165
	Bibliography	201
	Index	213

Illustrations

1. British trade routes, 1750–1800 — 4
2. "Crossing the Line," George Cruikshank — 7
3. "Johnny Newcome in Love in the West Indies" — 13
4. Title page of *Jamaica Magazine*, 1812 — 33
5. "Harbour Street, Kingston," James Hakewill — 36
6. "Plantain Walk," William Berryman — 45
7. Letter from Henry De la Beche to William Daniel Conybeare — 68
8. "The Hyena's Den at Kirkdale," William Daniel Conybeare — 69
9. Letter from Jamaica, P. L. Simmonds — 81
10. "Holeing a Cane-Piece," William Clark — 97
11. "Trelawney Town," from Bryan Edwards, *History, Civil and Commercial*, 1801 — 108
12. "Rachel Pringle of Barbadoes," Thomas Rowlandson — 152

Acknowledgments

THIS PROJECT would not have been possible without support from Florida State University and the Office of Proposal Development's Council on Research and Creativity, whose generous funding of research and publication costs was enormously helpful. Travel grants from the Office of the Provost and the Department of English facilitated my archival work at every phase of the project. I also would like to thank the various librarians and museum curators who have generously helped me in my research, especially the staff at the National Library of Jamaica and Tom Sharpe of the National Museum of Wales. Special thanks to Martin Rudwick, whose generous help in finding William Conybeare's illustration of Kirkdale Cave was much appreciated, as was James Cheshire's patience in supplying his map of British shipping routes. Numerous friends and colleagues have helped me at various stages of this project: Nadi Edwards, who first pointed me to *Hamel* so long ago; Carolyn Cooper, whose hospitality during my Kingston stays enriched the project in so many ways; my dear, dear friend Rachel Moseley-Wood, who brought me into the heart of her family, who made me laugh, and tried to teach me to stuuuuppse. Tim Watson is a collaborator extraordinaire; I am indebted to his generosity and very much appreciate all the critical insights he has brought to our collaborations. Meegan Kennedy has been a stalwart friend and helped me carry on—even when! My mom and sisters shared their strength and counsel during a hard, hard time, and I will always be grateful for their unquestioning support. And, finally, a dedication cannot convey all I owe to Matthew Kopka for his love, patience, provocative readings and rereadings, and willingness to share his knowledge of Caribbean history and his passion for the hard work of life.

Crossing the Line

Introduction
Why Creole? Why the Novel?

> This is an entertaining, we may say instructive, novel. The scene is new, and the manners described are also new. Our novelists had before colonized a great portion of the terrestrial globe with various inhabitants from the world of fiction; but until the present production, our West-India Islands have been colonized by acts of parliament with only real, substantial Englishmen. These islands are, however, yet almost *terrae incognitae* to us; we know as little, speaking popularly, of their history as of the nature of the country . . .
> —Review of *Hamel, the Obeah Man*, in *Westminster Review*, 1827

THE CARIBBEAN occupies a significant place—physically and imaginatively—in eighteenth- and nineteenth-century anglophone literary culture. Recent applications of postcolonial and critical race theories to canonical novels like *Oroonoko*, *Robinson Crusoe*, and *Mansfield Park* and to less iconic but routinely taught works like *Julia de Roubigné*, *The History of Sir George Ellison*, *Belinda*, and *Woman of Colour* illustrate our period's growing interest in relationships between fiction and geopolitics—particularly those evident in the discourses of slavery and abolition that permeated so much writing of the long eighteenth century. But even as recent criticism situates the rise of the English-language novel in relation to the expansion of Great Britain's Atlantic empire, much scholarship remains focused on works by metropolitan authors. Although this focus performs the necessary work of showing how novelists like Defoe and Austen shaped *British* identity in the period, it runs the risk of upholding the kind of metropolitan privileging uncovered in the narratives themselves, reaffirming, as it were, the centrality of metropolitan subjects and their responses to contemporary events in the Caribbean.

In order to expand the critical discussion of early nineteenth-century English language fiction—a move anticipated by the reviewer of *Hamel* cited above—*Crossing the Line* examines a group of novels by writers whose identities and perspectives were shaped by their experiences in

Britain's Caribbean colonies, white creoles.¹ Colonial subjects residing in the West Indian colonies "beyond the line," observes Thomas C. Holt, were perceived by their metropolitan contemporaries as far removed—geographically and morally—from Britain and "true" Britons.² Routinely portrayed as single-minded in their pursuit of money and irredeemably corrupted by their investment in slavery, white creoles had much to do to show they were driven by more than a desire for power and profit. *Crossing the Line* explores the integral role early creole novels played in this cultural project.

Read as a distinct body of fiction, early creole novels trouble traditional histories of the English-language novel and complicate our understanding of West Indian literary history. But my analysis of these works does more than broaden the scope of British prose studies and shift "the temporal boundaries of Anglophone Caribbean literature from its traditionally assumed twentieth-century origins,"³ necessary as such interventions are. Instead, my aim in *Crossing the Line* is to challenge our easy assumptions about the texts, their authors, and the truths they claim to reveal through fiction. Reengaging these narratives, recognizing their contributions to the novel's development and their role in (re)producing colonial culture, allows for a more nuanced understanding of the anglophone Atlantic world during the period of slavery and emancipation—and makes clear the dangers of relegating such works to a finished past.

In pursuing this aim, my project crosses—even transgresses—traditional lines charting literary chronologies and marking nationalistic literatures, even as I recognize the influence of narrative genealogies and nationalistic impulses. The four novels that anchor the study—three anonymously published works, *Montgomery; or, the West-Indian Adventurer* (1812–13), *Hamel, the Obeah Man* (1827) and *Marly; or, A Planter's Life in Jamaica* (1828), and E. L. Joseph's *Warner Arundell: The Adventures of a Creole* (1838)—challenge categories of genre, of historiography, of politics, of class, of race, and of identity, ultimately demonstrating the uncertainties generated by such taxonomic acts.

All of these fictions reveal the contradictions embedded in their constructions of the Caribbean "realities" they seek to dramatize, giving birth to characters and enlivening settings and situations in ways that shed light on the many sociopolitical fictions that shaped life in the anglophone Atlantic. In this, the novels demonstrate both the longevity of the impulse to ground colonial narratives' truth claims in empirical, experiential knowledge—a recurring feature in the "true relations" and "true accounts" of New World discovery literature from previous centuries—and the need to frame "the category of individual experience" in terms of "the aims of colonial expansion and developing market relations."[4] Given the shifting and unstable terms that shaped imperial ambitions and increasingly globalized economies over the course of the long eighteenth century, it is necessary to recognize the instability of the novel form broadly, and the creole novel specifically. As I discuss more fully below, these instabilities determined the production, circulation, and reception of texts set in the Caribbean. In recognizing what Elizabeth Maddock Dillon refers to as the "the shifting terrain of a globalizing economy," their authors engaged in constant (re)negotiations of form and content, the (re)production of ever new fictions to describe the new worlds they described.[5] Thus, in 1827 *Hamel*'s reviewer can present the West Indies to readers as "terrae incognitae," despite England's centuries'-old acquaintance with the region and claim the novel's novelty by virtue of the "new" scenes and "new" manners to be discovered in its pages. The discursive performances of the early creole novelists, in effect, operate as essential correlates to the colonial activities of "real, substantial Englishmen," validating the place/space of the West Indies by manufacturing and relating the "history" and "nature" of Britain's Atlantic colonies through fiction.

BEFORE UNPACKING the fictional performances at work *beyond* the line, it's necessary to acknowledge the early creole novel's indebtedness to actual, physical acts of *crossing* the line. Both phrases share a nautical origin, referring to the movement of ships and people over latitudinal lines like the Tropic of Cancer and the Equator as they sailed south and west into the Torrid Zones. Enslaved Africans, impressed sailors, Britain's second sons hoping to revive their fortunes in the West Indian sugar colonies: all were transported (often involuntarily) on vessels crossing the Atlantic from the Old Worlds of Europe, Africa, and Asia to the New Worlds of the Americas.

The journeys undertaken by British ships in the last half of the eighteenth century are plotted on the map below, each journey across the ocean traced in fine lines (see fig. 1).[6] Although the map's title, "British Trade Routes as Shown by Ships' Logs, 1750–1800," makes no specific mention of Britain's slave trading activities, the period it documents covers the half-century during which human trafficking between Africa and the British West Indies peaked—along with the private and state wealth amassed from the trade in slaves and sugar. Visually striking, the thin lines charting voyages that facilitated that traffic suggest both stasis and movement: thick, knotted strands emphasizing the most well-established and

4 *Introduction*

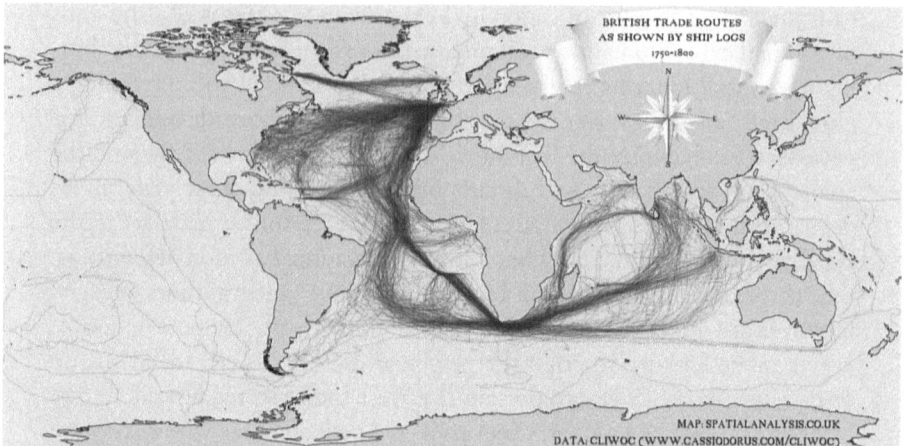

FIGURE 1. British trade routes as shown by ship logs, 1750–1800. (Plotted by James Cheshire using modern mapping technologies; courtesy of James Cheshire, Spatial Analysis)

often-traveled routes, loosely tangled swirls mimicking the currents and trade winds that determined ships' courses. In addition to emphasizing the sheer volume of oceanic, primarily transatlantic travel over a fifty-year span, the map emphasizes repetition and routine. This, however, isn't to say that mercantile trade routes were straightforward or predictable; indeed, as the map makes clear, reductive models of transatlantic trade between Old and New Worlds—its straight-edged triangularity—cannot capture the fluidity suggested by the curves and arcs, the multiplicity of lines crossed.

Even as the map makes clear that each ship's journey was part of a much wider system, a global network of commerce and trade, we must look elsewhere for a sense of the role of individuals' experience within that network—to see how the journey itself served as an introduction to life at the point of disembarkation. Accounts of systemic violence and its dehumanizing effects that defined life (and death) for the enslaved during the oceanic voyage abound, from autobiographical accounts like Olaudah Equiano's *Interesting Narrative* to historical studies like Marcus Rediker's *The Slave Ship*. Most often, as these accounts reveal, the violence inflicted on the enslaved came at the hands of white sailors and seamen. As Equiano describes them, the white men on the ship taking the ten-year-old Equiano from Africa to the West Indies were among the most savage people he had ever encountered: "I had never seen among any people such instances of brutal cruelty." But, he adds, brutality was "not only shown towards us blacks, but also to some of the whites themselves"; ships' crews were subjected to harsh physical punishments: floggings, keelhauling, summary executions.[7] Whether an individual wielded the whip, was brutalized by it, resisted it, or, like the child Equiano, witnessed its application, violence marked the experience of all who crossed the line.

Such violence, unsurprisingly, provoked acts of resistance that were violent in turn.[8] As Marcus and others have noted, enslaved people organized and participated in rebellions; crew members mutinied to overthrow maritime hierarchies. But whether resistance sprang from the ranks of the enslaved or from ships' crews—or, as happened on occasion, from alliances between members of those groups—it subverted disciplinary structures of shipboard life.[9] Moreover, the subversive potential realized in rebellious activity was engendered in part by the shifting terms that dictated the formation of individual and community identities at sea. People crossing oceans also crossed lines of ethnicity, race, language, and religion to form cooperative arrangements that were "far more complex than any simple division of black and white" suggests.[10]

Writing of the "anomalous intimacies" imposed by the "saltwater slavery" of the Atlantic crossing, Stephanie Smallwood points to the diversity among enslaved Africans—the human cargo often described as an indistinguishable mass, as in the infamous *Brooks* diagram of a slave ship's hold and in various abolitionist writings.[11] Even though these shipmates planted the "seed of community within the African Atlantic diaspora of which they now were a part," they did so only by putting aside the geographic, tribal, ethnic, and linguistic differences that had separated them prior to their forced journeys.[12] Africans and Europeans, enslaved, indentured, impressed, and free, all sailed to and from the West Indies serving alongside individuals born in the Americas, in East and South Asia, in the Pacific islands, in the Eastern Mediterranean, and elsewhere, working together as multinational, multilingual, multiethnic, multiracial bodies of sailors that made maritime travel possible. These motley crews, moreover, the seafaring communities whose members were drawn from every area of the globe, also presented those aboard with a sampling of the heterogeneous populations they would encounter and become part of once they arrived in the Caribbean.

All of this demonstrates the powerful forces and contingencies—the dismantled hierarchies and shifting power relations—that characterized life at sea and that gave rise to the fluid identities of those carried to the West Indies. Perhaps nothing depicts this fluidity and the attempt to contain it more than the "crossing the line" ceremony conducted as vessels passed over the Tropic of Cancer or the Equator on their way to the colonies. At that time, crew members and passengers who had never made the passage underwent raucous, violent, carnivalesque baptism rites that represented (for common sailors at least) a respite from the absolute authority of ships' officers. As E. L. Joseph describes such "nautical saturnalia" in *Warner Arundell,* when ships "passed the tropics, they were no longer subjects of any European power"; nor did crews recognize the captain's authority, for "while the ship is crossing the line" the rules of maritime law are suspended, the ship "being in neither latitude nor longitude.'"[13] Although this ritual was perceived by many officers as a "disagreeable practice" and condemned as "an absurd piece of folly," it was also recognized as a time-sanctioned rite of passage "of which the omission might be regretted."[14] Without the release of such "folly" (which was believed to improve morale and industry among the seamen), all manner of ills could arise, from the doldrums to melancholic fevers to ungovernable insubordination.

Reluctantly condoned, the mock trials, shavings, and duckings that commemorated the crossing, along with the oath administered by "King Neptune" (a role usually played by the most seasoned crewmember), emphasize the topsy-turvy, world-turned-upside down quality of the ceremonies: the oath-taker was free "not to eat biscuit while [he] could get wheaten bread, unless he preferred the biscuit"; not to kiss "the servant, when he could kiss the mistress, unless he liked the servant better, &c. &c."[15] (see fig. 2). Like the violence of shipboard life and the shifting subject positions that defined the experiences of multitudes of people crossing the line, the ceremonial suspension of order, the lawlessness, and the liminality contained in *Warner Arundell*'s et ceteras and visible in George Cruikshank's illustration can all be read as a rehearsal for what voluntary and coerced voyagers would find when they disembarked beyond the line.

For the enslaved, arrival in the West Indies most often meant a continuation of the horrors of the Middle Passage; for ships' crews, the journey continued as vessels charted new courses. Prospective residents coming from Britain and Europe held different expectations about their new lives, shaped not just by their recent experiences crossing the line, but by a multitude of images encountered before they had departed. These images, produced and circulated in the metropole, presented the Caribbean colonies in multiple and competing ways: as island El Dorados where enormous fortunes were to be made or, conversely, as "the grave of Europeans."[16] More often than not, the region was perceived and constructed

FIGURE 2. "Crossing the Line," by George Cruikshank, 1825. Cruikshank's depiction of the ceremony appeared in a series of illustrations devoted to life in the British navy. (© National Maritime Museum, Greenwich, London)

as a special kind of "no place" where disorder and misrule of the kind celebrated by the "sons of Neptune" during oceanic crossings was to be endured or embraced.[17] Most importantly for my project, those who survived and settled not only crossed the line, but according to metropolitan imagery, remained on the "other," wrong side of it. Like those born in the so-called New World, they became, in eighteenth-century parlance, "creoles."

Why Creole?

As I considered this study's title, I rehearsed various ways to describe the body of novels at its center: "nineteenth-century anglophone Caribbean," "early white West Indian," "colonial Caribbean." None of these descriptors, however, conveyed the contentious history and relevance of "creole," or demanded the need for historicizing and (re)negotiating the sociopolitical contingencies that went into the formation and fraught articulations of Caribbean culture during the period of slavery and emancipation.[18] When I refer to "the early creole novel," then, I do so self-consciously. In my study I draw on the sense of the word "creole" as it was used when the texts were produced. This older sense reflects an accretion of meanings from the earliest days of European colonial activity in the New World, embedded in nascent colonialist theories of racial difference. I also bring to bear current theoretical discussions of the nuances and complexities attached to the word by scholars like Kamau Brathwaite, Sylvia Wynter, Orlando Patterson, Edouard Glissant, Sidney Mintz, J. Michael Dash, Stuart Hall, and Sean Goudie. For this project, then, "creole" encompasses the early colonial sense of one who was born in or a long-term resident of the Caribbean; it also takes into account the various processes of "creolization," of the literal and figurative crossings by which such individuals came to see themselves as *culturally distinct* from the Old World populations of their origins."[19]

It should be noted from the start that both "creole" and "creolization" are unstable terms. "Creole," as primarily applied to individuals, meant (and means) different things in different settings, as Carolyn Allen demonstrates in her exploration of the word. Tracing its illusory origins yields various possibilities, one being an Ibero-American corruption of *criadillo* (from the diminutive for "servant" or "child," also carrying the sense of "bred, brought up, reared; domestic"), a term colonial writers in the eighteenth century attributed to enslaved Africans transported to South America, who applied it to their children born in the New World. Maureen Warner-Lewis presents another possibility, identifying the term's roots with the Kikoongo word for "outsider," a sense that, like the European etymology, reflects "creole"'s earliest use by enslaved peoples and subsequently by Europeans to differentiate Old and New World populations.[20] In anglophone and European writings of the long eighteenth century, the term's meaning continued to develop alongside Enlightenment natural philosophy to emphasize what Ralph Bauer and José Antonio Mazzotti refer to as a kind of "environmental determinism," so that "creole" came to include subjects who, though born in the Old World, had been transplanted to the New, "and, thus, been subject to its peculiar natural influences for an extended period."[21] In addition to remarking the operation of natural influences like climate and disease environment, metropolitan commentators pointed to cultural influences, routinely noting a West Indian ethos that distinguished creolized former Europeans, a point I develop more fully below. In almost all cases, Allen points out, "'Creole' is and expresses the result of the Atlantic crossing and colonization."[22]

Theoretical debates surrounding creolization today arise from the term's applicability to contemporary questions about racialized identities in Caribbean societies, questions that cannot be severed from their historical roots. Working from the model provided by Brathwaite's highly influential study of the development of creole society in Jamaica from 1770 to 1820, most scholars agree with the basic definition of creolization as a process of cultural change wrought by "the stimulus/response of individuals within the society to their environment and—as white/black, culturally discrete groups—to each other."[23] Beyond this basic formulation, reconsiderations of hierarchies and influence—racial and socioeconomic, political and material—have generated much discussion, particularly in relation to emergent Caribbean nationalism(s), decolonization, and post-independence societies, and to the formation of transnational identities and literatures. Questions attendant on processes of creolization, as the novels in *Crossing the Line* demonstrate, are evident from an early period.

But even as *Crossing the Line* draws on the conception elaborated by Brathwaite, it also addresses concerns expressed by subsequent critics. As O. Nigel Bolland cautions, models of creolization that (ultimately) privilege synthesis and blending result in an idealized, ironically homogenous conceptualization of creole culture. Wary of such assumptions, Bolland argues for an "understanding of creolisation as a central cultural process of Caribbean history," one that should lead to "a reconceptualisation of the nature of colonialism and colonial societies, as social forces and social systems that are characterized by conflicts and contradictions and that consequently give rise to their own transformation."[24]

Bolland's emphasis on the transformative power of conflicts and contradictions makes clear the need to recognize that the culture(s) reflected in and produced by the novels considered here, though identifiable as creole, are neither static nor monolithic. The bulk of the novels I examine in *Crossing the Line* were produced by *white* creoles, writers whose attempts to construct and uphold categories of racial difference tended to minimize, ignore, or—importantly—manage the power and persistence of African and black creole influences on West Indian life. They were produced, moreover, in a short-lived moment before novelists of the later post-Emancipation period would assert their own claims of local, experiential knowledge, and give voice to colonial subjects of color, as in the case of Michel Maxwell Philip's *Emmanuel Appadocca,* a post-Emancipation novel I discuss in my conclusion. The irony of white creole novelists' attempts to define enlightened creole culture appears in the narratives' documentation of the Afro-Caribbean cultural practices they wished to contain: their works provide us with a print record that, if read with care, can supplement the oral testimonies, archaeological evidence, and later West Indian fictions that supply histories of peoples marginalized within colonial print accounts.

We must read these early creole novels skeptically then, as Evelyn O'Callaghan puts it, to "investigate how race figures differently across cultural contexts and thus to advocate the examination, interrogation, and, where necessary, contestation of these categories."[25] We must also learn to decode the embedded trace histories of silenced voices that early creole fiction contains in order to perform the kind of literary archaeology described by Toni Morrison and advocated by Jenny Sharpe in *Ghosts of Slavery*, which entails ongoing reassessments of our period's racial inheritance.[26] Like it or not, these novels influenced later nineteenth-century Caribbean culture and continue to have much to say about more recent Caribbean literature.

Similarly, reading these texts in a transatlantic frame reveals the degree to which anglophone creole and British identities were dependent on rather than formed in isolation from each other. Just as critics like Thomas Holt, Catherine Hall, and David Lambert have shown that subjects in Great Britain used the West Indian "other"—black, brown, and white—to forge an identity based on Britain's geographical and cultural distance from its Caribbean colonies, so, too, did white creoles play off of contemporary notions of Britishness to define themselves as distinct—not peripheral—subjects.[27]

All of this suggests that, as Stuart Hall observes, creole identity was from its beginnings contested and fluid, rooted at the juncture points of the New World in physical, psychological, and cultural spaces where "creolisations and assimilations and syncretisms were negotiated."[28] The early creole novels I examine in *Crossing the Line* reveal that these negotiations were often violent, dramatizing the "fateful/fatal encounter . . . between Africa and the West" and exposing the tensions generated in the "contact zone" of the Caribbean colonies.[29] At the same time they reveal a fraught dialectic between metropolitan and creole constructions of the British West Indies, between Old and New World sensibilities in the tumultuous period leading up to and extending beyond so-called full emancipation in 1838. The perspective privileged in these works, moreover, reveals their white authors' consciousness of the "in-between," the "not quite" position they occupied, despite attempts to maintain a racial purity that—presumably—would guarantee their continuing membership in Protestant European civilization.

This consciousness was borne of longstanding attitudes held by Europeans toward colonial inhabitants, as mentioned above. Such attitudes, as Karen Ordahl Kupperman describes them, reflect the "powerful continuity in European response" to creoles, by the early nineteenth century an already three-hundred-year-old tradition of pan-European intellectuals and colonial policy shapers who viewed subjects living in the Americas as different from themselves and therefore degraded.[30] In the anglophone Caribbean, colonial subjects were differentiated by and from Britons "at home," particularly in terms of their perceived degeneracy. Moreover, perceptions of white creoles' differences from Europeans—despite their European antecedents—were central to European national identities founded on the construction of the colonies as geospatial places of difference.

As Lambert, C. Hall, Bauer and Mazzotti, and others have observed, notions of difference and degeneracy were explicitly tied to the perceived influence of slavery and the cross-racial intimacies that characterized the institution, particularly on white slaveholders. Writing of slavery's effect on white planters, one early twentieth-century historian echoed a longstanding argument that the institution "seems to have degraded the master even more than the slave."[31] This commonly held attitude—concerned primarily with slavery's effect on the plantocracy and (importantly) eliding the suffering of the enslaved—was certainly reflected in literary productions that grew out of increased metropolitan antislavery activity, as Wylie Sypher shows in his germinal study of West Indian "types." Often portrayed as bluff and backwards, provincial and passionate, white West Indians returning to England provided an easy mark in metropolitan works, from Frances Sheridan's Ned Warner in *Sidney Bidulph*, to Richard Cumberland's title character in *The West Indian*, to Maria Edgeworth's Mr. Vincent in *Belinda*. As antislavery campaigning intensified, however, images of naïve but good-hearted white West Indians gave way to those of avaricious tyrants whose unfeeling behaviors toward their passive, enchained victims threatened not only their souls but also the souls of complacent Britons who refused to agitate for abolition. As for black West Indians, despite well-known individuals like Ignatius Sancho and Olaudah Equiano, black characters featured in metropolitan fiction are very nearly effaced from the texts, like "the black" given to Sidney Bidulph by her creole cousin in Sheridan's novel and the anonymous servants brought to England from Jamaica by Sarah Scott's George Ellison. Even when black characters are more fully incorporated into the plot, like Juba in *Belinda*, they are often depicted as simpletons, easily duped and/

or sentimentalized victims to be pitied or laughed at by freeborn British subjects. Disdain for creole planters in no way translated into high regard for Afro-Caribbean subjects.

As the preponderance of metropolitan constructions of creoles grew less reliant on geographic and climatic differences between Great Britain and the Caribbean and more concerned with condemning the slaveholding foundations of white creole society, the West Indian became central to the process of constituting "the white, British, bourgeois subject." This subject, Lambert argues, "could be consolidated, and the 'problem of slavery' resolved, by disowning and repudiating those 'un-British' groups involved in slavery—the West Indian planters—and displacing the spaces of slavery to the margins of Britain's imaginative imperial geographies."[32]

White creole authors, as noted above, were often bitterly aware of the irony of their position—that direct or indirect involvement in the slave trade isolated them from their metropolitan counterparts even as the institution enriched the mother country.[33] Early creole authors and those sympathetic to West India interests worked to remind readers in England that the slave-driven economy of the Caribbean was the engine of Britain's empire. As St. Kitts physician-turned-poet James Grainger insisted in 1764, cultivation of the century's most lucrative cash crop—the theme of his West Indian georgic *The Sugar-Cane*—was "most momentous to my Country's weal!"[34]

For antislavery writers, shoring up ideals of British moral superiority on the foundations of creole turpitude involved not only the condemnation of chattel slavery but also of those aspects of creole culture deemed most insidious. Customs and manners shared across creole populations perceived as shaped by African and black creole cultures were the subject of much indignation and satire in the West Indies and in Britain. Prints like *The Torrid Zone; or Blessings of Jamaica* and *Johnny Newcome in Love in the West Indies,* as well as Lady Maria Nugent's often-cited journal entries disparaging the indolent speech patterns, lassitude, and dietary habits of Jamaican creoles, all point to concerns about what J. B. Moreton described as "negrofied" white creoles, and the strident metropolitan response to it (see fig. 3).[35]

The most dangerous signs of such corruption, according to commentaries on West Indian life and in the pages of creole novels, were the sexual predilections of white men like the Jamaican planter Simon Taylor (1739–1813) and overseer Thomas Thistlewood (1721–86). Thistlewood's journals record countless instances of his abusive relations with enslaved women as well as domestic details of his thirty-plus-year

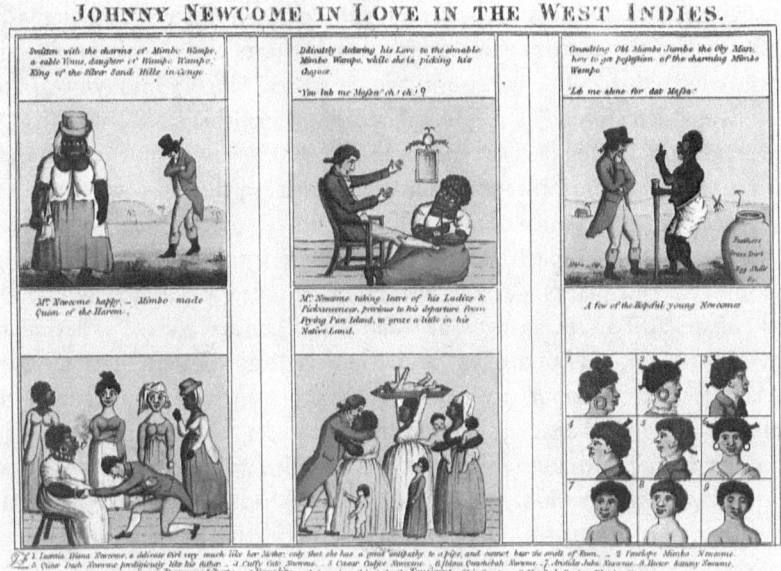

FIGURE 3. "Johnny Newcome in Love in the West Indies," one of many satiric prints featuring "Johnny Newcome," the generic name for a newcomer to the British West Indies. (Courtesy of The Lewis Walpole Library, Yale University)

relationship with Phibba, an enslaved woman and mother of Thistlewood's son.[36] Children like Thistlewood and Phibba's John provided visible evidence of coerced and, perhaps more rarely, voluntary cross-racial relations bemoaned by visitors like Janet Schaw and representatives of the region's ruling elite like Edward Long.[37] Fictionalized characters of mixed race appear in all of the novels examined in *Crossing the Line*, their "illegitimate" presence incorporated in the plot to provide evidence of white men's moral failings, to express sympathy with colonial subjects of color in their quest to attain "mulatto rights"—a hotly debated subject in the colonies and in the metropole in the period—or to provide a tragic figure whose madness or demise allows white creoles to display "pity and condescension."[38]

Why the Novel?

If it was easy for Britons in the metropole to decry the immorality of creole culture, it was less easy for white creole writers to mount a defense of such charges. In addition to revealing a compulsion to counter pervasive images generated by metropolitan antislavery writers, early creole novelists evince an awareness of the tenuousness of their position, particularly at the turn of the century when antislavery activists *and* slavery apologists acknowledged that the system, in the words of *Marly*'s anonymous author, was "detestable." The general acceptance of this stance was (itself) the product of a long antislavery campaign, of a sense as time passed that the passage of abolitionist and emancipationist legislation was imminent. In light of the abundance of nonfictional texts devoted to the "West India Question"—essays, parliamentary reports and proceedings, editorials, pamphlets, and prints—creole writers acknowledged that it would be difficult to add anything new, at least in nonliterary form.[39] The creole novel, however, *was* perceived (and conceived) as something new: a vehicle in which to couch political arguments, a form that purported to draw scenes and characters "taken from the life," as presented through mimetic description, but with room to dramatize its contents in ways that allowed writers to validate their colonialist position.[40] In short, there was "nothing," according to *Marly*'s author, "so effectual as the machinery of a novel" to "awaken the interest and engage the attention" of readers,[41] or to lay bare the constructed nature of the reality the novelists claimed to depict.

Casting political theory in novel form, as Tilottama Rajan points out in her study of English Jacobin novels of the 1790s, was a strategic decision, a means by which writers could "disclose the fictions used in the economy of the political world, both the theoretical and actual worlds."[42] Such works, Rajan adds, attempted to draw in readers through extratextual referents. Though Rajan refers here to readers of Jacobin fiction, the same can be said of the relationship between creole novels and readers encountering them for the first time: like readers engaging Jacobin politics through novels, readers of colonial fiction could be educated, led through a work's nuances to arrive at a more sympathetic understanding and appreciation of the white creole position—or so the novelists hoped.

The analogy between the Jacobin fiction of reform-minded novelists like William Godwin and Mary Wollstonecraft—produced in the wake of the French Revolution and influenced by the British Crown's response to (real or perceived) threats posed by seditious writers—and the work of creole novelists is more apt than it may at first appear. Creole novels were also produced at a particularly unstable moment in the history of the colonies; their authors, too, self-consciously adopted the novel form to reveal what they presented as fictions spun by their political opponents. Like the Jacobin novel, the nineteenth-century white creole roman à thèse had a relatively short lifespan, a roughly thirty-year period that saw waning economic and political influence of the West India lobby, numerous slave uprisings, and the end of British West Indian slavery. In the years before Emancipation, wide-scale uprisings—Bussa's Rebellion in Barbados in 1816, the Demarara Revolt of 1823, and Sam Sharpe's Baptist War of 1831-32 in Jamaica—made it clear that, with or without metropolitan intervention and its acceptance by colonial assemblies, the enslaved themselves had brought slavery in its pre-Haitian Revolution form to an end. Emerging from this tumultuous period, the creole novels I examine are marked by an awareness of impending and inevitable change as well as a desire to stabilize and, perhaps more importantly, *revise* Caribbean history as it was unfolding, a point I return to below.[43]

In highly self-conscious ways, then, early creole novelists labored under a double imperative: first, to represent "novel" subjects in new world settings, to repudiate what one of *Hamel*'s characters called the "old stupid world" of England and its ignorance of West Indian "reality," and, second, to substantiate that reality by claiming insider knowledge of creole culture, including a "just picture . . . of the present state of the Negroes."[44] The novel form—as defined in the previous century by practitioner and critic Clara Reeve—readily lent itself to both imperatives. Presenting "something new" and claiming to provide "a picture of real life and manners, and of the times in which [the novel] is written," creole novelists attempted to work within accepted parameters of the genre laid out by Reeve: to "represent every scene, in so easy and natural a manner, and to make them appear so probable, as to deceive us into a persuasion (at least while we are reading) that all is real."[45]

These attempts, of course, were not simply exercises in literary form, but represented creole novelists' contributions to a wider epistemological project to overturn "old," that is, metropolitan or European, presuppositions about white creole degeneracy, and to validate, in their place, white creole ways of knowing predicated on experience of life in the Caribbean colonies. This project, as Keith Sandiford argues in *The Cultural Politics of Sugar*, illustrates the "sweete negotiation" practiced by colonial writers whose texts try to allay anxieties generated at the intersections of textual (cultural) and material (agricultural) production in the West Indian colonies. The phrase, taken from Richard Ligon's *True and Exact History of the Island of Barbadoes* (1657), serves as Sandiford's central metaphor for the kind of desire underpinning colonial narratives of the long eighteenth century—including, I would add, creole novels produced in the early nineteenth century. "Drawing its energy principally (though not exclusively) from the economics of sugar production," writes Sandiford, "that desire subsumes within itself both the material artifacts and the ideological content of that production":

> These texts produce negotiation as a desire to win a tenuous and elusive legitimacy for an evolving ideal of Creole civilization, conflicted by its central relation to slavery and its marginal relation to metropolitan cultures. Each of these sources of conflict posed stout challenges to Creole pretensions: slavery aroused moral and economic objections crystallizing in abolitionist and anti-slavery polemics; traditional cultural preservationists (purists) back home continually interrogated the Creoles' desire for social credibility by raising the spectre of cultural pollution and political disintegration.[46]

Crucial as the negotiations that Sandiford tracks are, the early creole novelists I examine approached that cultural-epistemological project using somewhat different discursive strategies. Equally desirous to attain "elusive legitimacy," early creole novelists often simply laid claim to it, insisting that the imaginary scenes contained in their novels were "strictly consistent with fact."[47]

Such truth claims, as mentioned above, link these novels to the "true relations" of much earlier colonial accounts, but display a sharper, more obviously political edge, constituting a white creole rejoinder to the moral objections of abolitionists and to the skepticism expressed by "cultural preservationists" in Britain. In other words, in their attempt to smooth over the "ironic ambivalences and contradictions" that Sandiford rightly identifies as characteristic of creole writing, these novelists insist on the authority to write what they (and only they) know: only white creoles can accurately describe the situation in the Caribbean colonies; only authors familiar with daily life there can correct the falsehoods (or at best, naïve misinformation) presented in metropolitan works about West Indian subjects, whether white, brown, or black—particularly those produced by British emancipationists.[48] So these novelists suggest.

The claims for such authority were often underpinned by authors' displays of obvious familiarity with Caribbean locales. From *Montgomery*'s account of an expedition into the Jamaican bush during the Second Maroon War, to *Hamel*'s descriptions of Jamaica's Blue Mountains and the limestone cave systems in Portland Parish, to *Warner Arundell*'s depiction of the bustling sprawl of Trinidad's Port of Spain, local color speaks to the authors' intimate knowledge of West Indian scenes. At other times, truth claims based on what Tim Watson calls "eyewitness insiderism" are spelled out, as when *Hamel*'s narrator ends the obeah man's last speech by pointing out that he has translated rather than transcribed it. With more than a hint of condescension, the narrator explains that although Hamel's use of "the creole tongue" would be "sufficiently understood" by Hamel's creole auditors, it would be incomprehensible to metropolitan readers.[49] Through such acts of translation—of words and manners and scenes—creole novelists offered readers the benefits of their Caribbean experience, inviting them to share, even if vicariously, a privileged perspective that simultaneously exoticized life in the Torrid Zone for readers and rendered those drawn in to the narrative complicit in its epistemological work.

In actuality, the privileged perspective claimed by the novelists was limited. White creoles were not privy to all aspects of West Indian culture any more than were metropolitan visitors, military personnel, or colonial administrators serving temporarily in the West Indies, as is clear from the many insurrectionary acts carried out by enslaved people in the Emancipation period. But, according to the claims laid out in the novels, white creoles were nevertheless in the best position to convey West Indian knowledge and to represent Caribbean realities, especially to British readers with little to no experience of the region. Nowhere are such assertions more explicit than in the prefatory materials that accompany a number of the works. *Marly*'s author, for example, assures readers in the first edition's "Note to the Public" that a "Slave Driver" from Jamaica undeniably is qualified to "detail the actual occurrences which take place on a sugar estate"; despised though he might be in England, "he knows the truth, and might a true 'tale unfold'" to readers willing to overcome metropolitan political biases.[50] Like the other creole novels featured in *Crossing the Line*, *Marly* does not hide its plantocratic affiliations. More importantly, such asseverations of narrative authority—staked out crudely in *Marly* or in more sophisticated ways in *Hamel*, *Warner Arundell*, and *Old Port-Royal*—represent attempts to reproduce claims of local white rule and legitimize ruling-class control over the colonies' black and brown populations. Sometimes staged in conjunction with British colonial policy, sometimes in opposition to it, these efforts are characteristic of the early creole novel.

If it is easy to spot evidence of creole novelists' attempts to present "true" tales that conveniently legitimize white rule—to rewrite, in effect, an increasingly revolutionary Caribbean history in the moment of its production—it's more difficult to gauge the success or failure of their efforts. That said, there are clues about the novels' reception: with the exception of *Montgomery* and *Old Port-Royal*, both of which were printed in Kingston, all the novels were published in Great Britain,[51] indicating a willingness on the part of British printers and booksellers to undertake their production and distribution. Most of the novels, circulating on both sides of the Atlantic, were reviewed in British periodicals.[52] But although these reviews typically expressed appreciation for the "authenticity" of the novels' West Indian scenes, many also point out the novelists' partisan sympathies.[53] Abolitionist James Stephen, for example, readily acknowledged the accurate portrayal of the Jamaican setting in *Marly:* given the "graphic delineations of scenery and manners," he writes, "no man who has seen the West Indies" would doubt that the author had resided there.[54] But Stephen was quick to denounce the novelist's claims of impartiality on the West India Question as false, identifying the author as an "antagonist" who soon "drops his mask and appears in his true character, as a serious and zealous apologist of slavery, and champion of the colonial cause."[55]

Part of Stephen's indignation over *Marly*'s proslavery apologetics appears roused by the mode of presentation—what Stephen calls the "catching form of a novel"—and the author's decision to write "in the guise of a novelist."[56] Stephen's language, with its implicit charge of deceit, points to the ironies in creole novelists' attempts to present so-called facts through fiction, difficulties of form that Watson explores in his study of British writing in the nineteenth-century Atlantic world.

Tracking the shift in nonliterary West Indian texts "from realism to romance and back again,"[57] Watson identifies the "creole realism" at work in them. Despite "the attempt to narrate the story of the British colonies from the point of view of a planter class defined by [its] qualities of reasonableness and enterprise," Watson points out, the documentary record of the Caribbean told from the white creole point of view is forever turning into the literary genres that it eschews: sentimental fiction, gothic melodrama, and imperial romance.[58] As the dominant generic norms of the metropole—scientific, empirical, and commercial—increasingly were found inadequate to the work of defending and validating the West Indian position on slavery and emancipation, the creole plantocracy "turned more explicitly to the genre of romance to express its opposition to the colonial authorities and their ideological underwriters, the humanitarians and philanthropists of the abolitionist movement in Britain."[59]

For early creole novelists, this movement toward romance perhaps is less a turn than a self-conscious willingness to blur generic lines. Eighteenth- and nineteenth-century men and women of letters wrote across genres as a matter of course. Even so, the tangle of discursive modes through which their authors "tell their tale" constitutes an identifiable feature of the early creole novel, an interweaving of matter-of-fact authorial interjections, reports of local history, and sentimentalized plot lines that promulgate the authors' idealized vision of white creoles and their relationships with black and brown people, enslaved and free, whose lives and cultures the novels purport to document.[60]

Even as early creole novelists responded to metropolitan writers and borrowed from literary prose forms popular in Britain, from the sentimental to gothic sublime to picaresque adventure tales, they also express a self-consciousness about the novelty of their works, a belief that their narratives constitute a new kind of novel, located in the New World and expressive of "*Creole* society and *Creole* sentiment."[61] The general outline of these sentiments also demonstrates that the novels were in conversation with one another and with other nonliterary representations of creole culture. Indeed, the more deeply one delves into the colonial archives, the more one sees the circulation and repetition (nearly verbatim at times) of basic tenets of a creole epistemology that, with every iteration, reveals clear hegemonic ambitions, the influence of which was felt even in metropolitan productions.[62]

Even so, the blending of narrative modes, the porous boundaries between fact, fiction, history, political polemic, and reportage that distinguish early creole novels also generated ambivalence, at least on the part of British reviewers. The mixed nature of metropolitan reviewers' responses, undoubtedly shaped by the shifting ground of Emancipation debates, is clearly articulated in *The Atlas* review of *Hamel*. Because its commentary reveals the stakes involved in producing (and reading) a creole novel, it is worth citing at length:

> [W]hatever may be [the author's] faults, he is thoroughly familiar with the manners he has attempted to describe. It is not from books that he has learned his facts, but from a long and acute observance of the subjects of his story.
>
> The design of *Hamel* is to show the present state of society, black and white and mixed, in the island of Jamaica. Inasmuch as the book is very agreeable, and in many points able, it is to be lamented that it is a thorough *party* work. The author may be right in his views; had he, however, been dispassionate, we should have been much more inclined to trust him. It is particularly important to this country—it is essential to the happiness of a very large proportion of mankind, that the state and interests of the West Indies should be understood; and a work which gave us much new information that could be entirely relied upon, and gave it too in the lightest and pleasantest way, would be extremely valuable. We believe that very little real knowledge of these islands exists at home; there has been much misrepresentation, much private motive, much

hypocrisy, much cant, much interested zeal, much well-intentioned delusion at work. Every man who visits these countries exclaims, "How little they know of this at home!" Now we are angry with the author of *Hamel* for not doing all the good he had in his power.[63]

The review expresses open uncertainty about the novel's ability to provide the objectivity necessary to resolve the emancipation question, along with the desire for a "realistic" description of characters and situations. This realism, moreover, should be stripped of passion (in the immediate context of a debate that roused very deep passions). At the same time, the reviewer acknowledges that "real knowledge of the islands" can be conveyed through novelistic discourse and encourages its dissemination in that form.

More difficult to tease out, however, is a definitive response on the part of the reviewer to the overall conundrum presented by the early creole novel: which parts of the narrative reflect "facts" drawn from "long and acute observance," and which, as "fiction," are untrustworthy? This is an irresolvable but nevertheless worthwhile question to consider. Moreover, it's one that suggests that, for metropolitan reviewers at least, the creole novel could be aesthetically pleasing and interesting but remain politically unconvincing. In other words, metropolitan readers could allow themselves to be entertained by such exotic works, even instructed about the unfamiliar world they depict; at the same time—crucially—they could retain their footing on the moral high ground.

The fragility of this accommodation assumes greater ideological significance when we complicate our reading of the formal characteristics of the early novel and its creole iterations. Indeed, the value of the latter for twenty-first-century readers resides not just in their contribution to a genre defined by mimesis—which, as suggested above, laid a foundation on which creole novelists rested their wider truth claims. In addition to acknowledging their "creole realism" (to borrow Watson's phrase once more), we need to keep in mind the ways early creole novelistic discourse helped generate the West Indian "realities" they defined and defended through their fictions. As importantly, we need to acknowledge that constructions of West Indian life like those presented in the novels—whether or not accepted as "authentic"—are still being grappled with, as evidenced by Caribbean writers' and scholars' ongoing attempts to engage with rather than dismiss the colonial archives and the historiographies revealed there.

Read in this way, we can see that early creole novels participate in the public sphere that Raphael Dalleo describes, demonstrating "the various ways that writers have sought to speak to the region's social and political realities" (and, I would add, to individual readers) at particular historical moments.[64] This is not to say that the novels stop speaking once their moment of production has passed. Rather they generate continued/ing resonance because, as Ian Baucom paraphrases Frederic Jameson's theory of genre, they "survive the moment of their fashioning ... by carrying within themselves, as a sort of ghostly aftereffect, the signature ideologies of their formative moments, which they then rewrite onto the subsequent historical moments in which they are redeployed."[65]

This emphasis on ghostly aftereffects in Baucom's study of Atlantic modernity is complemented by his engagement with Walter Benjamin's philosophy of history. Time, he emphasizes throughout *Specters of the Atlantic,* "does not pass but accumulates"; in this sense, the "fatal Atlantic 'beginning' of the modern is more properly understood as an ending without end. . . . [H]istory," Baucom concludes, "comes to us not only as flash or revelation but piling up. Because this is, not was. Because this is the Atlantic, now."[66]

Baucom's sense of history's accretive character—the "now-being" of Atlantic modernity—infuses his examination of the interrelatedness of "Finance Capital, Slavery, and the Philosophy of History," as his subtitle indicates. Opening with a provocative analysis of the *Zong* massacre— the murder of 132 enslaved people thrown overboard from a British slave ship in 1781—Baucom analyzes the event and the emergent sociopolitico-economic framework that made it possible: the system of finance capital that fueled the Atlantic slave trade, the actuarial language of the marine insurance policy that provided Captain Luke Collingwood the rationale to order the murders, and the documentary and narrative records that repeated and recreated the atrocity.

The massacre unquestionably helped shape the late eighteenth-century contest between slave traders and abolitionists, but as Baucom stresses, the event, its preconditions, and its afterlife all reveal a struggle "not only . . . between competing theories of right (the slaves' right to human dignity and the slavers' right to trade), but one between competing theories of knowledge, a struggle between an empirical and a contractual, an evidentiary and a credible epistemology."[67] This contest, Baucom argues, extends and replays "the central epistemological drama of the long eighteenth century," in which, "as mobile property displaced 'real' property, and the imaginary value of stocks, bonds, bills-of-exchange, and insured property increasingly trumped the 'real' value of land, bullion, and other tangibles, the concepts of what was knowable, credible, valuable, and real were themselves transformed."[68]

Emerging from these transformed and transformative structures of knowledge, the novel represented a means by which Britons could make sense of them. Following Michael McKeon, Baucom points out that the British novel was a genre whose form embodied a "theory of knowledge" that displaced "a classical historical epistemology" structured around conceptions of factual evidence, and participated instead in an epistemological project reliant on notions of credibility.[69] As such, the novel form and by extension novelistic discourse, responded to and shored up knowledge structures defined by shared ideas of what was credible, probable. In this sense, the novelist testifies to "witnesses," what cultural participants agree *could* (have) happen(ed).

What does Baucom's reading of such epistemological shifts mean for a study of early creole novels? Elizabeth Maddock Dillon's study of the American origins of the novel provides a partial answer. In her reading of *Oroonoko,* a novel produced one hundred years before the *Zong* sailed from Africa, Dillon identifies early signs of the epistemic shift Baucom describes. Within Behn's narrative, she writes, we find "an important (and novelistic) shift of epistemes . . . that is related to the discovery of the New World"; but this shift "is the result of the new norms of a market-oriented colonial growth rather than the geographic fact of the American continent."[70] That Behn's text registers an "episteme of the novel that . . . is less empiricist than *contractual*" says much about the genre's development. As Dillon points out, the key concerns that have long been associated with the English language novel's origins—issues of nationhood and domesticity—must be read against a "larger, transatlantic scene of colonialism and market expansion," a scene that takes into account "the circulation of persons and relationships in the shifting terrain of a globalizing economy."[71]

The instability Dillon describes as the "shifting terrain" of emergent economic conditions of the seventeenth century not only helps situate the novel's history in a transatlantic, colonial frame, however. It also helps explain why—after three centuries of colonial activity and print culture rooted in "true relations" of the New World—the creole novelists I discuss insist on the novelty of their work, to assert the newness of the scenes and manners they describe. These writers, in other words, demonstrate the powerful dialectical relationship between empiricist and contractual epistemes; that that relationship demanded constant renegotiation; and that part of those negotiations were always articulated through the language of discovery because the West Indian islands and West Indian culture were constantly under construction.

The creole novelists, moreover, performed their reproductive work on the same discursive stage as that occupied by those abolitionist writers attempting to convey the trauma of the *Zong* massacre, who tried "not merely to make the past present but to render the unseen visible, to bear witness to the truth of what has not been (and what cannot have been) witnessed."[72] The early creole novelists, I argue, also attempted to "render the unseen visible" and to "credibly" describe what had not and could not have been witnessed by metropolitan readers who had never been to the West Indies, who therefore had no idea of the local conditions dictating events in the colonies. This acknowledgment is discomfiting perhaps but also necessary, especially given the temptation to dismiss the early creole novel for being on the wrong side of the line, the "wrong side of history." Indeed, this phrase itself tends to reinscribe providentialist notions "that history has a discernible direction," that the processes of its unfolding set clear boundaries between right and wrong—notions that, as David Scott argues, require us as readers to guard against the "facile normalization of the present."[73]

Too, we need to be aware of the teleological implications of such notions when examining early creole novels in light of the chronology of Emancipation. For even though much of the urgency surrounding the question of slavery diminished once Emancipation legislation passed in 1833, the plantocratic ideologies that dictated the material conditions of daily life for newly emancipated slaves and their descendants did not disappear with chattel slavery, as critics like Sylvia Wynter, George Beckford, Tim Watson, Diana Paton, and others rightly observe. And although the plantocracy (whether resident in the colonies or living as absentee proprietors in Britain) certainly did not seek the abolition of colonial slavery, as Nicholas Draper points out, "the structure and terms of emancipation were strikingly favorable to the slave owners as a whole."[74] In many cases, Draper observes, slave owners who received compensation money from the British government after Emancipation successfully joined the increasingly globalized "free" market of nineteenth-century finance capitalism. Even as some West Indian planters were "swept away by their inability to adapt to challenges originating both before and, especially, after Emancipation," many other (former) slave owners became "important contributors to the transformation of the British economy between the 1830s and the 1870s."[75]

Such transformations—the cultural, commercial, and political "legacies of slave-ownership"[76]—constituted the new reality of West Indian and global worlds that the early creole novelists anticipated. As for creole writers active in the immediate post-Emancipation era, they, like the (ex) slave-holders and their descendants described by Catherine Hall, "had a lot to say and a powerful impulse to tell, to give witness to various forms of testimony, to weigh in with their versions of the past and their expectations of the present and future"; they believed, continues Hall, "in the power of writing and they believed they could make a difference to how the past was understood and in so doing would shape the present."[77] All the novels discussed in *Crossing the Line* are marked by such historiographic tendencies; all are burdened by the weight of the most distinctive marker of Caribbean culture—an engagement (often through *dis*engagement) with the system of enslavement and local peoples' resistance to it.

Iterations of the seemingly binary relationship between enslaver and enslaved, particularly the insistent opposition of plantocratic benevolence and rebellion against the system upheld/justified by it, appear in each of the novels examined in *Crossing the Line*. Binary formulations, however, collapse under the weight of the dialectical process of creolization that Brathwaite describes, the ongoing stimulus/response between discreet groups and individuals that make up creole society. Nowhere is this collapse more evident than in the novels' representations of black and mixed-race characters. These characters, for the most part, are constructed in order to validate white creole identity and historiography, as suggested above. In some instances, however, their presence subverts race-based hierarchies. But whether the novels produce and perpetuate racialized stereotypes common in colonial (and metropolitan) discourse, or whether they challenge them, these characters reveal the complexity of creole cultures linked by undeniable intimacies across racial lines. From the straightforward depiction of the brutalized slave who disrupts the planter picturesque imagery of *Montgomery*, to the polyvalent depictions of interracial romance in *Hamel, Old Port-Royal*, and *Creoleana*, to questions of mulatto rights in *Marly, Warner Arundell*, and *Emmanuel Appadocca*, such intimacies reflect a recognition of the quotidian workings of West Indian social constructs that are absent in metropolitan works about the Caribbean, including those that explicitly address these subjects.[78]

But even as the novels' incorporation of such intimacies reveals the complexities of colonial societies, they seldom acknowledge the violence that shaped them. As is typical of much proslavery discourse, the novels deploy various strategies to play down what abolitionists emphasized as the "horrors of slavery." The simplest of these strategies, of course, is to deny such horrors existed, to insist instead that the enslaved recognized the benefits of their enslavement. The novels routinely incorporate anti-emancipation speeches made by loyal "servants," or slaves "in name only" who "have no want of freedom."[79] If freed, these characters ask, who will take care of them? Elsewhere, the novels seek to deflect attention from the rigors of coerced labor, including fieldwork, by emphasizing instead the difficult work performed by resident whites. Whether that work consists of the duties assigned to white bookkeepers (estate under-managers) like the title characters in *Montgomery* and *Marly,* or the emotional toil so integral to assertions of white people's greater sensibility—the "agonized feelings" and "labouring heart" exhibited by Montgomery,[80] the acute distresses of *Hamel*'s plantation mistress Mrs. Guthrie, or the sad decline of Warner Arundell's planter father—white labor, the narratives imply, is far more taxing than that of the enslaved.

Of course, the novels' depictions of black and brown characters suggestively point to strategies by which enslaved and disenfranchised people negotiated their daily lives, through the representation of their sexual agency, as in the case of *Old Port-Royal*'s Ellen Mansvelt, *Creoleana*'s Lucy, and *Hamel*'s Michal, or in the construction of characters able to outmaneuver and outwit their white "superiors," as in the case of the fictional Hamel, the enlightened mixed-race pirate Emmanuel Appadocca, and the historical trickster figure Rachael Pringle in *Creoleana*. As Brathwaite acknowledges, the interactions that constituted the process of creolization were shaped inarguably by the master–slave relationship; yet he also acknowledges—as the novels in *Crossing the Line* illustrate—that white creoles' insistence on upholding their society's racialized hierarchy opened subversive possibilities on numerous levels, from the kind of day-to-day resistance mentioned above to large-scale revolt. These possibilities prompted creole novelists to construct West Indian narratives that—even as they depicted major rebellions and individual acts of subversion—minimized and contained the complexities of cross-cultural, cross-racial contact.

ULTIMATELY, the novels featured in *Crossing the Line* attest to the indefensibility of the white creole position, however benignly portrayed, however romantically recalled. Perhaps this accounts, at least partially, for the relatively small number of early creole novels produced in the Emancipation era. But even as the early fictions I examine appear confined to the final quarter-century of British slavery, their influence extends beyond that moment of publication. As I argue throughout *Crossing the Line*, the early novels represent an attempt by their white authors—affiliates or members of a slave-holding elite—to write back to and overturn metropolitan notions of West Indian degeneracy that disallowed any possibility of a civilized creole culture. This attempt demanded that authors privilege a narrow vision of creole experience, a vision that for subsequent generations of West Indian writers became the impetus to write back to the pre-Emancipation ruling classes, to wrest narrative control from their predecessors and, in the process, to validate a much broader conception of creole experience than white creole writers had been willing to entertain.

With this in mind, I close *Crossing the Line* by considering several post-Emancipation novels that deal explicitly with Caribbean historiography: *Old Port-Royal* (1841), *Creoleana* (1842), and *Emmanuel Appadocca* (1854). Each of these works participates in a discursive mode familiar to readers of historical fiction. In their respective rewritings of creole history and reconstructions of creole subjectivity, Samuel Gray, J. W. Orderson, and Michel Maxwell Philip continue the acts of crossing so central to the earlier novels. With my reading of *Emmanuel Appadocca*—often identified as the first novel published by an Afro-Caribbean creole—I gesture ahead to a point in Caribbean literary history when West Indian writers of the late nineteenth and early twentieth centuries carved out a body of localized prose fiction "written by the West Indian about the West Indian reality."[81]

Although most scholars identify later novelists such as Thomas MacDermot, Claude McKay, C. L. R. James, George Lamming, and many others as filling in literary gaps between traditional Eurocentric literary fare and "what had traditionally been ignored," I argue that there is another layer of complexity to the strictly transatlantic dialectic between (anti)colonial and metropolitan writers. As I aim to prove in the coming chapters, early creole novels by white colonists also represent attempts to sort through the tangled crossings of colonial subjects and ideologies. More importantly, only by acknowledging the traces of early creole novels' ideological and epistemological work in subsequent periods can we see our way through to a space from which we not only can read the West Indian novel but also more recent Caribbean fiction.

We can, in other words, read the texts of colonialism, anticolonialism, and postcolonialism with a clearer understanding of their relationship. Most importantly, rereading the early creole novelists—recognizing their work in (re)producing colonial culture of the Emancipation era and beyond—provides a way to come to terms with the pasts and presents, the facts and fictions, of their making.

1 Hortus Creolensis
Cultivating the Creole Novel

OF THE pre-Emancipation creole novels examined in this book, only one—*Montgomery; or, The West-Indian Adventurer*—was published in the Caribbean. Written by "a Gentleman Resident in the West-Indies" for "upwards of 25 years," *Montgomery* is set primarily in 1790s Jamaica, then the largest and most productive of Great Britain's Atlantic sugar colonies.[1] The novel, printed at the newspaper offices of the *Kingston Chronicle,* appeared in three volumes, the first two in 1812 and the third in 1813. According to Frank Cundall, the early twentieth-century scholar of anglophone Caribbean print history, the author of *Montgomery* was likely a "Scotchman," drawing from autobiographical experience to present a picture of white creole life that "may be taken as historically correct."[2] The novel is of interest, suggests Cundall, "as being from the pen of one who wrote sympathetically both of the manners and morals of the inhabitants of Jamaica, with the example of St. Domingo before his eyes, and of the question of the gradual abolition of slavery; and, often in the form of post-prandial conversation, gives views on the condition of life in Jamaica generally and forms on the whole a true account of life on the sugar estates and pens at that period."[3]

Cundall's brief assessment provides a useful springboard for my reading of the novel, as does Kamau Brathwaite's later description of *Montgomery* as an obviously partial documentation of Jamaican life due to the absence of any sustained treatment of black or brown people, enslaved or free. The latter do appear, as Brathwaite notes, but despite—or because of—the hero's ameliorist tendencies, "the fact remains that no slaves appear in the novel who are or can be viewed with more than 'pity and condescension.'"[4]

Read together, these commentaries—one emphasizing the novel's accuracy, the other its inadequacies as a realistic depiction of West Indian slave society—capture the conundrum white creole writers sought to resolve through the novel form. Tasked with demonstrating that dependence on institutionalized slavery did not diminish white colonists' potential as enlightened partners in achieving Britain's economic and cultural aims, *Montgomery*'s author must confront the paradoxes of the plantation system and white creoles' position in it. Of course, many West Indian texts take up this challenge, performing acts of "sweete negotiation" that Keith Sandiford identifies in his study of colonial narratives. As Sandiford's reading of works like Richard Ligon's *True and Exact History . . . of Barbadoes* and William Beckford's *Picturesque Tour of . . . Jamaica* illustrates, if white slaveholders hoped to refute charges of West Indian degeneracy, it was necessary for them to construct persuasive counter-narratives to emancipationist depictions of Atlantic slave societies.

Montgomery contributes to this project but stands apart from other colonial prose as the first *novel* to engage the connections between "literary production and the more secular business of sugar production."[5] As discussed in the introduction, white creole writers were drawn to the novel form as a promising tool to carry out the aesthetic and sociopolitical labor required to overcome what most white West Indians viewed as antislavery propaganda. More specifically, *Montgomery*'s author looks to the tropes and conventions of the sentimental novel—popularized decades earlier by writers like Samuel Richardson, Sarah Fielding, Henry Mackenzie, Sarah Scott, and Laurence Sterne—to construct a Jamaican-born man of feeling, a protagonist whose sympathetic and exemplary character is tried and proved by his West Indian adventures.

As this chapter demonstrates, however, the very conditions that give rise to *Montgomery*—its situatedness in Jamaica, its status as a Caribbean artifact penned by a long-term resident and printed by a colonial press devoted to shoring up slave-owner interests—pose particular, site-specific problems for the author's construction of creole sentimentality. Simultaneously bound by the novel's formal demands to draw scenes and characters "as nearly after life as possible" (which, the author insists, "ought to be the case in every performance of this sort") and to provide moral instruction to West Indian readers by stimulating "a love and emulation" of "whatever [is] amiable and praiseworthy in human nature,"[6] *Montgomery* must accommodate the uneasy relationship between West Indian processes of cultivation and enculturation, between the hero's ambitions as a prospective West Indian planter and his and the author's work as sentimental cultivators of creole morality.

The terms of this negotiation, I argue, were determined by conceptions of culture and civilization taking shape over the course of the long eighteenth century. As Raymond Williams reminds us, prior to the dominance of a globalizing modernity and its concomitant -isms (colonialism, capitalism, imperialism), the term "culture" most typically functioned as a "noun of process," the "culture *of* something—crops, animals, minds."[7] Coincident with the rise of English nationalism and expansion into the Americas, the term assumed a host of "new and elusive meanings," variously articulated as "'the arts', as 'a system of meanings and values', or as a 'whole way of life'" associated with a particular "civilized" population.[8] In the anglophone Caribbean these strands of meaning proved inextricable from one another. As *Montgomery* reveals through its depiction of the Plantation—capitalized to indicate, as Antonio Benítez-Rojo puts it, "not just the presence of plantations but also the type of society that results from their use and abuse"[9]—*agri*culture and culture-building were performed simultaneously, in conjunction with and dependent on each other.

Throughout this chapter, I present *Montgomery* as a case study of the dialectical workings of these processes, as a dramatization of tensions produced by their interdependence. Such a reading demands close scrutiny of the novel's West Indian setting as place and space, a locale comprising material and ideological sites where culture operates as noun of process (the large-scale cultivation of export crops by enslaved workers) and, for white creoles, as overarching sign of polite and enlightened planter society. More often than not, however, the novel's representations of Jamaican scenes and characters and the hero's sentimental responses to them expose the transformative violence endemic to the Plantation's agricultural/cultural operations.

Such violence underwrites multiple scenes depicting the hero's shifting position in Jamaican society, whether detailing his experiences working as a low-level employee on a large sugar estate, wandering in solitude through charming tropical scenery, or weeding a flower garden to demonstrate his devotion to the creole heiress he woos and marries. Such scenes, which I discuss more fully below, not only adhere to the demands of novelistic realism by reproducing the quotidian violence enabling the Plantation's transformation of land and people on its behalf; they also expose the discursive violence required to wrest Henry Montgomery's West Indian adventures into sentimental shape.

The instances of day-to-day and systemic, of material and aesthetic violence in the novel are staged most often on sites devoted to West Indian cultivation—of land, of men, of manners, and of romance. Before turning to the novel's treatment of creole place, though, I want to look at another, extratextual but absolutely central site of cultivation: *Montgomery*'s place of publication, the printing offices of the *Kingston Chronicle*. At the time of *Montgomery*'s appearance, the *Kingston Chronicle* was under the editorship of Andrew Lunan, brother of John Lunan, editor of another of Jamaica's daily newspapers, the *St. Jago de la Vega Gazette* in Spanish Town, and author of *Hortus Jamaicensis*, the botanical compendium that gives this chapter its title. The *Kingston Chronicle* was supported by a network (often familial as in the case of the Lunan brothers) of printers, editors, booksellers, and contributors affiliated with or members of Jamaica's slaveholding elite.[10] Like other regional arms of the colonial press, Jamaica's print industry was central to the production and dissemination of local "knowledge," its material output—from daily newspapers like the *Chronicle*, to the Proceedings of Jamaica's House of Assembly, to *Hortus Jamaicensis*, to the first Jamaican novel—shaped and defined colonial life in various ways. In undertaking their work of cultural dissemination, these printing businesses operate as "site[s] of authority" and sites of cultivation. Taken together, they perform multiple roles, as Julie Codell observes of other colonial presses: "[a]gent of change, of hegemony, of resistance, and of many other inflected ideologies and opinions in between." The press, she continues, "voiced many colonial experiences to and from readers who inhabited a real and a virtual Empire 'at home' and 'abroad.'"[11] My reading of the Jamaican press in relation to *Montgomery* emphasizes the anxieties underlying iterations of the real and virtual, and explores how those tensions affected the press's production of agricultural and cultural knowledge.

After situating *Montgomery* in the context of Jamaican print culture, I turn to the novel itself. Here, too, constructions of the real and the virtual appear as part of the novel's formal structure: realistic descriptions are woven into the West Indian narrative at the same time its plot unfolds through a discursive mode privileging white sensibility and refinement. In this, *Montgomery* can also be read as a site of cultivation, a self-consciously didactic text given over to the inculcation of sentimental virtues among its West Indian readers. *Montgomery*'s author repeatedly turns to the conventions and literary tropes associated with sentimental culture, from spectacles of suffering and sympathy to scenes of the pathetic and the picturesque. In the end, however, the novel's textual (re)production of physical settings where those spectacles and scenes play out—whether on the estates and pens where agricultural activity is paramount, or in the beautiful-terrible wilderness of the Jamaican bush—makes it clear that the violence of the Plantation is unavoidable, ever-present.

As importantly, these passages demonstrate that violence is indispensable for the novel's sentimental didacticism. Without it, Henry Montgomery's exemplary sensibility would have nothing against which to define itself. The textual representations of Montgomery as he bears witness, both seeing and testifying to the violence inflicted on enslaved people, are transformed by his sympathetic responsiveness into displays of white West Indian sensibility—images to counter constructions of white *in*sensibility that featured so prominently in antislavery rhetoric. Thus, even as the novelist incorporates instances of brutality as realistic elements of West Indian life, they create the conditions that give rise to the hero's virtues; displays of these virtues in turn legitimize the novel's claim of improving creole customs and manners. *Montgomery*, in other words, emplots the transformative violence necessary to the ideological work of the sentimental creole narrative. In so doing, this first Caribbean novel lays a foundation on which subsequent creole novelists will write through the problem-space—that "ensemble of questions and answers around which a horizon of identifiable stakes (conceptual as well as ideological-political stakes) hangs"—of Emancipation-era colonial fictions.[12]

Printed for the Proprietors

Montgomery, as mentioned above, is arguably the first novel composed and printed in the anglophone Caribbean,[13] appearing alongside a variety of materials offered by the *Kingston Chronicle*'s proprietors for the edification and entertainment of white West Indians.[14] In addition to the main work of putting out a daily newspaper, for example, the *Kingston Chronicle* offices published works such as John Rippingham's *Jamaica Considered in Its Present State, Political, Financial, and Philosophical* (1817); Alexander Campbell's *Sermon Preached in the Parish Church of St. Catherine's, Jamaica* (1819); two scientific treatises by the Jamaican apothecary Alexander Watt, *New Theory of Optics* and *New Theory of Physical Astronomy* (both appearing in 1825); and the *Proceedings of the Society for the Encouragement of Horticulture and Agriculture, and the Arts Connected with Them in Jamaica* (1825).[15] The wide range of material suggested by this partial catalog provides insights into both Jamaican colonial life and pre-Emancipation social relations: Lunan and the authors publishing with him are held up as representatives of enlightenment rationality and arbiters of creole morality. They were clergymen, council members, planters, and professionals: a "Society of Gentlemen."[16] The fact that their works appeared in print (often by subscription) reinforced these claims, making them "real" by providing documentary evidence that their sense of white creole entitlement and their efforts to institutionalize white privilege were justified.

The push by white creoles to (re)define themselves via a local print industry was crucial if they were to succeed in validating their society as enlightened and progressive. By the first decades of the nineteenth century, for example, resident and absentee planters were quick to describe slavery as a "cruel, and apparently unnatural system."[17] That description, however, was nearly always accompanied by the insistence, backed by self-declared knowledge of the actualities of West Indian life, that a "complication of difficulties" mitigated against general emancipation.[18] Aside from arguments warning of economic ruin and lost colonies, punctuated by obligatory allusions to the recently declared Republic of Haiti, white planters and their allies presented readers with a central and indisputable "fact" of their own manufacture: enslaved people were incapable of understanding and undertaking the responsibilities of "freedom"; they remained "altogether ignorant of the modes of civilized life"—despite having "a civilized race" (the planters themselves) "always in view."[19]

The colonial press played a key role in the (re)production of these so-called facts in its fight against Emancipation. An active site of cultivation, it was, as Codell observes, dedicated to the building of "an imaginary empire, at the same time that its nature was assumed by readers to be the 'real,' a transmitter of 'true' events."[20] The Kingston press responsible for the local production of imagined and real in pre-Emancipation Jamaica and of *Montgomery,* transmitted two seemingly disparate but ultimately complementary kinds of knowledge: practical instructions for resident planters and white estate employees desirous of improving the productivity of their land and labor force, and samples of enlightened good taste presented for readers wishing to improve their moral and aesthetic sensibilities.

The contents of the *Jamaica Magazine*—a miscellany published by the *Kingston Chronicle* offices from 1812 to 1813—provides a representative illustration of the press's double duty.[21] Edited by Andrew Lunan, the *Jamaica Magazine* offered readers a variety of material, as its title page attests (see fig. 4).[22] Alongside extracts from British and European sources, news of "Discoveries and Inventions in Science and the Arts" and ladies' fashion reports from the metropole, Jamaican readers found items that "possessed the natural advantage of local interest on many colonial topics,"[23] including planting advice to and from proprietors and estate overseers, "Principal Occurrences in the Island" (marriages, deaths, descriptions of earthquakes and violent storms, horse-racing results, shipping

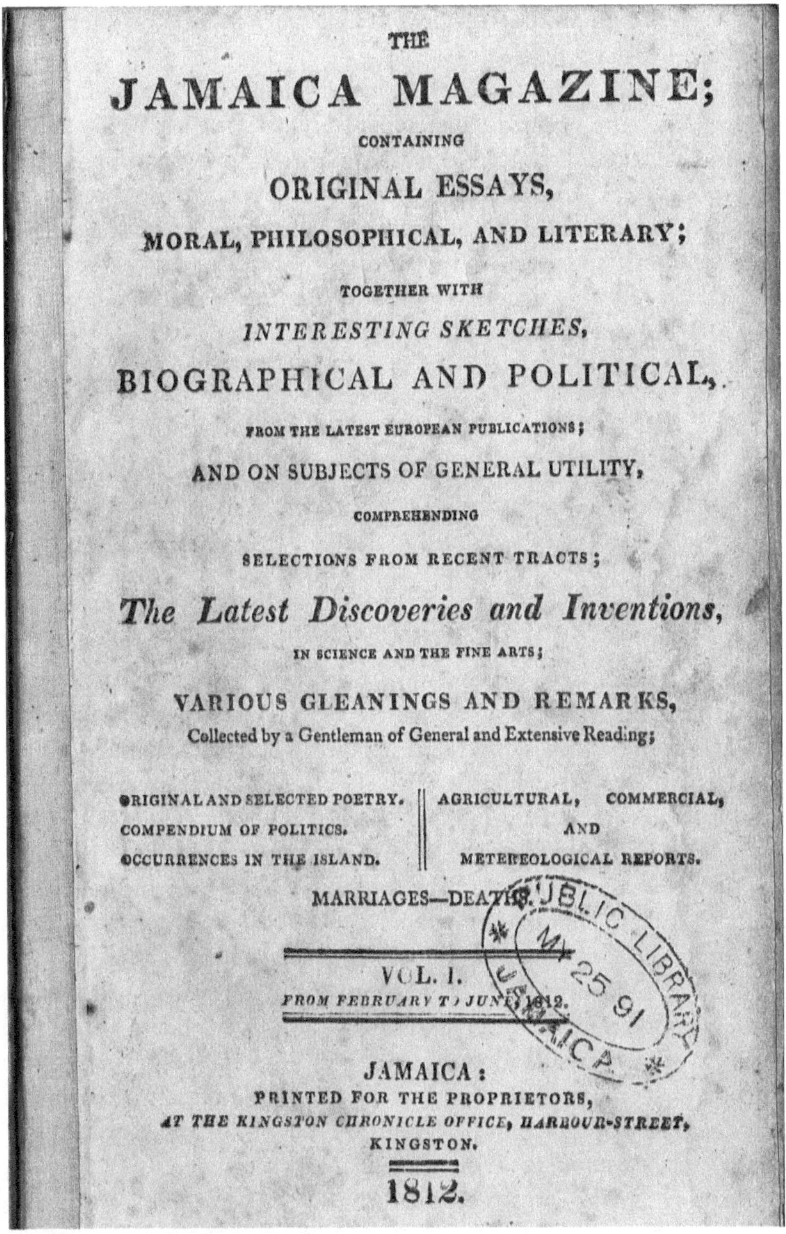

THE JAMAICA MAGAZINE;

CONTAINING

ORIGINAL ESSAYS,

MORAL, PHILOSOPHICAL, AND LITERARY;

TOGETHER WITH

INTERESTING SKETCHES,

BIOGRAPHICAL AND POLITICAL,

FROM THE LATEST EUROPEAN PUBLICATIONS;

AND ON SUBJECTS OF GENERAL UTILITY,

COMPREHENDING

SELECTIONS FROM RECENT TRACTS;

The Latest Discoveries and Inventions,

IN SCIENCE AND THE FINE ARTS;

VARIOUS GLEANINGS AND REMARKS,

Collected by a Gentleman of General and Extensive Reading;

ORIGINAL AND SELECTED POETRY.	AGRICULTURAL, COMMERCIAL,
COMPENDIUM OF POLITICS.	AND
OCCURRENCES IN THE ISLAND.	METEREOLOGICAL REPORTS.

MARRIAGES—DEATHS.

VOL. I.
FROM FEBRUARY TO JUNE 1812.

JAMAICA:
PRINTED FOR THE PROPRIETORS,
AT THE KINGSTON CHRONICLE OFFICE, HARBOUR-STREET,
KINGSTON.

1812.

FIGURE 4. Title page of *Jamaica Magazine*, 1812. The *Jamaica Magazine*, like *Montgomery*, was published at the offices of the *Kingston Chronicle*. (Courtesy of the National Library of Jamaica)

news), and "Original Communications" like poetry and other literary fare composed by island residents.[24]

Whether locally produced or "gleaned" from the "latest European publications," the magazine's contents were presented to show that despite the physical distance from Great Britain, proprietors—of news offices, of estates, and of human beings—appreciated the same virtues lauded in the metropole. White creoles, in short, were not the degenerates that abolitionists painted. As the *Jamaica Quarterly Journal, and Literary Gazette*—another miscellany produced by the *Chronicle* offices from 1818 to 1819—proclaimed on the title page of each issue:

> While the Manners, while the Arts,
> Which mould a Nation's soul,
> Still cling around our hearts,
> Between let Oceans roll:
> Yet still from either beach
> The voice of blood shall reach
> More audible than speech
>   "WE ARE ONE."[25]

The transatlantic bonds celebrated here assume an ironic cast, of course, when read against complaints of metropolitan interference in West Indian affairs. In some instances, these complaints were articulated in calls for independence that invoked the North American colonies' successful break from British governance. Most typically, indictments against metropolitan "interference and menace" were provoked by calls for "the milder treatment toward the negroes" by "persons and writers in the mother-country," indictments that circulated via the machinery of the colonial press and filled the pages of both the magazine and the journal.[26]

As David Lambert argues, "the controversy over slavery was fundamentally bound up with the contested articulation of white colonial identities between colony and metropole."[27] Very often this contest was cast in terms of West Indian degeneracy, of the moral dissolution of Europeans residing in the tropics and their creole descendants. From Charles Leslie's *New History of Jamaica* (1740), to J. B. Moreton's *West India Customs and Manners* (1793), from the many "Johnny New-Come" prints, to Lady Nugent's journal, numerous West Indian commentaries fulminated against creole depravity.[28] The primary readership of these works was located in the metropole; they were printed and circulated in cities like London, Edinburgh, and Glasgow that, although they contained sizable communities sympathetic to the colonial cause, were home to fewer readers possessing firsthand experience of West Indian life. In contrast, the Jamaican printers, editors, and booksellers—on-site purveyors and defenders of white creole culture—operated at a local level, engaged in efforts to combat the negative images of creole society.

Andrew Lunan's Harbour Street offices, where the *Kingston Chronicle,* the *Jamaica Magazine,* and *Montgomery* were printed, provides a case in point. Numerous other printeries and mercantile businesses as well as the courthouse and the customs house were located on Harbour Street, one of Kingston's principal thoroughfares—a site where creole culture was performed on a daily basis. James Hakewill's *View of Harbour Street* presents a still-shot of this performance (see fig. 5).[29] One of only two images of West Indian urban life in Hakewill's *Picturesque Tour of the Island of Jamaica* (1825), this particular view appears distinct from the artist's renderings of Jamaica's tropical scenery and orderly sugar estates. But, just as Hakewill's picturesque images of waving cane, rusticated bondspeople, and stately great houses obscure the day-to-day operations of estate life—a point I develop more fully below—the Harbour Street scene reveals little of urban contributions to the Plantation's work. Hakewill's letterpress, for example, identifies Harty's Tavern on the right side of Harbour Street as a licensed "public entertainment." The nature of its business, writes Hakewill, is signaled by the flag flying above it, dominating the center of the image. But other business activities were conducted at Harty's, including the sale of enslaved people. Routinely referenced in advertisements in newspapers like the *Jamaica Royal Gazette*—whose offices were also on Harbour Street—Harty's was a well-known meeting point where prospective buyers and sellers congregated, before or after crossing Harbour Street to gather news from the Commercial News-Rooms, or to purchase a book from Lunan's shop, or to visit the Sussex Hall Freemasons lodge, also located on Harbour Street.[30]

Harbour Street, in other words, represents a nexus, a site where colonial subjects converged to act out the business of the Plantation. And even though Hakewill doesn't mention Harbour Street as a hub of the local print industry—the place where printers, newsagents, booksellers, and editors like Lunan, William Smart, George Strupar, Frank Treadway, William and Alexander Aikman (father and son), and the De Cordova brothers worked[31]—the material produced there was part of the plantation machinery, shaping daily life just as surely as the merchants, planters, army personnel, and enslaved people who appear in the Kingston streetscape. As for the *Kingston Chronicle* proprietors, their role in producing two miscellanies and the first novel in the anglophone Caribbean in such

FIGURE 5. "Harbour Street, Kingston," from James Hakewill's *A Picturesque Tour of the Island of Jamaica from Drawings Made in the Years 1820 and 1821,* 1825. (Courtesy of the National Library of Jamaica)

a short time suggests that they and their Harbour Street neighbors were working with a sense of common purpose, manufacturing and maintaining a textual-colonial order in the form of news, government documents, and essays on plantation management, alongside evidence of an "elegant literary taste" that they considered "one of the most infallible signs of the progress of civilization and polished manners among a people."[32]

Given the West Indian context and the imperative to simultaneously naturalize and formalize the relationship between white creole culture and agriculture, to nurture an aesthetic sensibility compatible with its origins in plantation production, the *Jamaica Magazine* editors relied on an apt metaphor. The miscellany's varied contents—"composed of something suited to every taste"—are presented to readers in the inaugural issue as "an irregularly laid out garden"; "mingled promiscuously, and blooming without order or arrangement," its display of literary blossoms encompasses "the fairest and sweetest which the taste and industry of the editors (or, if the reader pleases, . . . *gardeners*), can cull from the wider *plantations* to which they have access."[33] Here the explicit connection between *gardener* and *plantations* marked by the editors' typographical underscoring reveals the broader implications of their wordplay. Just as John Lunan addresses his Jamaican botany *Hortus Jamaicensis* to an "imagined community" of (self-identified) refined planters whose "leisure time" and daily business can be yoked to the "agreeable study" of botanical science—thereby raising a "superstructure" testifying to planters' "good taste and discrimination"—the magazine figures the enchanting disorder of Jamaica's tropical landscape in its cultural labor of imposing order and discipline on the Plantation.[34] Read together, such discursive moves constitute exercises in power, a demonstration of the processes by which the island's self-proclaimed literary elite work to reimagine the Jamaican landscape, "to reconstruct history and reconceive Caribbean subjectivity." The attempt, however, also reveals "multiple, intertwined knots of conflict" that bind nature and culture together and threaten to destabilize the magazine's ideological project.[35]

One such knot of conflict appears in the *Jamaica Magazine*'s "Observer" column, a regular feature of the miscellany whose author dedicates himself to promoting signs of civilization and good taste on behalf of the proprietors. The Observer routinely invokes the sentimental virtues lauded in didactic novels and periodicals of eighteenth-century Britain—fitted, of course, for the magazine's creole audience.[36] The Observer's commentaries—praise for the virtuous conduct of a coffee planter's daughter, denunciations of white colonists who fail to keep the Sabbath, for example—demonstrate an awareness that whereas some of his fellow creoles do not need instruction per se, many others could benefit from a course in moral improvement. A "Gentleman of General and Extensive Reading," The Observer routinely draws on his familiarity with sentimental culture and conventions, presenting readers with scenarios designed to address long-held and widely circulated assumptions about creole degeneracy. Like *Montgomery*'s author, The Observer seems determined to confront the question that is clearly spelled out in the novel: Is "the prevalence of vicious manners . . . really so universal in the West Indies . . . as to endanger the morals of every young man who went thither?"[37]

As suggested by the expansive literature devoted to assessing the West Indian character, degeneracy seemed a foregone conclusion. Even commentators from the colonies and those sympathetic to the colonial cause routinely condemned the moral laxity of white creoles, as when planter-historian Edward Long condemns his fellow proprietors for their devotion to black and brown mistresses, or when J. B. Moreton echoes Long's criticisms in his *West India Customs and Manners*, a work I discuss more fully below.

The Observer's response to this fraught question takes the form of an epistolary exchange between him and "Juvenis," a young Scotsman newly arrived on the island. Juvenis, according to the "letter" shared by The Observer with his readers, is the son of respectable parents who, despite their distressed circumstances, have provided him with a liberal education. Given the lack of opportunity in Great Britain, Juvenis has come to Jamaica hoping to improve his fortunes. Newly employed as a "sub-BOOK KEEPER" on a large sugar estate, [38] Juvenis is confronted with scenes of dissipation and excess, tormented by the profligacy of his fellow whites. "At first," he writes,

> I wished to disburthen my heart to them with an undisguised simplicity:—they would listen to my story with a pretended sympathy, and then burst into a loud laugh, and endeavour to turn all I had said into ridicule. . . . [I]f I felt an involuntary commiseration at beholding the scenes of wretchedness and suffering which occasionally presented themselves to my view, I was treated with scorn and contempt—was called fool, JOHNNY NEWCOME, &c. and was told, "that I would KNOW A LITTLE BETTER by and bye."[39]

Unfolding his "unfortunate case" to The Observer, Juvenis hopes to receive encouragement, or at least evidence of "that sympathy which I know not elsewhere, in this region, to look for."[40]

Despite the young man's pointed appeal and The Observer's claim that he "cannot but sympathize with Juvenis," the reply is brief and to the point. Ignoring Juvenis's reference to "scenes of wretchedness and suffering" that provoke his commiseration for the enslaved, The Observer narrows his response to engage questions of individual character and agency. Whatever situation a young man finds himself in, The Observer insists, he should (if honorable) be able to maintain that character, regardless of the actions of others. Nor, The Observer continues, should Juvenis allow "partial views of human nature" to "inspire general prejudices and distrusts." In short order, The Observer advises Juvenis to pursue another line of work, one more "congenial to his talents, his inclinations, and his feelings."[41]

The Observer's one-paragraph reply to Juvenis—followed immediately by advice on "the most effective mode of destroying the red ant, or preventing them having access to bee hives"[42]—carries more than a suggestion of impatience. Possibly a strategy to minimize the discomfiting implications of Juvenis's distress, the perfunctory reply offered by The Observer echoes the derisory advice of the young man's peers—that he will "KNOW A LITTLE BETTER by and bye." Certainly The Observer's dismissal of Juvenis seems at odds with the *Jamaica Magazine*'s mission to cultivate delicacy and refinement, to encourage creole readers to fulfill the "duties of morality" routinely put forth in the magazine's pages.

Despite the brevity of Juvenis's appearance in The Observer's column, the circulation in the West Indian press of a young man whose sentimental make-up alienates him from the work of the Plantation points to Juvenis's literary kinship with *Montgomery*'s Jamaican-born protagonist: both are educated as "gentlemen," both make an Atlantic crossing to Jamaica from Scotland to pursue a career in planting; both are presented as models of a male sensibility that alienates them from other participants of the plantation economy. Both characters, moreover, come into public view in 1812; both emerge from Lunan's *Kingston Chronicle* offices; and both speak to the importance of local experiences that simultaneously define creole culture and civilization and threaten to impede its inculcation.

Indeed, even though it's uncertain which character appeared first, it's tempting to read Juvenis as an embryonic Montgomery, The Observer column a rehearsal for the novel's fuller treatment of the contest between virtue and vice, a struggle often presented as the defining feature of white West Indian experience. Whether or not Juvenis is a prototype of *Montgomery*'s creole man of feeling, the similarity of their circumstances highlights the shared cultural work of the Jamaican miscellany and the novel. Both publications are complex cultural artifacts rather than simple reproductions of contents manufactured in Britain and Europe in the case of the *Jamaica Magazine,* or simply an imitation of British sentimental fiction in the case of *Montgomery.* Both protagonists—unlike West Indian characters appearing in metropolitan narratives—present the difficulties faced by the sensible white man as real, the act of resisting the expected transformation of virtue to vice as laudable. But whereas Juvenis's story is abbreviated—he doesn't appear in subsequent issues of the magazine—Montgomery's trials are displayed on the much larger stage of a novel, embellished by a full complement of sentimental conventions.

These conventions are drawn from a half-century-old trove of British sentimental fictions, of course. But even as *Montgomery*'s author lays bare the novel's debt to British literature of sensibility, the preface emphasizes "the novelty of such a work." Unlike the metropolitan productions that preceded it, *Montgomery* features "West-India scenes and West-India characters"; its author directly addresses readers who are "acquainted with, or resident in, that part of the world." Such a pointed invitation for West Indian readers to derive "some benefit, in a moral point of view" from the novel, to engage in efforts to "ameliorate manners, and exalt and do justice to whatever [is] amiable and praiseworthy" in human nature reiterates the interplay between the specific setting of Jamaica and the cultivation of creole sentiment.[43] The novel's validation of the polite and the amiable, of the "estimable qualities of the heart," in other words, corresponds to the sympathy that Juvenis seeks from The Observer—but that The Observer fails to provide. *Montgomery* fills the sympathetic void.

Improving the Improver

In 1790, right around the time that *Montgomery*'s author transports his hero from Scotland to the island of his birth to pursue "the planting line," J. B. Moreton published *West India Customs and Manners* in London. Proffering advice to a young man preparing to leave Great Britain for Jamaica, Moreton assures his addressee that the information contained in *Customs and Manners* is based on his personal experiences as a bookkeeper on an estate in the Jamaican parish of Clarendon. In addition to listing the symptoms of yellow fever, advising against swimming in shark-infested waters, and delineating the malpractices of medical quacks, Moreton provides a description of the white residents the young man will encounter on the island. White creoles, explains Moreton, are well-known for their "contrarious" characters. They are "open-hearted, generous, kind and hospitable to excess," but also "proud, vain, . . . lazy, dull, and indolent, . . . and volatile as air where drinking, whoring, gaming, or any kind of dissipation invites."[44]

The adjectives Moreton deploys to summarize the white creole character are found in countless commentaries published in the metropole, as discussed in my introduction. But Moreton's critique of white West Indians also reveals the "contrarious" nature of his own dispositions, particularly when he describes what was considered the most troubling evidence of creole depravity, the sexual relationships between white men and women of color. "It's quite usual," he informs his readers, "for a Creole gentleman after dinner to send to the field for one of his favourite wenches, who is instantly hurried home and conveyed to his chamber, . . . piping hot and drowned with perspiration, in which condition he enjoys the savoury object; after which . . . she returns to labour till night: thus he takes one almost daily in rotation, and roves with as much ease and dignity as a plenipotentiary through raptures of delight."[45]

Here it's difficult to determine which stereotyped character is the real object of Moreton's ridicule, the so-called creole gentleman or the enslaved woman who is the object of his desire. But even as Moreton denounces the sexual predilections of white creoles—the most worrisome sign of what he calls their "negrofied" characters—he attaches no such significance to the sexual behavior of temporary visitors to Jamaica, himself included.

Advising the prospective emigrant about "unlawful amours," he acknowledges that in spite of personal "fortitude and firmest resolutions," the young man is "frail flesh and blood" and will doubtless "have connections with the tender sex."[46] Such moral lapses on the part of the European, however, do not signal degeneracy, as in the case of the creole; rather these liaisons are temporary concessions to the torrid climate, which, Moreton explains, "excites desire, and makes men and women more amorous and lascivious" than in temperate zones.[47] Whereas Moreton condemns the creole for irrational and excessive libidinousness, the temporary resident receives gentle censure followed by advice on the best method of treating the venereal infection the young newcomer inevitably will contract. All the while expressing the dangers of becoming "naturalized to the country," Moreton guides his reader through the process of establishing liaisons with local women of color, from the initial step of attending a mulatto ball, to meeting and bedding "the finest girls in the island."[48] The women Moreton refers to are famous, he says, for preferring white men, a "fact" that makes them appropriate objects for "sport." "Mongrel wenches," he explains, are taught by their mothers from "their youth up . . . to be whores."[49] "When the ball . . . is over," he enthuses, a young man can escort her to his "lodging, and taste all the wanton and warm endearments she can yield before morning."[50] Again, Moreton claims to write from experience, proudly declaring, "I have spent many merry nights at such balls."[51]

Clearly, Moreton's descriptive account of West India customs and manners—part self-righteous screed against West Indian immorality and part guide for the adventurous sex tourist—is far different from *Montgomery*'s sentimental attempt to improve West India customs and manners. Devoting an entire novel to the task, *Montgomery*'s author points to numerous examples of good-hearted, morally upright creoles, from the patriarchal Mr. Goodwin, who encourages the white men in his employ to marry, to the humane and kind overseer Mr. Edwards, who tenderly nurses Montgomery through a bout of yellow fever. For those West Indians and Johnny Newcomes who do need reforming, the character of Henry Montgomery is offered up as a model for emulation.

Sentimental novels, of course, seldom feature immoral protagonists. But unlike earlier men of feeling like Sarah Fielding's David Simple or Henry Mackenzie's Harley, whose adventures take place in the familiarized context of Great Britain, the island-born Montgomery, having spent his childhood in Scotland, is bound for Jamaica. The anxieties peculiar to this colonial site, generated by descriptions like Moreton's, with its litany of temptations encountered by young white men crossing the line, the evils of slavery, and the degeneracy of the West Indian planters, are distilled in the novel's description of Montgomery as he nears the end of his Atlantic voyage. As Jamaica's physical setting looms larger, he asks a fellow passenger, a planter returning to the colony, to advise him on the issue. The planter's response is far from reassuring. After detailing a process of moral decline worthy of Moreton, he bluntly concludes: "[I]t is melancholy to think that an ingenuous and amiable youth ... possessed of a virtuous sensibility of heart, should become a martyr to gross and profligate habits. ... [H]ad I a son of this description," he concludes, "I would choose some other profession for him than the planting line."[52]

The author's displays of Montgomery's "virtuous sensibility," of course, are presented as evidence of the possibility of living a virtuous life—even after crossing the line to reside in Jamaica. In this respect, Montgomery follows a pattern established by another, much earlier man of feeling who travels to Jamaica to improve his fortunes, Sarah Scott's George Ellison. But whereas George Ellison is an "accidental" slave owner—an Englishman whose virtuous industry as a sugar and spice merchant secures his fortunes and his marriage to a creole widow in possession of a "considerable plantation, cultivated by a numerous race of slaves"[53]—Montgomery comes to Jamaica to learn the business of planting. He enters the estate system not as a wealthy proprietor, like Ellison, but as a junior bookkeeper, the lowest position that white men occupied in the plantation hierarchy.

As the scenes depicting the early days of Montgomery's employment unfold, his naivety about the place he occupies in this hierarchy becomes clear, particularly in the scenes set on Retreat Estate, the large property where he first works. He soon learns that the differences between his expectations and the duties assigned to him are irreconcilable, a lesson he communicates to Crabfield, the insensitive white overseer who manages Retreat. As Montgomery tries to explain to Crabfield, the business he wants to learn is "that of a husbandman, or farmer."[54] As such, Montgomery wants to follow "agricultural pursuits," not perform the menial offices assigned to him by Crabfield. Certainly "reckoning and keeping account of the poultry, sheep, and hogs, attending the plantain walks and other provision grounds,"[55] though part of the actual routines assigned to estate bookkeepers, don't conform to Mongomery's notions of husbandry, shaped as they are by the discourse of improvement that rationalized Britain's western expansion from its beginnings.

As Richard Drayton points out, throughout the early modern period, husbandry—the "Mother of all other Trades and Scientificall Industries"[56]—was perceived as comparable to religion in its capacity to improve, a belief obviously shared by the Cromwellian Walter Blith, who noted in his *The English Improver* (1649) that "God was the first and original Husbandman."[57] But the ennobling conceptions of husbandry Montgomery carries with him to the New World are profoundly different from what he finds on Retreat. His initial experiences of the plantation, its operations, and organization are marked by a growing awareness that the Plantation system is, to use Sidney Mintz's description, "unlike anything known in mainland Europe."[58] Contrary to the romantic images Montgomery entertains about being a gentleman farmer, his discoveries on Retreat—the "specialization by skill and jobs, and the division of labor by age, gender, and condition into crews, shifts, and 'gangs'"[59]—are rendered even more distressing by the *discipline* required to maintain the extractive agro-industrial complex designed around the cultivation and export of sugar. This discipline, Mintz observes, "was probably its first essential feature."[60]

Set against this backdrop, much of *Montgomery*'s drama revolves around the title character's efforts to reconcile the irreconcilable: his sensibility to the Plantation's discipline and the violence that attends it. Unlike colonial productions that set out to obscure colonial violence by transforming the plantation machine from "an engine of impoverishment and devastation" to "an organic agent of enrichment," *Montgomery* confronts it head on in a scene displaying the brutal punishment of an enslaved man who crosses Montgomery's path. Although the scene's focus on the "cruel treatment of the slaves" isn't unique in locally produced fiction (as shown in Juvenis's allusion), it appears more often in the work of antislavery activists than of writers sympathetic to the West Indian ruling classes like *Montgomery*'s author.[61] This particular passage, moreover, is marked by an aesthetic discourse—the "imperial" or "planter picturesque"—that typified colonial writing of the period.[62] But whereas most examples of the planter picturesque exhibit West Indian scenes as "an aesthetically determined setting which occludes the true historical relationship" between the land and landowning slaveholders,[63] *Montgomery*'s picturesque elements demonstrate the novelist's attempt to navigate the fault lines of that relationship.

As mentioned above, the novel's emphasis on the discrepancies between

Montgomery's expectations and the life he finds on Retreat generate the text's sense of dislocation. Like Juvenis in the *Jamaica Magazine,* Montgomery's character is immersed in "scenes at which his heart revolted," his sympathetic nature depicted as one constrained by "the society of beings whom he could not love."[64] The only relief the novelist affords his hero comes when he performs the "most pleasant" of his bookkeeping duties: "overlooking . . . the plantain walks." This task, we're told, provides Montgomery the opportunity to engage the Jamaican landscape through the (to him) familiar lens of the picturesque. Moving through "various charming scenery," Montgomery's heart is filled "with a pure but pensive delight."[65] The waving "clusters of the bamboo cane," the "lofty trees," along with the "murmurs of [a] cascading stream" and "the cooing of . . . wild doves," provoke "sweet contemplations" that "spread a momentary gleam of happiness over [Montgomery's] soul."[66]

Montgomery's emotional reaction to such a setting, of course, signals his sensibility; the natural beauties of the plantain walk and the hero's appreciative response are artfully represented to trigger a similar response in the reader. More importantly, such artifice creates for Montgomery and the sensible reader a comforting distance from the brutalities of the slave-based plantation economy and the indignities the hero suffers on the estate as he works under Crabfield, whose very name suggests antipathy toward the idyllic beauty of the plantain walk. Immersed in its aestheticized (and anaesthetized) space, where the author places him "beneath . . . a beautiful orange tree" growing "near the brink of a murmuring waterfall,"[67] the figure of Montgomery operates, temporarily at least, as an ornament to the scene, much like the bookkeeper depicted in William Berryman's watercolor (see fig. 6).

But, as Brathwaite observes, even in such an idyll, the "reality of slavery will intrude."[68] Unlike Berryman's sketch, which remains a static and softened image of Jamaican estate life, the novel's subsequent passages reveal the undercurrents at work in representations of the plantain walk, the significance of that particular site for subjects integrated into the workings of the Plantation. Those subjects, including the novelist and the majority of *Montgomery*'s West Indian readers, would understand how the plantain walk figured into the machinery of the estate, how, from the earliest days of England's slave colonies, the need to cultivate food for enslaved laborers was acknowledged by planters, as was the necessity of allotting them the time "for the Culture of their own Plantations." These provision grounds typically included "a small Plantain Walk"[69] in recognition of the plantain's nutritional qualities and its reputation as "the best of all the

FIGURE 6. "Plantain Walk—Bookkeeper—Watchman and Hut—man with casks of water / greattoe [*sic*] in stirrup," William Berryman, ca. 1808–1816. Berryman produced numerous watercolors and sketches during the eight years he spent touring Jamaica; he died in England, however, before he could fulfill his ambition to publish a series of engravings of travels around the island. (Courtesy of the Library of Congress, Prints and Photographs Division)

Indian food for negroes," one that "makes them the most able to perform their labour."[70]

The well-maintained plantain walk, however, signals more than the planter's astute husbanding of an "excellent resource."[71] The plantain walk and provision grounds also function as discursive markers of plantocratic "civilization" and "culture," touted as a boon offered by planters to their enslaved workers. The credibility attached to such self-referential beneficence is suggested by the *Monthly Review*'s assessment of Grenadian planter Gordon Turnbull's *Letters to a Young Planter*, which notes the planters' "indulgence" in allowing the enslaved to cultivate their own food: the author, writes the reviewer, "particularly inculcates a mild, humane, and careful treatment of the slaves, not forgetting even the poor cattle. We are much pleased with this proof of his benevolent disposition."[72]

But the pleasure Montgomery finds in his favorite duty, itself rooted in his appreciation for the plantain walk's natural beauty, turns to pain when his "sweet contemplations" are interrupted by the appearance of "an object" entirely antithetical to his musings: "a wretched emaciated negro crawling along the ground, as if hardly able to support himself. He was covered with filth and rags, and had a number of frightful sores about him!"[73] Montgomery, "struck with horror," is momentarily paralyzed—as befits a man of feeling. But the inclusion of this character and the language conveying Montgomery's horrified response is not new to pre-Emancipation literature. Textual representations of the mutilated bodies of the enslaved are a common feature of antislavery and ameliorist writing of the long eighteenth century, from Aphra Behn's *Oroonoko* to Crevecoeur's Letter IX in *Letters from an American Farmer*, from William Blake's illustrations for John Stedman's *Narrative of a Five Years' Expedition, Against the Revolted Negroes of Surinam* to Robert Wedderburn's *Horrors of Slavery* and Mary Prince's *History*.

The description of Montgomery's encounter, however, is unusual because it is *not* part of an abolitionist work aimed at metropolitan audiences to showcase the barbarity of tyrannical slaveholders. Rather, it constitutes a key passage in a novel published in Kingston by a long-term white resident of Jamaica, affiliated with members of polite creole society like the resident proprietors and readers of the *Jamaica Magazine*.

The authority to perform the cultural work these white West Indians share—to insist on the one hand that print artifacts of white creole culture constitute evidence of an already achieved state of civilization and to acknowledge that the virtues associated with that culture must be taught and nurtured continuously through the discourse of improvement[74]—is based in large part on the novelist's insider status, his claims of intimacy with West Indian life, as discussed above. Certainly the hero's plantain walk encounter draws on this familiarity, the didactic power of the scene magnified by the author's ability to tap into the host of meanings that the setting would hold for West Indian readers.

But the persuasiveness of this encounter—its success in proving Montgomery's sensibility and (thus) the possibility that virtue can rise above the brutality of the "old," unameliorated system of slavery practiced by Crabfield—depends ultimately on the figurative labor performed by the anonymously rendered slave. Just as the success of the sugar estate required actual people to perform the material labor of planting, cultivating, harvesting, and processing the sugar cane. Indeed, in *Montgomery*'s plantain walk scene, the figure of the slave performs double duty: his lacerated body provides spectacular evidence that the process of civilizing white creoles is unfinished business, and it provides the occasion for the novel's hero to display the refined humanity necessary to forward that business to its teleological end.

The novel's exploitation of the image of the brutalized slave—the work it performs by emphasizing the negative example of those responsible for his "unhappy condition" (the "reality of slavery" that Brathwaite notes) and by showcasing the protagonist's virtuous sensibility—exacerbates the tensions introduced by an accompanying failure of picturesque imagery. In *Montgomery*, the startling encounter transforms the setting of the plantain walk from soothing idyll to a site/sight of horror. The violence of this transformation, moreover, demands a reconfiguration of West Indian space, a discursive shift from the seemingly benign planter picturesque to the perfunctory interrogatives of a judicial inquest: "Who do you belong to?" (A neighboring plantation.) "What brings you here?" (I've come to die.) "But, what made you leave home?" ("O! Massa, no take me up and send me home—let me dead here softly.").[75]

Called on to abandon a system of meanings that, for Montgomery and the sensible reader, has been destabilized by the man's appearance, the novel presents the exchange between the "emaciated negro" (the "witness") and Montgomery (the "judge") in forensic terms. In so doing, the cross-examination provides both verbal and physical testimony, as the slave answers Montgomery's queries and exhibits his "dreadfully lacerated" body marked with "severe wounds" from a cutlass. The man's body in particular presents troubling evidence—a visible record of the punishments inflicted on him—held up for Montgomery's judicious inspection.

Unsettled by what he sees, Montgomery presses his questions, asking why the overseer on his master's estate has flogged him so mercilessly, and why the watchman of Retreat Estate has so severely wounded him. Both punishments, the man tells Montgomery, were meted out because he was accused—wrongly, he insists—of theft: in the first instance, he was accused of cutting "grass belong to buckera for sell," ostensibly for his own profit; in the second of pilfering plantains to assuage, as the narrator translates the slave's account, "the imperious cravings of hunger."[76]

Montgomery's reactions, however, indicate the narrative's lack of concern over whether or not the man is a thief (i.e., the reliability of his *verbal* testimony). Rather, the dying fugitive's *body* of evidence demonstrates that an act of inhumanity has been committed (or at the least, sanctioned) by white men on the estate. Indeed, when Montgomery reports the incident to Crabfield, he does so in terms that assume the now-dead man's guilt, despite his having told Montgomery that the "watchman tell lie upon me": the novelist and his contemporary creole readers, in other words, are not called on to determine whether or not "a poor negro, . . . impelled perhaps by hunger, cuts a few canes, or pilfers a bunch of plantains," but to bemoan the "fact" that a white man has ordered such a brutal punishment.[77]

The crisis here of creole inhumanity appears in metropolitan abolitionist writing as well. But in *Montgomery,* as in other creole texts, it is magnified by the conditions that generate a particularly creole narrative. That is, despite the scene's sentimentalized, even formulaic language, it reveals the unsentimental actualities of daily life on the estates—simultaneously validating the narrative authority granted by the author's twenty-five years in Jamaica, and giving the lie to claims of West Indian benevolence. But even as the dying man's bodily text operates as the "realistic" occasion for a novelistic celebration of white sensibility, it exposes the picturesque aesthetic—an aesthetic more often than not held up as a hallmark of sentimental culture—as insufficient in the Jamaican setting.

This failure is articulated in no uncertain terms by the hero himself. "'God of mercies!'" he exclaims. "'What, alas! to an oppressed, degraded being like this is the perpetual spring which reigns in this genial climate?—what signifies the bounties of nature, the fertility of the soil, the numberless sylvan beauties scattered around, to one fettered by the chains of a cruel bondage? he is not permitted to enjoy them—to him they are but a blank—a dreary blank.'"[78] Montgomery's passionate outburst overturns, even negates the conventions of planter discourse that, as in *Hortus Jamaicensis,* transforms the Jamaican bush into a tropical cornucopia, overflowing with "the indescribable beauties of nature" and the "fruits of the wonderful vegetable treasures which the hand of the Almighty has so abundantly scattered around."[79]

But even as the encounter with the dying slave forces, as it were, Montgomery's (and the reader's) acknowledgment of the disjunctions between the beauty of Jamaica's landscape, the actualities of estate life, the picturesque aesthetic projected onto both, and on white creoles' participation in the plantation machine that dictates daily life for the enslaved who labor on it, the novel in no way sustains the critique. Rather, the consternation Montgomery displays confirms that the "planting line," at least as practiced on estates like Retreat—"lovely by the hand of nature, but made horrible to the sight by cruelty and tyranny"—is not for him, and that the cruelty and tyranny of the plantation system is most keenly felt by the creolized man of feeling.[80]

The novel's unself-consciously ironic insistence that Montgomery, not the enslaved people he encounters, suffers "the most degrading slavery" during his employment on Retreat Estate,[81] is only one expression of Montgomery's exemplary sensibility. Soon after the plantain walk scene, the novel's plot unfolds on another site of production as the novelist moves his hero away from the diurnal operations of the sugar estate and into scenes of creole romance and domesticity. This move is accompanied by Montgomery's vocational transformation: unfit for planting, he leaves Jamaica for a short period and returns an Anglican clergyman, chosen by the Bishop of London to use his experience of the West Indies to save creole souls. But even though descriptions of Montgomery's religious work contribute to the novel's display and inculcation of white West Indian morality, the project of reconceiving Caribbean subjectivity also requires a material foundation. In the next section I discuss the site where that foundation is laid: the ornamental tropical garden.

Montgomery's Garden of Love

The garden at the heart of Montgomery (and *Montgomery*) is located on Citron-Vale, the estate of Mr. Woodford, a West Indian proprietor whose daughter captures the hero's affections. This "little" garden, as befitting the novel's move into romance, is a far different site than the thousands of acres under cane that dominate so much of the Jamaican landscape, and Montgomery's first sight of it occurs under far different circumstances from those of his initial encounter with the plantation machine on Retreat. Strolling with the Woodford family on the grounds of Citron-Vale, Montgomery learns that Maria and her two sisters each have a "little flower garden."[82] Of the three "parterres" pointed out to him, Montgomery is drawn to Maria's. Montgomery's appreciation of the "choice and tasteful arrangement of flowers" in Maria's "little plat," of course, signals a shared sensibility of the kind featured in countless sentimental romances of the long eighteenth century and that anticipates the novel's epithalamic conclusion.

But the garden also allows the novel to shift the terms of Montgomery's relationship to the Jamaican landscape, to obscure the horrors of the plantain walk and the disciplinary regimes of Retreat Estate that previously defined it. Having liberated himself from the "degrading offices" he was compelled to perform under Crabfield's supervision, Montgomery assumes the role of a secret gardener, using the site of Maria's flower garden to express his devotion. Learning that Citron-Vale's gardener has been too busy to keep Maria's flower plot in order, Montgomery turns to the task, transplanting Jamaican wildflowers and tending the bed without Maria's knowledge:

> He assiduously employed the greater part of the day in plucking the weeds . . . , smoothing the earth, pruning the roses, myrtles, and other shrubs, and placing fresh mould about every plant in it. . . . He gently brought the wild and wandering . . . plants to embrace, cut off the old and useless twigs, and thus gave it neatness and shape. To complete his labour, Montgomery formed a little seat within this fragrant bower, of earth, covered with fresh sods of the Bahama grass. He then gave Caesar, the gardener, a piece of money, as a bribe not to tell that it was he who had done all this.[83]

The depiction of Montgomery's physical labor in this domesticated and domesticating scene sets him apart from more stereotypical West Indian adventurers, white men arriving in the colonies whose aim, as Bryan Edwards observed, is simply "to acquire a fortune" and who thus "consider a family an encumbrance" and hold marriage "in but little estimation."[84] Montgomery, on the other hand, values the sanctity of "virtuous love" (without which "a society would soon be little better than a horde of savages") and marriage (which is "absolutely necessary to the well-being of all civilized nations").[85] Marriage among white men, the novel insists, operates "as a curb to vice," capable of "soften[ing] the feelings and humaniz[ing] the manners" of men who otherwise would "sink into a . . . semi-barbarous state, through gross habits, and a want of that sweet intercourse with the amiable part of the other sex, which is so conducive to happiness and civilization."[86]

Not all white women on the island are "amiable" of course, and the novel, as do other descriptions of creole life, contains representations of "bad" white women—though the latter are not nearly so common as opportunistic black and brown women who "naturally" are determined to ensnare white men and usurp the legitimate reproductive labor that should be taking place in white families. Fortunately for Montgomery (and the white heroes of *Hamel, Marly, Warner Arundell, Old Port-Royal,* and *Creoleana*) there are among the island beauties angelic (white) creole women whose sensibility and sympathetic taste both provide a civilizing model for other creole women, and present a proper object of desire for the novel's protagonist; his inclination in turn provides instruction for white men whose illicit desires need rechanneling.[87]

In this, the tropes of sentimental romance deployed by *Montgomery*'s author signal the centrality of "obsessively 'correct' pairings disciplined by totalizing notions of color" that Deborah Wyrick identifies in nineteenth-century colonial prose.[88] Part of a much wider colonial project, one undertaken by colonial administrators in the metropole as well as in the colonies, this "white-on-white domesticity" was framed, as Ann Stoler describes it, "in opposition to more prevalent sorts of unions on which colonialisms thrived."[89] The marked distinction between the latter—what the novel describes as the "mohametan intercourse" engaged in by Crabfield and Montgomery's fellow bookkeepers on Retreat Estate—and Montgomery's "pure" love for the planter's white daughter clearly facilitates the mediation of the "discrepancies between prescription and practice" through its valorization of white endogamy as the desired norm of white creole familial society.[90]

As important as it is to recognize this norm as the teleological end of creole romance, it is equally important—at least in *Montgomery*—to acknowledge not only the disjuncture between prescription and practice, but also their interdependence. In other words, Montgomery's role as romantic hero (held up as a model for white men in the tropics to emulate) is predicated on displays of his sensibility; that display, in turn, sharpens rather than obscures the contrasting display of the insensibility of others. Without characters like Crabfield, whose vices include the repeated sexual exploitation of enslaved women, neither Montgomery's virtues nor the picture of white domesticity conjured by his romance with Maria can be represented as central pillars on which white creole culture and civilization rests.

Even though Montgomery's reworking of Maria's ornamental garden runs counter to the signs of white men's degeneracy, the literal and figurative/cultural labor staged in the "little plat" demonstrates the various subtle (and not so subtle) ways that the garden upholds the operations of the Plantation machine even as it appears to occlude it. Maria's flower garden is, after all, on the grounds of Citron-Vale, and is thus "placed in intimate and unsettling proximity to the plantation"; so situated, it becomes, as Nair describes such spaces, "not simply a private seat of nature, but a cultural and economic site with global impact."[91] When, for example, Montgomery usurps and "improves" the labor of Caesar, the slave tasked with maintaining the house grounds, Caesar's work is devalued, obscured by Montgomery's efforts. Just as earlier the novel subordinates the actual enslavement of Africans and African-descended creoles to emphasize Montgomery's figurative slavery under Crabfield, in the garden scene the privileging of Montgomery's labor over Caesar's—on a site that is at once the center of Citron-Vale and isolated from it by what is grown there and why—reveals "how the reconstitution of nature and imperialist normative practices has . . . material effects on human subjects."[92]

For Montgomery, the material effects of his gardening are quantifiable: when Maria discovers that he has secretly been improving the "little plat she called hers,"[93] she expresses delight at how lovely the garden has become under his tillage. The sexual overtones attached to such labor and such delight suggest that Montgomery's return on his sentimental investment will be sizable. Not only does the scene foreshadow the sexual and reproductive labor Maria will bring to the marriage, but also the money and property suggested by the beauties of Citron-Vale.

There is another laborer in Maria's garden, the man whose work—though temporarily replaced by that of Montgomery—is indispensable to the cultivation of white endogamy: Caesar. Caesar's significance is suggested by his presence in both garden scenes, at the beginning of the courtship narrative as described above, and at the novel's end, when the now-married couple returns to Citron-Vale for a farewell visit, one of the last scenes that takes place in Jamaica. After wandering the sites where they first met, pausing "to survey objects, and contemplate spots, familiar to remembrance," Montgomery and Maria reach the garden. Looking around, Montgomery's gaze focuses on a wildflower that he had plucked from the Jamaican "wilderness" and secretly transplanted into the flower plot because Maria had once admired it in the early days of their courtship. "It had grown tall, and spread considerably"; yet, Montgomery observes, it "was neatly pruned, and not a weed grew near it. An emotion of delight thrilled through the heart of Montgomery, while his eye rested on the fragrant object, and by an involuntary impulse he pressed his Maria to his bosom and kissed her!"[94]

The chaste kiss and exchange of tears that immediately follow—"messengers of the heart" that signal true and pure affection—emphasize the distinction between the illicit (and vicious) sexual excesses of Retreat Estate and the proper union of Montgomery and Maria's marriage. But the scene also underscores the role of Caesar, who appears before the couple, "with his hat in his hand," revealing that in Montgomery's absence he has assumed responsibility for the garden's well-kept appearance. His acts of improvement, as much as Montgomery's, have rendered the garden a fit stage for the display of virtuous white love.[95]

But the enslaved gardener's presence allows for more than the opportunity to reiterate the superiority of idealized, pure love over the sensuality of degenerate white men who have, through their illicit interracial relationships, renounced claims to civilization. It provides the occasion to reinforce the lines of racial difference rather than simply condemn the crossing of them. As a black slave, Caesar is incapable, the narrator explains, of appreciating the purity on display before him. Love in "the African breast"—"if it may be so called"—is uncontrolled and unregulated.[96] It "bursts forth at once, like a violent blaze, impatient of restraint, and kindling into new fervour" at the sight of the object that inspires it: "The delicacies, the restraints, the timidity, the awe, the respect, which, [sanguine] love excites in the virtuous and cultivated mind are but little known" to the "savages" whose love is little more than sensual appetite, without sentiment, or "dignity, and with but little of esteem or of friendship."[97]

The emotional inability to experience refined attachment or "virtuous love" is invoked here as part of the wider rationale against emancipation on the one hand, and arguments for the need to work hard at instilling virtue among the white population on the other. But without Caesar's *inability* to appreciate the kind of love Montgomery and Maria display, the white couple's sensibility would not be evident; "sanguine love" needs other-love to define itself against. Caesar's appearance and labor is necessary to the performance of idealized white endogamy, both in terms of the literal work he performs in Maria's flower garden and the cultural work that he contributes to as the foil to Montgomery's creole man of feeling. In this, Caesar occupies a position very much like the nameless slave of the plantain walk who provokes Montgomery's emotional, sensible, humanitarian response, clear signal of his own civilized character.

54 *Hortus Creolensis*

Conclusion: "A March in the Woods"

As discussed above, *Montgomery*'s attempt to offer up a model of white creole civilization through various (and ongoing) transformative acts of cultivation depends on the literal and figurative exploitation of laboring black subjects. Caesar and the anonymous slave on Retreat Estate are clearly tied to (in a sense, tamed by) the plantation, whether constructed along the lines of the picturesque model recovered in scenes of Citron-Vale, or the supposedly anomalous countersite represented by Crabfield's Retreat. There is, however, another black presence invoked by *Montgomery*'s author, a presence, moreover, that threatens to undo the cultural labor performed by Caesar and the plantain walk slave: the Jamaican Maroons.

Montgomery's account of the Second Maroon War of 1795–96 occupies an interesting position within the narrative, a (momentary) suspension of the sentimental romance's progress. Convinced that Maria Woodford is beyond his reach and that his own sensibility renders him unfit for estate work, Montgomery prepares to "bid adieu to this *calling* [i.e., planting] for ever" and return to England.[98] At the moment of his departure, however, he is enlisted in the military campaign against "A Revolution" of the Trelawney Town Maroons. The account of the Maroon War relayed in the form of Montgomery's journal of an expedition into the island's interior, seems removed from scenes set on the estate and in Maria's garden. The journal entries are sometimes brusque, the prose unfolding more quickly than the rest of the novel. Even so, the hero's account of a "march into the woods" in pursuit of the Maroons recalls the picturesque treatments of earlier scenes. Passing through deep mountain woods, for example, Montgomery is moved to cite a passage from James Thomson's "Summer," an apt choice given that it forms part of a lengthy description of the exotic spoils of Britain's West Indian colonies.[99] But whereas Thomson celebrates British mastery over a mid-eighteenth-century colonial landscape, Montgomery's journal touches a different nerve. Even as Montgomery waxes poetic about what first appears like the "fit abode of peaceful solitude and contemplation," his journal entry suddenly turns to gothic mode, as he recounts the terror of white soldiers suddenly confronted with "the vestiges of savage warfare!"[100]

After moving through a "sylvan glade" recently occupied by the Maroons—as shown by their abandoned huts, "a few scattered patches of ground [that] seemed as if lately cleared and planted," and "heaps of ashes, where plantains, yams, &c. seemed lately to have been roasted"—

Montgomery's party enters "a den of death," a "dangerous defile, where a party of whites had already been defeated by a maroon ambush."[101]

Here the militia company looks with horror on "the unburied skeletons of the victims who had fallen, most of whose heads had been cut off and stuck on the stumps of trees. . . . Some of these, it [was] suspected, had been wounded, and fallen alive into the hands of the savages, who doubtless [caused] them to die a death of protracted tortures, attended by every horrible insult!"[102] The "terror and alarm" on the soldiers' faces, which Montgomery attributes "chiefly to the appaling [sic] spectacle . . . and the concomitant images it was calculated to conjure up" provide a stark contrast to the descriptions that precede it, including the attempt to assert British dominance over the Jamaican landscape through the recitation of Thomson's jingoistic poem.[103] Montgomery's immersion in a colonial landscape at once horrific and fascinating, grotesque and beautiful, in other words, emphasizes the distance between the metropolitan poet, extolling the products of colonial labor from a "safe" distance, and the novelist's hero, whose experience results in a macabre unraveling of Thomson's verse.

The "appaling spectacle" here recalls the spectacle of the mutilated slave on the plantain walk; both scenes describe the impact on the landscape of agricultural activity not explicitly related to monocrop production. But whereas cultivation of the plantain walk is sanctioned and regulated by slaveholders, touted as evidence of planters' humane treatment of the enslaved and a demonstration of their managerial efficiency, the cultivation practiced by the Maroons signals their independence from the plantation economy.[104] Perhaps more importantly, the difference generated by the presence/absence of black bodies in each scene tells its own story. The physical presence of the dying slave is central to the plantain walk scene, as discussed above, his mutilated body in plain sight. But although the skeletal remains of white soldiers certainly contribute to the spectacular display described in Montgomery's war journal, it is the *seeming absence* of the Maroons that generates the greatest anxiety. The Maroons, in other words, are there and not there. Mention of "lately cleared and planted" ground and ashes where foodstuff "seemed lately to have been roasted" invests the text with an uncanny admission that the Maroons simultaneously are located in a past-tense space *and* occupy the soldiers' present, in the shadows, invisible. This constitutes a different, more troubling form of erasure than that evident in descriptions of slaves whose suffering is subordinated to the anguishes of Montgomery's laboring heart. For even though the hero's account of the Maroon War ends with a summary of its eventual outcome—the surrender of the Maroons—he also imparts a warning about possible "future wars" with this "sly and subtle" enemy. And even though the novel never again mentions the Maroons, the resistance they and other rebellious subjects embody within the plots of creole fiction carries the potential to disrupt the performance and production of white creole "civilization" in ways impossible to ignore.

As befits the first early creole novel—published in the Caribbean by a long-term resident—*Montgomery* displays a number of characteristics that appear in subsequent creole fictions, from attempts to dramatize and privilege experiential knowledge of the Caribbean, to the compulsion to prove the validity (or even the possibility) of white creole culture for metropolitan readers. In attempting this cultural work, however, *Montgomery* also displays the peculiar anxieties generated by its creole characters and scenes. Written from the position of one familiar with the plantation machine, its discipline, its brutality, and its far reach, the novel provides evidence of the fragility of a white creole culture that tries to obscure these actualities. This fragility, as I have argued throughout the chapter, is fully displayed in those scenes that document the many and varied acts of violent transformation involved in the quotidian routines of the estates, whether the physical violence necessary to transform Jamaican wilderness into an arena of agricultural production or to coerce the laborers necessary for that work.

The novel also participates in another kind of transformative violence—the discursive rearranging performed by early creole print culture in its attempts to translate colonial violence into more benign articulations of a civilized, already improved society. But, like the colonial newspapers and literary magazines produced on Kingston's Harbour Street by the early West India press, *Montgomery* cannot avoid engaging Caribbean place and space, sites and sights where violence—though partially obscured—is inescapable. Ultimately, then, *Montgomery*'s cultural work, the literal and aesthetic acts of transformative cultivation it attempts, reproduce the very inconsistencies and contradictions it seeks to smooth over. Whether or not the novels that follow *Montgomery* are better able to perform this work is the subject of the following chapters.

2 "A Permanent Revolution"
Time, History, and Constructions of Africa in Cynric Williams's *Hamel, the Obeah Man*

LIKE *Montgomery*, Cynric Williams's *Hamel, the Obeah Man* is very much a product of creole place and space, sites described, at least in part, in the same gothic overtones that contribute to *Montgomery*'s accounts of estate brutality and Maroon warfare. But Williams's engagement with place isn't driven by the desire to display the virtuous sensibility of the novel's title character or the sufferings he endures. Rather, the relationships between setting and characters in *Hamel* are characterized by the ability (or inability) to read West Indian sites through the lens of enlightenment rationality. Like other proplanter writings that constructed binary formulations pitting Western reason against African unreason to justify institutional slavery, Williams's novel emphasizes the superiority of an enlightened worldview over superstition. But in this novel, the primary contest played out between primitive superstition and sophisticated skepticism pits Roland, an unscrupulous Methodist missionary, against Hamel, the African leader of a slave revolt in Jamaica and a practitioner of obeah.

Conventional West Indian accounts of obeah—described as a form of "witchcraft or sorcery" practiced by "natives of Africa" who "brought the science with them from thence to Jamaica"—cited its practice as evidence of enslaved people's superstitious ignorance.[1] Western rationality, in contrast, was the province of the enlightened white planter class. In *Hamel*, however, Williams situates the title character's Africanness not in opposition to enlightenment ideals, but as central to a parallel system of beliefs about time, history, and culture—different from Eurocentric values, but not necessarily and always inferior to it, as the relationship between Hamel and the novel's white characters (good and bad) illustrate. This construction sets *Hamel* apart from other West Indian writings, both fiction and nonfiction, particularly in the way Williams acknowledges the possibility—albeit in his perception, limited—of black culture, specifically African culture.

Hamel, in other words, is no *Montgomery*. Instead of a white creole man of feeling, readers find in this novel, as Brathwaite described the obeah man nearly fifty years ago, "a black man of African culture at the center of and in control of what should have been a Euro-oriented document of the colonial Plantation."[2] Hamel is, Brathwaite writes in the 2010 reissue of the novel, "a cool black nation-language African free-slave, w/ an Islamic name to boot."[3] While Brathwaite has persistently noted the novel's "deeply race conscious and colour-prejudiced" ideology, he also points to the importance of the attempt by "a white writer, during the period of slavery . . . to go beyond the superfices of the 'System' and . . . enter into the imagination of at least a single slave."[4]

In this chapter I explore and contextualize those "superfices" to consider how far (or, indeed, whether) Williams is able to move beyond them. I focus particularly on the centrality of early nineteenth-century conceptions of time, its "progress," and its relationship to history and culture in the period of slavery after the Haitian Revolution, when those conceptions are challenged by an African present/presence. Such constructions of time and history, of course, are intimately tied to and revealed by the discourses of slavery and abolition that Williams and other early creole novelists contributed to through their fiction. That relationship was noted by contemporary reviewers, who pointed out *Hamel*'s kinship with historical novels like those of Sir Walter Scott. As the reviewer for the *Westminster Review* remarked, even though *Hamel* "does not describe historical incidents, it in reality belongs to that class [historical novels], embodying in picture the manners of the present creole inhabitants, which another half century will probably see materially changed."[5] In other words, in addition to teaching "history, manners, and morals, by means of the novel"—what the *Atlas* reviewer of *Hamel* considered "one of the most important inventions of modern times"[6]—Williams's novel actively engages in the nostalgic preservation of a historical moment that has not yet taken place: the final days of institutionalized Anglo-Caribbean slavery, already undergoing a process of romanticized (re)production.

This (re)productive process both relies on and generates the narrative's unsettled and unsettling tone, established in the novel's opening pages and maintained throughout. Undergirded by precisely detailed descriptions of setting as well as more generalized evocations of loss and foreboding, Williams's novel represents a turn to "the historical romance of the cultural periphery, of which Walter Scott's *Waverley* [1814] is the prime example."[7] It is, as Tim Watson notes, a narrative that "emphasizes transformation, 'collapse', and loss . . . perfectly fitted for a white creole understanding of the pre-emancipation Caribbean."[8] Upsetting this perfect fit, however, is the overarching plot's reliance—as it moves through a threatened rebellion, to the dissolution of that particular threat, and finally to the narrative's reestablishment of plantocratic authority—on Hamel, that "cool black nation-language African free-slave, w/an Islamic name to boot." Hamel—Williams's constructions of his Africanness, his prescience, his place both inside and outside history—all speak to the fraught dialectics between various Eurocentric constructions of Old and New Worlds.

Unlike *Montgomery*'s sentimental didacticism, its display and cultivation of white morals and manners in the Caribbean, Williams's text responds to tensions generated by what Angelika Epple calls the "epoch of *exclusive Eurocentrism* in historiography."[9] For most historians of the time, she writes, "the history of humanity was a development toward the better. Human progress included the transformation from stupidity to wisdom," which was very often "equated with the transformation of black into white races."[10]

This historiographic tendency—the production of a Eurocentric "world history" that relied on reconstructive acts to reify notions of a directional, progressive historical trajectory—was not limited to works (re)constructing the histories of humankind or nation-states, however. As Martin Rudwick observes in *Worlds before Adam,* the new science of geology that emerged over the last decades of the eighteenth century "became the first truly *historical* natural science."[11] It did so, he continues, "as a result of deliberately transposing methods and concepts from the human sciences of history itself."[12] Geologists of the period, Rudwick notes, came to see "that the earth's deep or prehuman geohistory could in principle be reconstructed almost as reliably as, say, the history of the ancient Greeks and Romans."[13] Enlightenment geologists' discovery of "deep time," moreover, did not simply challenge Mosaic readings of the earth's age; it required new ways of interpreting the earth's "records," adding geological meaning to the already familiar geographic sense of Old and New Worlds.

Acknowledging the historiographical work shared by the natural and human sciences in the early nineteenth century provides instructive insights into *Hamel*'s engagement with "universal" history and the local present of the novel's Jamaican setting. More specifically, my reading focuses on the ways *Hamel* is caught up in this emerging historiography, its violence, and on what it means to the creole project of (re)constructing West Indian history. The centrality of an African obeah practitioner, who, by the terms of Hegelian notions of universal history, should be relegated to its "imaginary waiting room,"[14] suggests Williams's ambivalence and conundrum.[15] Occupying a position both inside and outside the putative progressive movement of history, Williams's Hamel reflects and (ironically) resists contemporaneous Eurocentric representations of Africans and African Caribbean culture. At the heart of these representations are white creole attitudes—very often shared by people in the metropole—toward black people's (in)capacity for self-rule and the ways such attitudes reflected and buttressed early nineteenth-century conceptions of the progress of (white) history and (white) civilization.[16] In Williams's novel, however, Hamel disrupts history's flow in his attempt to effect a "permanent revolution" on the island, and (re)orders its progressive, if gradual movement by renouncing his revolutionary aims, thereby ensuring a restoration of plantocratic rule. He is constructed as both threat to and savior of white creole time.

The dilemma created by the obeah man's dual role recalls competing representations of the single historical incident drawn into and specifically alluded to in the novel's plot: the Haitian Revolution. As I discuss in this chapter's conclusion, Hamel's planned rebellion assumes the character of a generic insurrection and, at the same time, recalls a particular event—Haiti writ small, revised and contained by Williams, albeit uneasily. But in 1822, the year in which *Hamel* is set, Haiti is more than a site where enslaved people rose up against their enslavers in a massive rebellion; it is an independent state, populated and governed by self-emancipated African and African-descended black citizens, newly unified under Jean Pierre Boyer, the republican president who had recently conquered Spanish Hispaniola. By 1822 histories dealing with Haiti were no longer limited to colonialist accounts of the revolution, as most had been in the 1790s, but were now records of a *national* history. Whereas accounts of the St. Domingue uprising (as it was then called) had been produced almost exclusively by European and white writers, counter-narratives circulating through the colonies and Europe after the Republic of Haiti was established in 1804 were being produced by Haitian historians for a Haitian audience.[17] For Williams, participating in the novelistic-historiographic project that is *Hamel*, the cautionary work of the novel is not limited to warning about insurrection, but alerts readers to the idea that history itself is up for grabs, that the *"people without history"*—people, ironically for Williams, like his hero—are writing themselves back in.

Gradualism and *Hamel*'s Subterranean History

In 1822 and 1824 two observers recorded their perceptions of Jamaican life in the years immediately preceding the publication of *Hamel*, asserting their objectivity in doing so. The first commentary appears in *A Tour through the Island of Jamaica*, by Cynric Williams, the authorial persona created by *Hamel*'s author. Arriving in December 1822, the *Tour*'s narrator travels around the island, encountering various West Indian types along the way. One such figure is the opinionated planter Mr. Mathews, who provides a lesson in reading history for the narrator's edification: "[A] dispassionate review of history will teach [us], that revolutions in the manners and condition of mankind are the result of ages, the mind being gradually and almost imperceptibly prepared for them."[18] Acknowledging this "fact" of history's operations, Mr. Mathews continues, is crucial if the West India Question is to be resolved and the safety and best interests of all colonial residents assured: "If it were possible to put our slave population a few stages in advance in civilization . . . I would most willingly give my slaves that boon, accompanied by their freedom; but their immediate emancipation, with their present ignorance . . . would be destruction to us all, masters and slaves."[19] Equating sudden emancipation with the destruction of the West Indian colonies comprised one of the most frequently repeated arguments offered by West Indian proprietors in the debates of the 1820s. Thus, when Williams's Mr. Mathews offers up his "disinterested" assessment—tinged with regret that it's not possible to hurry the slaves along the path of civilization and freedom—he touts the credentials of a long-time resident with a clear understanding of the present (i.e., primitive) state of African and Afro-Caribbean subjects.

Such assertions are not confined to long-time resident planters, however. A second observer, Henry Thomas De la Beche, shares a similar truism in his private correspondence with his friend William Daniel Conybeare. Unlike Mr. Mathews, however, De la Beche's assessment reveals his ambivalence: "[I] as sincerely regret as you can do that I have any concern with the West Indies," he confesses to Conybeare (deferring to Conybeare's abolitionist sympathies), but, he continues, "I am still afraid, that the consequence of the angry feelings of the contending parties will be, that neither the Colonists, Abolitionists, nor English Government will long have any thing to do with this most beautiful Island, but that it will be subject to all the horrors of a revolution effected by semi-barbarous people."[20] Rhetorically distancing himself from the contention of the emancipation debates, De la Beche attempts to persuade Conybeare not only that he is a "well wisher to the slave population," but also that he is a disinterested commentator, a challenge given the reason for his trip to Jamaica.[21] As Conybeare well knows, De la Beche had undertaken the journey to the West Indies to inspect Halse Hall, the 4,482-acre sugar estate worked by 207 enslaved people that he inherited at the age of five.[22]

But De la Beche had other "business" in Jamaica, which he describes earlier in the same letter: "I have already coloured geologically a considerable portion of the Map of Jamaica, . . . which if I die here you must continue to examine as also my geological notebooks, and make what use of the whole you think best."[23] In addition to owning Halse Hall, De la Beche was building his reputation as a geologist. An active member of the Geological Society of London and fellow of the Royal Society, he was on the way to becoming a founding figure of British geology; later in his career De la Beche would be appointed Director of Great Britain's first national geological survey, and would serve as one of the nation's first government-appointed scientists. He did not die in Jamaica during his year-long visit, nor did he die, like fellow absentee proprietor Matthew Lewis, on the return journey. Instead he survived to continue his geological field work—funded by proceeds from Halse Hall until the sugar market collapsed—and to publish his *Notes on the Present Condition of the Negroes in Jamaica* in 1825.[24]

Given his membership in a scientific community that measured geohistory in terms of its unfolding over an "unimaginably lengthy period of time," De la Beche's belief that the legal status of the enslaved should be "gradually bettered, and not suddenly" isn't surprising.[25] Too, his declaration of impartiality in the *Notes* reflects his empirical training as a scientist and the accompanying ideologies that enshrined notions of the superiority of white people over people of color. The practice of justifying race-based slavery through scientific argument—an instance of the period's scientific racism—was widespread in the eighteenth and early nineteenth centuries, a demonstration of the ways science served "the needs of an embattled ruling class."[26] In this case, science and the ruling class are embodied by a single representative—De la Beche.

As scientist *and* planter, De la Beche tries to negotiate his undeniable conflict of interest, insisting that he is motivated by a "sincere desire to ascertain facts" about the daily life of (his) enslaved laborers. The *Notes*, he assures readers, contain only evidence that has "come under my own personal observation."[27] The evidence of these facts, moreover, lead to one conclusion, the same offered by the less scientific, but equally "sincere" Mr. Mathews: more time must pass before the enslaved are ready for freedom. Together, Mr. Mathews's and De la Beche's comments reveal how well the conceptualization of a progressive universal history that posited white civilization as the *telos* of its supporting narratives fit the "enlightened self-interest" of individual planters, the plantocracy as a whole, and an imperial science operating in the colonies and metropole.[28]

More startling, though, is the language of gradualism—described by Elizabeth Heyrick as "the very master-piece of satanic policy"[29]—that permeated *anti*slavery writings. It was enshrined in the very name of the institution that was the face of antislavery activity in Britain: the Society for the Mitigation and *Gradual Abolition* of Slavery, also known as the Antislavery Society. The clearest expression of the society's views, shored up by Enlightenment rationality and historical progressivism, was put forth by the society's leader, Thomas Fowell Buxton, in a motion presented to the House of Commons in May 1823. In pursuing legislative action on the slavery question, Buxton reassured his audience, the society meant "nothing rash, nothing rapid, nothing abrupt, nothing bearing any feature of violence." Indeed, if successful in passing the motion, he added, slavery "will never be abolished: it will never be destroyed"; rather, "[i]t will subside; it will decline; it will expire; it will, as it were, burn itself down into its socket and go out. We are far from meaning to attempt to cut down slavery, in the full maturity of its vigour. We rather shall leave it gently to decay—slowly, silently, almost imperceptibly, to die away, and to be forgotten."[30] Despite its conciliatory language—which infuriated immediatists like Heyrick as well as many Caribbean planters and colonial assemblies who decried any perceived gesture of metropolitan interference in West Indian affairs—Buxton's motion was rejected. In its stead conservative Foreign Secretary George Canning recommended various ameliorative measures in order to effect "a progressive improvement" in the character of the enslaved and thereby "prepare them for participation in those civil rights and privileges which are enjoyed by other classes of His Majesty's subjects."[31]

The persuasive power of such rational language—Buxton's slow fade and gentle decay, Canning's gradual ameliorism, Mr. Mathews's "almost" imperceptible revolution of manners and condition, along with race scientist Thomas Winterbottom's explanation that "[e]very permanent, characteristic variety in human nature is effected by slow and almost imperceptible gradations"[32]—reflect the shared assumptions, the common ground of a belief in the superiority of Western (more specifically, British) civilization. Discourses of the natural sciences proved handy for colonial administrators, abolitionists, and planters alike since it allowed all parties to position themselves as rational arbiters of the slavery question, but it did not require the jettisoning of beliefs in the superiority of white people. The terms of the discussion, in other words, need not focus on physical, biological traits distinguishing black and brown colonial subjects from white subjects—after all, as mainstream science had proved for rational thinkers, even the extremes of skin color "were . . . linked by infinite gradations of tint."[33] The telling, crucial distinction between races for early nineteenth-century enlightened policy makers, as the commentary above reveals, was the measurement of a people's state of civilization—the benchmark for which was British imperial culture.

Evidence for the primitive state of black people, in contrast, was provided by descriptions of violent insurrections and rebellious plots (real or imagined) by "semi-barbarous people" in the Caribbean. As I have argued elsewhere, these events—in addition to the literal violence that attended or threatened to attend them—were represented as disruptions of human history's gradual unfolding, much in the way that geologists read cataclysmic events like earthquakes as punctuating the immensely long and broadly progressive timeline of geohistory.[34] In other words, in these early decades of the nineteenth century, the violent phenomena that were acknowledged markers of geo- and human history's unfolding are described through a shared lexicon. As Noah Heringman points out the language of romantic revolution and of geological science operated dialectically, resulting in a kind of geological romanticism or a poetics of geology.[35]

As in the literal and figurative garden described in *Montgomery*, in *Hamel* the relationship between realistic and metaphoric images of natural phenomena is complicated by the novel form itself. When Williams's heroic young planter Oliver Fairfax tells his future father-in-law about the impending uprising, for instance, he draws his analogy from geology: "the very ground trembles beneath our feet," he warns Solomon Guthrie; "we are walking on a volcano ready to burst into flames."[36]

But Williams's geological imagery isn't limited to metaphor. In *Hamel* it forms a central part of the novel's mimetic descriptions of physical setting. Unlike the planter picturesque discussed in chapter 1, Williams's representations of Jamaica's topography rely on immersive, vividly detailed descriptions of a landscape with no explicit connection to planting, the plantation machine, or its disciplined time keeping. A marked contrast to the regular beauty of "improved" estate lands, the physical setting laid out in *Hamel*'s opening chapters plunges the reader, along with the mysterious "stranger" who appears in the novel's first paragraph, headlong into a landscape in the process of being violently transformed by nature: steep inclines and sharp descents into the "depths of ravines ploughed by torrents . . . manifested, by the ruin and confusion along their channels, the headlong passion to which they were sometimes subject."[37] Earthquake tremors—"not uncommon" in Jamaica, as the stranger remarks to himself[38]—accompany hurricane winds, the force of which is presented in realistically dramatic detail: "no sound but that of the elements raging as if to produce a second chaos, thunder and wind, the roaring of the augmented waterfalls, the rumbling of the rocks which they loosed from their beds, the creaking and crashing of falling trees. . . . [T]he lightning . . . illuminated the scene with its partial flashes, now here, now there: it gleamed only on mountains uncultivated and uninhabited . . . on naked precipices and foaming torrents, or on the giant trees of the forest quivering beneath the blasts of the hurricane."[39]

As it turns out, the storm's violence does operate on a figurative level, the raging elements (like Fairfax's volcano) matched by the rumblings of imminent insurrection. This significance, however, is revealed only later, after readers learn that the stranger, Roland, is a Methodist missionary intimately involved in the large-scale uprising that Fairfax's metaphor alludes to. But in the opening chapters, before we know of the revolt and Roland's activities—or of the degree of Williams's anti-missionary feelings—the description of earthquake and storm speaks to the intensely material foundations of the island itself.

More important for my reading of *Hamel*'s representations of history and time, this materiality goes deeper than describing the external effects of the hurricane, a meteorological phenomenon commonly associated with the Caribbean. It also renders topographical markers that document the island's long, nonhuman history of such events. In other words, the vivid description of hurricane and earthquake is more than a specimen of New World exotica. In its suggestion of a "second chaos," of an "uncultivated and uninhabited" primordial place, Williams sets up the novel's engagement not just with "world history" but with deep time as well.

Questions of deep time—measuring what geologists of the early nineteenth century agreed was the earth's immensely long history—were central to the developing science of geology, as were questions about how to read and interpret the "monuments" and "relics" of the earth's past, from fossil remains to the layered strata visible in cliff faces. The nearly consensual acknowledgment among geologists and the "knowing" public of geological time's vastness, of course, served to underscore the relatively brief history of humankind. But despite perceptions of the enormous difference between the spans of geo- and human history, accounts of both deployed similar discursive strategies when reconstructing past events, explaining present conditions, and forecasting the future. Parallels between these accounts, moreover, reveal how "time" was perceived and represented in creole writings like *Hamel,* how such constructions fueled gradualist discourse and helped marshal arguments against immediate emancipation, and how, in turn, they shaped perceptions of the novel's New World setting and productions of its (geo)history.

An obvious point of entry to a discussion of the parallels—and intersections—between literary and geological writings in the Jamaican context is to consider that point literally. That is, to begin with a consideration of physical points of access into the substrata of the island itself: the cave systems that are one of Jamaica's most remarkable geological features. Given the significance of caves and caverns in the island's pre-Columbian and colonial history, Williams's decision to use such a setting for many of the novel's key scenes isn't surprising. Suggestively named places like Runaway Bay, Spaniard's Hole, Seemenomore, and Two Sisters caves attest to their local reputation as places of refuge, for Taino Indians pursued by the Spanish, for Spanish colonists pursued by the English, for self-liberated slaves pursued by colonial planters of all stripes. But the caves also were contested spaces, their identification as such confirmed throughout the oral and print culture of the period. Williams, for example, draws on this tradition in the *Tour* when the narrator presents a "transcription" of a "true, genuine creolian anecdote" about a conflict between two slaves: Cato, self-liberated ex-slave and outlaw, and Plato, a slave who is promised freedom in return for Cato's capture.[40]

The battle between the two men is described in terms similar to stories about Three-Fingered Jack Mansong, a real-life slave-turned-highwayman of the 1780s, made famous for metropolitan readers by numerous accounts circulating in Britain at the turn of the nineteenth century.[41] As in the stories about Three-Fingered Jack, Cato takes refuge in the hills and caves of Jamaica's limestone districts; and like Three-Fingered Jack, Cato is defeated not by white authorities, but by a black man who converts to Christianity in order to obtain "a counter charm, or an equivalent obeah" to that of African practitioners.[42] The final physical battle between the two men takes place at the entrance to Cato's cave, from which Plato summons Cato to fight. Although Cato is defeated physically, he curses Plato for his betrayal, prophesying that his freedom will be short-lived: "Before the moon which shone on our matchets [*sic*] in that night of our battle shall rise again as big as it then was, . . . we shall meet where the

67 *"A Permanent Revolution"*

white man's ahpetti shall be no more worth than mine; and where the Great Master shall say who is the better man. Remember!"[43] The story moves to a rapid close, with the narrator's suggestion that Plato's superstitious belief in Cato's prophecy contributes to his death a month later.

The *Tour* moves on without further reference to Cato, Plato, or the cave.[44] But the tale clearly resonates for Williams, who returns to the "genuine creolian anecdote" in *Hamel,* taking core details—the outlaw's cave, its associations with rebellion, obeah, curses, and prophecies—and spins another more complex narrative around this peculiarly significant Caribbean site. In *Hamel* the subterranean abode of the obeah man becomes much more than the setting of a rebel's defeat and capture, but a place where Western conceptions of geological deep time and human, linear time converge in provocative ways. Reading Hamel's cave alongside two contemporary speleological events, one taking place in Jamaica, the other in England, clarifies this convergence—and, as I argue in the following section, demonstrates the novel's broader engagement with history, time, and place.

AT SOME POINT between May 13 and July 29, 1824, Henry De la Beche took time out from observing operations at Halse Hall to make "two or three trips" to conduct geological research. As he wrote to Conybeare, "white limestone covers an immense proportion of Jamaica," and although "organic remains are exceedingly rare," the limestone districts were "full of fine caverns." He had "not yet found any bones in them," he confided, but he was hopeful: "The large and beautiful cavern called Portland Cave in the Parish of Vere, presents the following section which is not unlike Buckland's caves"[45] (see fig. 7). "It is uncommonly hot in this cavern, more particularly when several torches are lighted," he continues, "but I will nevertheless see if I cannot dig into the stratum of clay. I may perhaps turn out the remains of some monstrous beast."[46] After returning to England half a year later, De la Beche read his "Remarks on the Geology of Jamaica" to fellow members of the Geological Society of London.[47] At that time, he didn't repeat his half-joking ambition to unearth fossil remains of a "monstrous beast"; he did, however, retain the comparison of Portland Cave to "Professor Buckland's cave."[48]

The allusion, as Conybeare and his London audience would have recognized, refers to the Kirkdale caves, made famous by the well-known theologian and Oxford geologist William Buckland. In 1822 Buckland had presented his analysis of fossilized bones found by quarrymen in a North Yorkshire cave, which he identified as belonging to an antediluvian

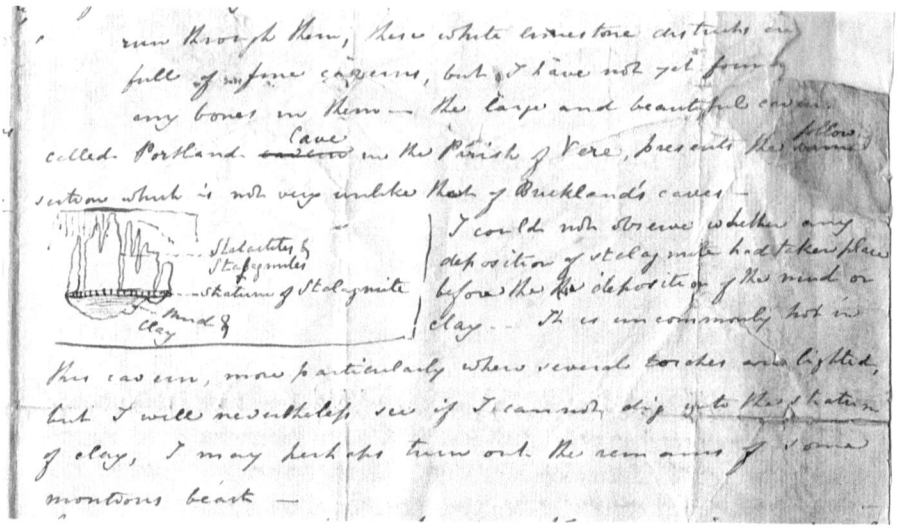

FIGURE 7. Letter to William Daniel Conybeare from Henry De la Beche, July 29, 1824. (Courtesy of the National Library of Wales)

species of hyena. Explaining to members of the Royal Society how the bones were found embedded in silty deposits between layers of stalagmite, Buckland argued that they revealed the "state of habitation in [England] in the period immediately preceding the [biblical] Deluge." The Kirkdale caves, Buckland enthused, provided a "natural Chronometer" for both the "Antediluvian Period" and the "Postdiluvian," thus proving that "the latter must have begun at or about the point of time assigned to it by our common Chronologies."[49]

De la Beche's reference to Buckland's findings in his survey of Jamaica—"a remote, and, if I may so speak, a *new* geological country"[50]—goes deeper than alluding to the old and familiar (North Yorkshire) to explain the new and unfamiliar (Jamaica). "Buckland's caves" were significant not only because they seemed to provide material evidence of a deluge, but also because they provided an exemplary model for reconstructing geohistory. As Rudwick explains, when Buckland presented his findings to the Royal Society—including a vivid rendition of Kirkdale's "whole [antediluvian] ecosystem . . . involving herbivores and carnivores as well as the scavenging hyenas"—he had, in effect, "fulfilled [Georges] Cuvier's aspiration to 'burst the limits of time'"[51]: Buckland's enquiries, extolled Humphrey Davy, president of the Royal Society at the time, had established a "distant epoch . . . in the history of the revolutions of

FIGURE 8. "The Hyena's Den at Kirkdale, near Kirby Moorside in Yorkshire, discovered A.D. 1821 [by W. Buckland]." William Daniel Conybeare's illustration caricaturing Buckland's exploration of Kirkdale Cave was accompanied by verse. (© The British Library Board)

our globe," a "fixed point, from which our researches may be pursued through the immensity of ages."[52] Buckland's (and De la Beche's) friend Conybeare acknowledged this contribution in a now-iconic image, which depicts "Buckland as having penetrated from the present world into the antediluvian past, or at least as having found a 'spy-hole' through which to see it as it really was"[53] (see fig. 8). In fleshing out the narrative of Kirkdale cave, argues Rudwick, Buckland reconstructed history and made "the deep past knowable in the present, . . . in effect, traveling in deep time."[54] By invoking Kirkdale, De la Beche alludes to the possibility that Portland Cave was another such time portal and that, armed with "the necessary implements" to conduct further researches, he too would be able to (re)construct a fixed point in Jamaica's geohistory.

Like De la Beche, who records in words and images his attempt to travel in deep time via the "natural Chronometer" of Portland Cave, Williams's depictions of Hamel's caves represent an attempt to reconstruct and, in effect, to restructure time and history. Williams, of course, does not deal explicitly with geohistory. Rather he conveys a sense of the profundity, solemnity, and mysteriousness of deep time, which is in keeping with various iterations of gradualist rhetoric. This sense is magnified in the scenes that unfold in Hamel's subterranean sanctuary. The site's significance is established early, when Roland scrambles up a precipice and crosses a dangerous chasm to shelter there from the hurricane described above. Like De la Beche—satirized in a contemporary publication as "an able explorer of the bowels of the earth"[55]—Roland surveys a "lofty cavern hewn by the hand of nature in the otherwise solid lime-stone rock," stalactites hanging from its roof, and "vomitories" opening into passages that "extended farther than he was disposed . . . to penetrate."[56] His gaze also takes in the cave's "rather curious contents": a "bonjaw" (banjo), a bamboo rod curiously "tattooed from end to end," and a clay pot carved with "rude figures"; stores of salted fish, "jerked hog," and rum; a cache of weapons; and a collection of hair, feathers, and mysterious powders readily recognized even by a "stranger" like Roland as the paraphernalia associated with obeah.[57]

As a "Chronometer" this cave tells a history through its "relics" and "monuments": cultural artifacts, provisions stored for future use by runaways or rebels, weapons to aid insurrections, even a fossil-like record of skulls—"some perfect, some which had been broken apparently with a sharp pointed instrument, and many of them serving as calabashes or boxes to hold the strange property of the master of the cave."[58] The master of the cave, we soon learn, is Hamel, the obeah man, whose familiarity with the cells and labyrinthine passages is evidenced by his sudden unannounced appearance before the missionary. Wakened from a troubled sleep, Roland's startled query ("In the name of God or Devil . . . who or what art thou?") and Hamel's calm rejoinder ("Master—what you will. . . . What you please,—a Negro") set the tone for their subsequent interactions.[59] The subversive irony of Hamel's answer becomes clear as the two characters reveal their "nature": Roland's religious hypocrisy and venality are increasingly visible as the novel's mysteries unravel; Hamel's role in their unraveling, moreover, affirms the obeah man's claim that "There is nothing in these mountains, in this island, which is concealed from me."[60]

Hamel's authority, first established in this underground scene, can be likened to the assertion of Buckland's authority in Kirkdale. Just as Buckland's mastery in reading the geological record enables him to "burst the limits of time" so Hamel's awareness of what goes on *in* the mountains, *in* the island, indicates his ability to read deeper than mere surface signs.

The omniscience Williams grants his hero, moreover, seems predicated on an awareness of conflicting configurations of history. When, for example, Roland attempts to assert the superiority of his religion over that of Hamel and his ally Combah (African-born prince and would-be King of Jamaica), Hamel calmly rebukes him: "Master Roland, ... we say nothing against your religion, nor your God; we had a religion before we knew yours; such as it was, it is."[61] This is not to suggest that Williams privileges Hamel's obeah over Christianity. He does, however, privilege Hamel's rational assertion that not only are there other belief systems, but that Hamel and Combah's religion is at least as valid as Roland's methodistical enthusiasm. More importantly, the obeah man's rational tolerance buttresses the claim of obeah's antiquity, which, it appears, extends so far back into the past that it is timeless: "as it was, it is."

On the one hand, this aspect of Hamel's "Africanness" exoticizes him, much in the way that early Western anthropology "invented" the "other" through a "temporal vocabulary that distances the exotic from the familiar."[62] Such temporal othering—a process rendered more vivid by the scene's underground setting—suggestively links the obeah man with the earth itself, his intimacy with its material architecture, his "earthiness," contributing to the novel's romanticized representations of his powers. But that process also allows the enlightened reader a kind of archaeo-anthropological view of African culture. The cave is both time machine and time capsule, and Hamel—as constructed by Williams—operates as both time traveler and curator, presiding over ancient "mysteries of the enslaved Coromantins," preserving the knowledge of Old World African culture, and collecting local, at-hand materials used in his creolized expressions of African/African Caribbean culture in the present of the novel.[63]

In this sense the novel does not simply relegate the obeah man and his practices to a "'primitive' past" nor does it participate in the systematic "denial of coevalness" that, according to Johannes Fabian's critique of modern anthropological writings, contributed to the construction of Western scientists' "Other."[64] Instead, Williams emphatically places Hamel, his Africanness—including both his religious activities and "self-liberation ethos"—at the center of the novel's contemporary setting.[65] For Hamel's activities, although attached to notions of antiquity (as with his ancient religion), are not *confined* to the distant past of deep time evoked by the scenes set in Hamel's cave. Rather, for Williams and other white creoles, Hamel is very much part of the idiosyncratic "local present" of 1820s Jamaica, his insurrectionary plot modeled on actual attempts by enslaved people to liberate themselves (or, rather, on colonial accounts of such efforts).

Against this backdrop, we can read the movement of the novel's plots in terms of parallel chronological lines, unfolding simultaneously in horizontal layers, much like the geological strata studied by early nineteenth-century geologists like De la Beche: on the surface of the Jamaican landscape, the young planter Oliver Fairfax, also Hamel's "owner," attempts to reclaim his patriarchal estate and pursue his romance with the white creole heroine, Joanna Guthrie. Below in the cavernous spaces commanded by Hamel, the obeah man plans the revolution on which "his own soul was bent: his arts, his influence, his every energy . . . devoted to the extermination of the Whites, or to their expulsion from this island."[66] In a sense, these narrative strands—in which the "African" layer unfolds underground—recall Gayatri Spivak's reformulation of Foucault, providing a tantalizing glimpse of the "subtext of the palimpsestic narrative of imperialism," a form of "subjugated knowledge" taken from "a whole set of knowledges that have been disqualified as inadequate to their task or insufficiently elaborated: naïve knowledges, located . . . beneath the required level of [Western] cognition or scientificity."[67] But as Williams lays them out in his novel, Hamel's activities are no mere "subtext"; nor are his "knowledges" presented as inadequate or naïve. We see this in the cave scenes, with Hamel controlling ingress and egress—moving, planning, strategizing from the caverns and passages that become identified as "his abode," his "sanctuary." In denominating Hamel the "proprietor" of the caves, a word play on the more typical slave-owning "West India proprietor," Williams emphasizes such ironic inversions.

Of course, my reading is not intended to obscure the constructedness of the novel's African characters. Williams's depictions of African and African creole cultures, including descriptions of the cave's contents, may be based on a degree of familiarity, but certainly not true intimacy. But within the bounds of the novelist's constraints, Hamel's presence makes this particular cavern an "African" space impervious despite Roland's intrusion. Indeed, unlike Portland Cave, in which "hundreds of people" have scrawled their names "upon the wall with charcoal" and to which De la Beche assigns new significance for geological "scientificity," Hamel's cave attests to the limitations of white knowledge.[68] When Fairfax demands to know the location of the obeah man's "secret hiding-place, some cave, which I know not, among the rocks, where runaways come to hear their fortunes and to buy charms of you," Hamel subtly challenges his authority, replying that such knowledge would be dangerous to his white master, that Fairfax would lose himself "among the windings."⁶⁹ Like Jamaican planter-historian Edward Long's description of the numerous passages in Green Grotto cave, most of which "had never been explored by any human being," the chambers and passageways of Hamel's cave are fathomless to the uninitiated.⁷⁰ As such, it is a space in which the "natural" order of white knowledge over black knowledge, white authority over black authority, is overturned, the world-turned-inside-out as much as upside-down.

Order suggests sequence as well as authority. The plantation system's order is predicated on both, ruling the enslaved labor force by imposing temporal structure/order on the quotidian operations of estate life. Daily routines, although adapted to meet agricultural cycles—planting and harvesting, wet and dry seasons—nevertheless followed strict schedules to facilitate the overarching discipline of the plantation machine that Mintz describes and that I discuss in chapter 1. There the day is treated as a temporal line bookended by dawn and dark, punctuated by the blow of conch shell or crack of the whip.⁷¹ In the world of Williams's novel, however, Hamel's position in such a linear scheme is ambiguous at best. Certainly the regimentation of the estates does not infiltrate his underground demesne, where he conducts his (invisible) revolutionary "business" concurrent with that of the plantation. Not that Hamel is subject to the estate's discipline when he is above ground, given his position as the watchman on Fairfax's estate. In this position, he tells Roland, his "business . . . is sometimes to go round the lines of my master's estate, sometimes to look after runaway Negroes, to watch the provision grounds, to hunt wild hogs."⁷² The degree of mobility Hamel enjoys in this sanctioned role—to keep watch over people and property—facilitates his secret, subversive work as an obeah man, not least of which is to orchestrate events according to his own conceptions of time and history, to "make manifest what is in the womb of time"—the revolution—at his own pace.⁷³

Of course, Hamel's orchestrations (as he acknowledges) rely on the credulity of his followers and, in Roland's case, of his enemies. Williams's anti-missionary sentiment is palpable, a fact that did not escape contemporary reviewers who noted the character's exaggerated villainy: Roland, wrote *The Atlas*'s reviewer, is "one of the most unredeemed scoundrels that ever did or did not exist."⁷⁴ And although Williams's anti-missionary zeal assures Hamel's victories over Roland, the novelist's desire to allay anxieties about rebellion requires him to limit the obeah man's ability to bring his plans to fruition. But even Hamel's failure is nuanced, depicted as a sign of the obeah man's ability to read time and to project future events by the evidence of past and present moments.⁷⁵ Thus, when Hamel learns that Fairfax has returned to the island after a lengthy absence, he recognizes that the moment for a successful revolt has passed: the rest of the novel is dedicated to Hamel's capitulation, not just to Fairfax but also to the plantocratic ordering of time and history.

Despite his ultimate abdication, Hamel's role in troubling conceptions of deep time and orderly history, highlighted by his cave's double office as chronometer and revolutionary headquarters, is reaffirmed in the novel's final scene. With the threat of imminent revolution contained through Hamel's intervention, with Combah and Roland dead (the latter buried in Hamel's cave), and Joanna Guthrie, Fairfax's love interest, safely returned to the young planter after being abducted by the rebels, the obeah man prepares to leave the island forever. First, however, he reveals to Fairfax and Joanna's father the secrets of the cave, the scene's language simultaneously mystifying and demystifying its significance for Williams's and Hamel's "plots":

> A more extraordinary labyrinth cannot be conceived. In some of the passages were chasms scarce three feet wide, down any of which an unguarded stranger must have fallen, as it were into a bottomless pit, for the Obeah man assured them he had never been able to fathom their depth.... We have formerly described some of the apartments in this strange abode, around which the Obeah man had always laboured to weave a net of mystery, by tales of enchantment and prophetic warnings, to keep all intruders from prying into his secrets; and we need say little more of the rest of them. Provisions of all sorts abounded—weapons, gunpowder, spears, a score of muskets, which had been used of late, and even two small brass cannon, which Hamel confessed he had, many years before, got from a Spanish bark which was wrecked on the coast.
>
> "It is all yours," said he to Mr Fairfax. "Use it, and defend your property, and your wife that shall be. No Negro, no man but myself, knows the intricacies of this cave at all."⁷⁶

After laying open "all the natural and artificial contrivances of his dwelling" Hamel ends the tour by leading his companions to the cave entrance above Jamaica's Rio Grande River, where Roland—and the reader—first encountered the obeah man. Having come full circle, as it were, the novel gestures again to the possibility of "a second chaos"—not threatened by the raging elements of nature as in the novel's opening scenes, but by the workings of human agency. Looking down from the heights of the cavern opening, Hamel and his companions see "far off at sea a large canoe filled with Negroes."⁷⁷ These men, he explains, are the followers of Combah (and, as such, once allied to Hamel), rebels now escaping "to the land of freedom"—Haiti—accompanied by Haitian fighters who had arrived earlier to assist in the revolt. "They will make up a pretty tale," Hamel prophesizes before offering a succinct and suggestive assessment of the revolution that did not happen: "but they might have conquered."[78]

"[L]ook at Hayti. . . . Look Still at Hayti": The End of *Hamel*

Hamel's revelations and prophecies, provoked by the sight of the canoe pointing toward Haiti, his suggestive yoking of history's production (making up a pretty tale) and revolution (albeit a failed one) reiterates the historiographical conundrum posed by the Haitian Revolution for white creole culture.[79] This (non)event, as Michel Rolphe Trouillot describes it, "entered history with the peculiar characteristic of being unthinkable even as it happened."[80] Williams's specific reference to Haiti in the novel's closing pages signals a confrontation with the paradoxical (a)historicity of the Haitian Revolution—but it is not the first time the novel weaves that revolution into its fictionalized plot. For Williams's novel raises not just the influence of the newly established Haitian Republic for white Anglo-creole culture in 1822, when the novel is set; it also looks back to and invokes what J. Michael Dash has called the "founding moment of the Haitian revolution,"[81] the Bois-Caïman ceremony during which the enslaved of St. Domingue sanctified their resolve to rise up against the white planters.

According to Antoine Dalmas, who published his *Histoire de la revolution de Saint-Domingue* in 1814, the rebels "had a kind of celebration or sacrifice in the middle of an uncultivated woods on the Choiseul plantation, known as Caiman, where the *négres* gathered in great numbers" on the eve of the uprising in August 1791.[82] Dalmas's description of the site of the ceremony—"uncultivated woods"—sets the tone for his description of the rebels themselves:

> A black pig, surrounded by objects they believe have magical power, each carrying the most bizarre offering, was offered as a sacrifice to the all-powerful spirit of the black race. The religious ceremony in which the *négres* slit its throat, the greed with which they drank its blood, the importance they attached to owning some of its bristles which they believed would make them invincible reveal the characteristics of the Africans. It is natural that a caste this ignorant and stupid would begin the most horrible attacks with the superstitious rites of an absurd and bloodthirsty religion.[83]

Dalmas's inscription of African savagery, the grotesquerie embedded in the description of the sacrificial scene along with its emphasis on superstition and ignorance all affirm the "horrors" of St. Domingue. Dalmas's language, though, draws on longstanding European and white planter attitudes that explicitly link African and African Caribbean religious practices with rebellion, whether vodou in Haiti or obeah in the Anglo-Caribbean. From Tacky's Revolt in Jamaica, to Makandal's plot in Haiti, from Matthew Lewis's description of a planned rebellion of St. Mary's parish to De la Beche's description of the conspiracy organized by Obeah Jack: every rebellion, says *Hamel*'s Solomon Guthrie, has an obeah man.

As importantly, in numerous accounts of such rebellions a key element of the colonialist script is an oath-taking ceremony like that described by Dalmas and by De la Beche in a journal entry of April 7, 1824, which recounts a projected rebellion at Buff Bay, where "The celebrated Obeah Jack . . . administered the great 'swear', at the same time giving [the rebels] a mixture of human blood, gunpowder, and rum to drink."[84] Williams, too, provides his novel with such a ceremony in a scene that links religious ritual and political expediency. The ceremony described in *Hamel*, moreover, takes place in the cellars of a ruined plantation—another subterranean space that, like Hamel's caves, provides a "spyhole" through which to (re)read Caribbean historiography and (re)assess the role of the early creole novel in its reproduction.

This scene occurs soon after Hamel's first encounter with Roland but before the reunion with Fairfax that leads him to abandon the rebellion. At this point, Hamel's plans appear to be on the brink of success: he has subdued Roland, forcing the missionary to attend a secret nighttime rally and follow through on a promise to solemnize Combah's coronation as King of Jamaica. At the appointed time, large numbers of prospective rebels gather at an abandoned coffee plantation to hear Roland's sermon. Although his recent encounter with Hamel has cooled the missionary's commitment to the uprising, he addresses the congregants, speaking from the ruined floor of the plantation house. Roland's "harangue"—a provocative display of immediast rhetoric—isn't the only religious activity taking place, however. As Roland exhorts his followers, "loud demoniac" laughter rises up from below, reminding the missionary that "his Obeah rival was at work."[85]

As in the cave scene that first dramatizes the conflict between Roland's methodistical enthusiasm and Hamel's enlightened obeah, Roland's position here against his rival is precarious at best. Indeed, at the moment Roland's sermon reaches its peak, the floor on which he stands gives way, and he falls from the sight of his audience to land in the middle of a second "African" space, where Hamel "and a chosen few" are preparing to take a blood oath to swear allegiance to their revolution. Surrounded by "a dozen or more wild-looking negroes, most of them naked to the waist," Roland reacts in horror and disgust, convinced, like Dalmas in his account of Bois-Caïman, that the African celebrants are reveling in the rites of a "bloodthirsty religion."

Roland's reaction—exaggerated by Williams's anti-missionary fervor—conforms in many ways to the colonial scripting of obeah mentioned above, characterized by the dismissive rhetoric deployed in most anglophone accounts of African religious practices. So embedded was this rhetoric that Lewis could convey his derision in shorthand: "[A] plan has just been discovered . . . for [the slaves'] giving themselves a grand fête by murdering all the whites in the island. . . . Above a thousand persons were engaged in the plot, three hundred of whom had been regularly sworn to assist in it with all the usual accompanying ceremonies of drinking human blood, eating earth from graves, &c."[86]

As Diana Paton notes, these colonial accounts of obeah—codified in the legislative acts outlawing the practice in Jamaica and throughout the Caribbean after Tacky's Easter rebellion of 1760—participated in a wider "history of *religion* as a race-making term with multiple, complex, and power-laden meanings":

> In the Roman Christian world *religio* (the root of the contemporary word *religion*) was a term that articulated truth claims, defining the boundary between "true" religion and "false'" superstition and paganism. Since the European Enlightenment, this boundary-marking aspect of the term has continued in the frequent contrast made between *religion* and terms such as *witchcraft, magic, superstition,* and *charlatanism,* all of which have been applied to obeah. Thus, the concept "religion" has acted as a race-making category: a marker of the line between supposedly "civilized" peoples (who practice religion) and "primitive'" peoples (who practice superstition or magic).[87]

On the whole, colonial accounts of obeah strive to maintain the binaries described by Paton, particularly as they work to affirm the racialized foundations of empire and plantation economics. *Hamel,* however, complicates them, for in the novel's oath-taking scene, Roland, not the African practitioners, is portrayed as ignorant and superstitious, rendered irrational and "primitive" by his terror. Reduced to a "shuddering suppliant," the missionary begs Combah to free him before he is forced to swear the oath of allegiance or witness "atrocities" that operate for him as "an acknowledgment of the power of Satan."[88] "You are premature," answers Combah, assuming the voice of reason: "What atrocities do you speak of? What have you seen or done? We are speaking of an oath: our ceremonies are awful, but not atrocious."[89]

Whether or not *Hamel*'s flipping of the typical racially inflected binaries constitutes a real departure from the colonialist script, and whether or not it is intentional—subservient to Williams's intention to demonize missionary "interference" in Jamaican affairs—the discursive opening created with Combah's words shifts the focus from any apparent religious rivalry to the significance of the oath itself. Carol Greenhouse, drawing on the work of Michael Herzfeld, argues that oath-taking ceremonies deploy a "symbolic vocabulary" that evokes "local constructions of the past in highly specific ways, as well as the local sense of unease in the present."[90]

Williams's novelistic representation of the oath ceremony presided over by Hamel draws on this symbolic vocabulary on two levels. First, by invoking the long history of associations between obeah and rebellion, Williams captures and perpetuates the "local sense" of present unease experienced by white creoles as they uncovered plots like Obeah Jack's Buff Bay revolt, reported by De la Beche and kept alive in accounts like Dalmas's description of Bois-Caïman in his *Histoire*. Second, because the construction of that local white creole past and local present relied on constructions of the "other"'s local past and local present—a dependence indicated by the centrality of obeah oaths in colonial accounts of insurgency—the novel (inadvertently) acknowledges the power of the oath for the African participants.

Like the "story of the Bois-Caïman ceremony" that "symbolizes the place religious practice had in the slave insurrection" and that reveals how "in one way or another, religious practices facilitated the process of its organization,"[91] *Hamel*'s incorporation of the "great 'swear'" underscores its symbolic and utilitarian functions. Too, Williams's obeah man and his fellow rebels can be counted among those who view "the present as the deterioration of a nobler past," their oath as an attempt to "ritualize gestures of mutual reassurance," by participating in the "secret mysteries of the enslaved Coromantins" and swearing allegiance to each other and their cause.[92] Here the fact of enslavement unsurprisingly posits—even for Williams—the local, New World present of 1820s Jamaica as a degeneration of an idealized (because "free") Old World African past. But the "ritualized gestures" comprising the oath ceremony not only reflect Williams's localized response to untenable local conditions; it also forecasts a soon-to-be black Jamaica modeled on the neighboring black kingdom of Haiti. In other words, with one foot in an Old World African past and one in a New Caribbean present, Williams's "Africans"—like the Bois-Caïman celebrants—straddle place and time.

Thus Williams's oath scene—Africanized and exoticized as it is—complicates the novel's engagement with competing conceptions of time in the 1820s, including those that fueled the debate over gradual versus immediate emancipation. Clearly Williams constructs Hamel and his would-be revolution as untimely, premature. But Williams also writes suggestively of the obeah man's capacity to challenge—if not to burst—the limits of time. Indeed, the novel's end circles back to the oath-taking ceremony as Hamel rejects Fairfax's offer of gold in return for not having carried out his revolution and for saving Joanna. Rather than gold, the obeah man explains, "I would have the conviction of having devoted myself, at least, with my companions."[93] In the absence of this conviction and in the face of what he describes as his betrayal of the rebels' oath, he cannot remain on the island, not because he feels threatened by those whose plans he has ruined, but because he has "ruined [him]self in the estimation of those to whom I had *sworn* fidelity."[94] Because Hamel no longer has a place in the local present of Jamaica, in other words, he leaves, with the sail of his canoe pointing eastward. To Mr. Guthrie's query, "[W]hither are you bound?" Hamel simply replies, "To the land of my birth—my mother's country."[95]

In the end, then, Hamel is bound for and bound to Africa, with the understanding that "the hour of Hamel will shortly arrive!"[96] In Williams's construction the immediacy of the obeah man's declaration suggests that he speaks of his death, but in expressing desire for that hour, and/or for a return to his birthplace, the language also points to an idealized future that is present and past at once—the hour, perhaps, of the black man's triumph. Describing a motionless Fairfax and Guthrie watching Hamel sail away, gazing "without regarding the time they so misapplied," until his boat is reduced in their vision "to a speck"—distilling time's passage to a pinprick—the novel remains both fixed and unsettled in temporality, history, and revolution.[97] Thus, it is and is not able to go "beyond the superfices of the 'System'" that constrains Williams and his "hero."[98]

3 "Lost Subjects"

The Specter of Idleness and the Work of
Marly; or, A Planter's Life in Jamaica

WHEN P. L. Simmonds arrived in Jamaica in December 1831, he wasn't sure where he would find work—only that Jamaica represented possible advancement for a young white man from Cornwall. Within a week he had been hired as a junior bookkeeper on Fort Stewart Estate, "kindly welcomed by the Overseer (or as the Negroes call him the Busher) Mr MacGregor, a more gentlemanly amiable young man I never saw."[1] A few days later, he set out to grant his sisters' "wish to know what [his] daily occupation is" on Fort Stewart Estate, a large property about four miles inland from Annotto Bay on Jamaica's northeast coast. Although we don't know how long Simmonds stayed on Fort Stewart, whether or not he returned to his family in Cornwall as "a Rich Jamaican Planter," or whether or not the "Fever . . . carr[ied] [him] off first," his descriptions of the daily routine on a sugar estate worked by more than four hundred enslaved people provide the details his sisters requested (see fig. 9):[2]

> After dinner I put by in the Store the Cheese and what cold meats may be remaining—I then give out Clothing to the Negroes, Nails to the Cooper and other things occasionally I have to read the Funeral Services. Every Monday morning I give out a Bar of soap to the Washerwoman to wash all the Book keepers Clothes—Starch you are obliged to buy for yourself and it comes expensive. I also on Monday give out Coffee, to serve for the Week—Butter is a great rarity yet they use it for every thing in Cooking, for roasting a Fowl & to fry Meat. They have no Dripping—I am obliged to be saving with Butter as our Cask is nearly out—Whenever I am at the Stores I am sure to have plenty of the Slaves begging for one thing and another, "Massa gib me a [leeka] drink. Buckra me very ill gib me a leeka rice to make [???]. Massa gib me a leeka leeka Butter, Buckra gib me a leeka drink of Santa [drink made from rum, sugar, and fruit juice]—gib me a leeka dry salt to yam [nyam, to eat]—and if I refuse

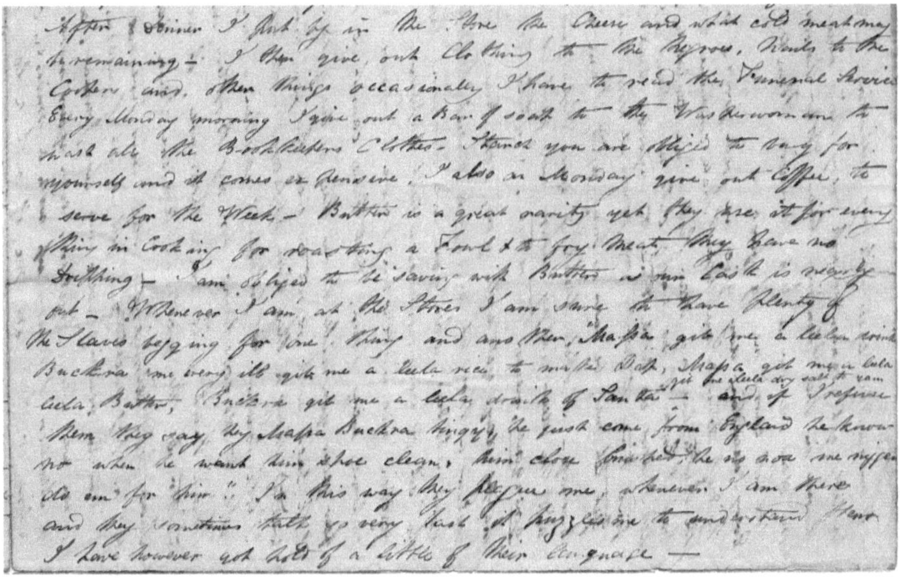

FIGURE 9. Letter to Serena Simmonds from her brother P. L. Simmonds, dated January 1822. At his sister's request, Simmonds writes to describe his daily routine as a junior bookkeeper on a large Jamaican sugar estate. (Courtesy of the National Library of Jamaica)

them they say hey Massa Buckra stingy, he just come from England he know no when he want him shoe clean, him close brushed, he no [know one?] nigger do em for him." In this way they plague me whenever I am there and they sometimes talk so very fast it puzzles me to understand them. I have however got hold of a little of their language—

For readers of *Montgomery* or of *Marly; or, A Planter's Life in Jamaica*, published three years before Simmonds's arrival, none of the details in his letter would be surprising. There are differences, of course, most notably the absence in Simmonds's private letter of the novels' political overtones and their obvious aim to instruct a wide audience about white creole culture and culture building in the early nineteenth century. But in terms of the descriptions of a junior bookkeeper's routine—from dispensing medicines in the estate hospital or hot-house, to rationing corn for feeding hogs and poultry, to keeping "spell" in the boiling-house, "which is to sit up all night while the Sugar is making to see that none is stole"[3]—all of the accounts convey the authors' awareness that their employment renders them subordinate to the disciplinary regimes of the estate hierarchy.

Moreover, the work performed by white employees is perceived by them as something completely unfamiliar to metropolitan readers. As Ronald Campbell, the young George Marly's friend and fellow bookkeeper complains, "[T]he people at home entertain curious ideas of the state of those who come here. They think, as I was led to believe it, that the people here lived an idle life, rioting in all the luxuries of a tropical climate." This idea, he continues, is every bit as mistaken as the pity he had been encouraged to feel for "the poor negroes" forced to perform "laborious work" by "unfeeling white people": "Little did I think," Campbell concludes, "that I myself should have to undergo more fatigue each day, than the negroes whom I pitied."[4] Even though Simmonds's letter does not directly compare his work with that of the enslaved people he superintends, he and the fictionalized Montgomery, Marly, and Campbell see the "labourious, nay, almost degrading" work of the junior bookkeepers as more arduous and more demanding than anything required of the enslaved.[5] As Simmonds assures his sisters: "I have plenty to do, no idleness here."[6]

Like Frank Cundall's description of *Montgomery* as a generally "true account of life on the sugar estates and pens at that period," Karina Williamson's introduction to the Macmillan Caribbean edition of *Marly* points to such minute descriptions of white employees' duties as evidence that the novelist draws on actual experience of estate life, something that Simmonds's letter appears to corroborate.[7] I am less interested, however, in reading accounts of bookkeepers' tasks as evidence of "eyewitness insiderism"[8] than in exploring how that insiderism (re)produces racialized notions of labor; with how and why the work performed by anonymous enslaved and free black people is contrasted with and subordinated to the work—physical, emotional, and cultural—performed by the novel's white characters.

Contrasting white and black labor is a key rhetorical strategy of white West Indian writing of the slavery period. *Montgomery,* as discussed in chapter 1, participates in this convention by privileging the sentimental work of the hero's "labouring heart" over the productive labor of the enslaved. *Marly,* however, even as it gives an occasional nod to the kind of sentimentalism operating in *Montgomery,* emphasizes a willingness to engage in productive labor as the truest measure of a people's progress on the road to civilization. The novel's depiction of enslaved people's lack of such volition provides evidence of the need for a "moderate course of ameliorism" that will see the enslaved guided slowly but surely toward a market economy that they will be "free" to enjoy. The path toward such freedom, of course, will be laid down by enlightened white planters like Marly.[9]

Marly's decision to remain on the island, like his embrace of ameliorism, is key to the novel's prescription for an improved colonial model. A local community of resident paternalistic planters, the novel promises, will outlast the institution of slavery and ensure a smooth progression into the post-Emancipation future, a period when it will manage and profit from the labor not of slaves, but of an improved, "liberated" black peasantry. This teleological end, of course, hinges on the novel's conclusion: the restoration of the young Scotsman to the estates left to him by his grandfather, his marriage to a creole heir, and the assumption of his role as the new patriarch of the landed creole family established by the "first of the Jamaica Marlys."[10]

In its broad outline, the novel reads much like a conventional quest narrative, but young Marly's "progress" is punctuated by digressive set speeches presented as a kind of supplemental education the would-be planter receives before succeeding his dead grandfather. Not only must he learn the daily routines of estate labor, the narrative suggests, but Marly also must weigh the relative merits of a number of sometimes competing views of "Creole society and Creole sentiment"[11]: from a Methodist missionary who explains the "natural" antipathy of white people toward black people, weaving in a denunciation of Bartolomé de las Casas for advocating the African slave trade in the New World and thus forestalling a superior method of colonization by white settlers; to the musings of an "eccentric" overseer who theorizes about "whitening the black race" through successive generations until—even in Africa—the black race disappears; to a lengthy oration by Marly's former classmate, a "brown gentleman" educated in Edinburgh and reunited with Marly in Jamaica, who expresses dismay over proposed metropolitan legislation to emancipate the enslaved rather than granting civil rights to mulatto proprietors.[12] In what is by far the lengthiest of these "harangues," the respected and well-traveled Mr. Broadcote promotes ameliorism and gradual emancipation as the surest way to protect West Indian interests in the increasingly competitive world sugar market. By the time Marly recoups his properties at the end of the novel, he has ostensibly sorted through these various lessons in plantership—though his process of thinking through them is implied rather than described in any detail.

Although the presentation of such a multitude of perspectives is useful in displaying the heterogeneity of white creole society, for some readers it undermines *Marly*'s success in both novelistic and polemical terms. As Barbara Lalla puts it, the disjunctions between *Marly*'s plot and the speeches that interrupt it mark the novel as a failed text: it "does not achieve gripping characterization by portrayal of individual struggle for selfhood, as distinct from a struggle for purely physical and social success"; moreover, the character Marly "conveys relatively little imagination and emotional sensitivity."[13] Ultimately, Lalla argues, the novel's contradictions arise "because civilization in 'imperial' discourse presupposes a dialectic of domination and subordination as a construct for order; in the Jamaican setting, this construct overrides the romantic revolution of contemporary British literature."[14]

I would argue, however, that unlike *Montgomery*'s and *Hamel*'s authors, the author of *Marly* is much less concerned with his protagonist's "struggle for selfhood" and "romantic revolution" than with his endorsement of a new, improved colonial order, characterized by ameliorist and gradualist policies as stated by Mr. Broadcote and promoted by abolitionists and planters alike in the 1820s. Marly's willingness to embrace "novel" idea(l)s—and, by implication, to move beyond "old school" plantership—helps explain the author's decision to present his proplanter message in narrative form, even though he is not, he confesses, "altogether alive to the mysteries of *fiction*."[15] For twenty-first century readers, of course, approaching *Marly* as a novel work reveals much about its moment of production and our own moment of consumption. Indeed, despite "obvious defects" like clumsy plotting and lengthy polemical orations,[16] *Marly* illustrates the intensity and persistence of the early creole novel's concerns with production and consumption: of literature, of colonial identities, and, not least in *Marly,* of (agri)cultural goods and labor(ers).

These concerns appear at the forefront of the novel, raised in the prefatory material accompanying the first and second editions, both published in 1828.[17] In the first edition's address "To the Public" and in the "Preface to the Second Edition," the author offers a fairly straightforward explanation of the decision to produce (and hopefully sell) a novel: readers overwhelmed with nonfiction works about the Emancipation debate will, it's hoped, pick up the novel and more readily sympathize with "Creole sentiment" couched in the mode of realist fiction than could be hoped from an increase of "essays and letters" that are "already . . . too numerous."[18] Employing the "catching form of the novel" and writing in the "guise of a novelist,"[19] the author anticipates greater "success" than could otherwise be expected. But promulgating proplanter sympathies in novel form was not unique to *Marly*, as the examples of *Montgomery* and *Hamel* demonstrate. For my reading of *Marly*, however, the author's peculiar conception of the form is even more critical than his decision to employ it: "to awaken the interest and engage the attention of the mass of readers," he explains, "there is nothing so effectual as the *machinery* of a novel."[20]

"Machinery" here carries the obvious sense of literary devices and conventions available to the novelist. But the word also conveys a sense of mechanization, of industrialized systems and their organization, of processes fitted to and for particular purposes. In other words, by invoking the machinery of a (creole) novel, *Marly*'s author calls to mind another machine of the Atlantic world, the plantation machine. As discussed in the introduction and in chapter 1, the mechanics of (re)production at work in early creole novels and on the large sugar estates generate numerous tensions along with their constructions of colonial settings, people, and experiences. In *Marly* and *Montgomery* especially, these tensions are embedded in the cultural/agricultural nexus, playing out in the novel's descriptions of daily estate life.

But whereas *Montgomery*'s tensions often are located in the interruptions of picturesque elements by brutal reminders of the actualities of plantation slavery, *Marly*'s are rooted in depictions of industry and idleness, in representations of differentiated labor performed by white and black characters enmeshed in the plantation machine. These representations, in turn, reflect the insistent belief held by some sectors of white creole society that improved West Indian prospects in the waning days of a colonial system of slavery, dependent on protectionist policies, could be achieved not simply by regulating and managing labor and laborers, but by improving them.[21]

Such improvements in the case of *Marly* cannot be plotted out according to the terms and conventions of contemporary British romantic literature, with its focus on the individual's coming of age; indeed, the prospective bildungsroman unfolding in *Marly* is not so much that of an individuated protagonist as of the machine itself. This is borne out by the novel's final chapter, in which Marly's quest is quickly and formulaically resolved once he publicly reveals his identity as the Marly heir, proves his legal right to his grandfather's estates, and proposes marriage to the daughter of the scheming attorney who had tried to cheat him of his property. Marly slips comfortably into his role as a wealthy West Indian planter, and, "in a very flattering manner," is fully embraced "by the society, of which he was to form a part."²² Once installed, the narrator informs us, Marly is ready to perform the work of improvement necessary to ensure the survival of the Plantation.

Before his position as a resident proprietor is validated by the resident white community, however, he is acknowledged by the enslaved people who will work under his gaze. Heralded by "a large body of negroes," Marly is delighted by the display of devotion:

> A more joyful set of countenances could no where be seen, far more so than if they had been told that they were free, for the most of them never desired their freedom, and at the present moment none thought of it. They were happy to see the man upon whom they had a claim for every thing which they considered valuable in life, and who, in the present state of their society, was their natural protector, for to no other source than to him could they look for help in the time of need.²³

The image of infantilized slaves, of course, is part of the fantasy of a smoothly operating estate running at peak efficiency. Marly values his inheritance not only as a mature property "in excellent condition" (he has recently taken a tour and assessed its state), but also as one that holds the promise of even greater profit under the supervision of the model slaveholder he promises to be and worked by happy slaves who have no thought of freedom. Of course, descriptions of Marly's earlier experiences as bookkeeper suggest he understands that the contented slaves of Happy Fortune are not representative of all enslaved people. He has seen and heard of "incorrigible runaways," "idle, disorderly, and dissolute" slaves, even ungrateful slaves who have attacked or murdered their masters.²⁴ Despite such examples from other estates and other proprietors, Marly unquestioningly accepts the "homage" of his slaves, a tribute befitting their complete dependence on him.²⁵

Such confidence in the willing service and unquestioning gratitude of enslaved workers is not uncommon in proslavery writings; but neither is it universal, particularly among absentee proprietors like Henry De la Beche and Matthew Lewis. Describing a "homecoming" scene similar to the celebration of Marly's restoration, Lewis observes the slaves' response to his arrival at Cornwall Estate, one of two properties bequeathed to him by his father in 1816 (the year Marly arrives in Jamaica). "The shouts, the gaiety, the wild laughter," the "strange and sudden bursts of singing and dancing" as the enslaved welcome Lewis, however, are perceived by him with a sense of unease, prompting him to wonder "whether the pleasure of the negroes was sincere."²⁶ Sincere or not, Lewis confesses, "there was something in it by which I could not help being affected."²⁷ Lewis comes to terms with such discomfort not by becoming "naturalized to the country," but by leaving the island and slavery behind, along with any sense of personal responsibility for the welfare of the enslaved laborers who work his estates.

Marly's author, no doubt, would attribute Lewis's pangs to his status as a newcomer, his opinions on arrival, like Marly's (and his friend Campbell's cited above), shaped by the abolitionist sentiment prevailing in the metropole. But whereas Lewis fails to come to terms with his disquiet during his residences in Jamaica, it takes Marly only one day on the job as bookkeeper on Water Melon Valley Estate "to lose his former favourable opinion of the Negroes being a much calumniated race, and to resort to the one formed by persons daily conversant in their management."²⁸ A quick study, Marly sees the necessity for such a hands-on education in managing the enslaved workforce, supervising their labors, and running an estate. And even though, unlike most of his contemporary bookkeepers, Marly rapidly ascends the estate hierarchy—the main events of the novel cover only a year—he makes the most of his time as "a practical student," "noting in his memory every thing which was passing forwards" related to estate management.²⁹ In this way, the novel suggests, Marly comes to possess not only an intimate knowledge of the daily operations of a large sugar property, but something the fictional Montgomery and real-life absentee owners like Lewis do not lay claim to: a "knowledge of the negro manners" that enables Marly "to please" the enslaved "in their own way."³⁰

Their own way, in the immediate context of Marly's wedding and homecoming celebrations, is to order rum for the celebrants. But, as the novel's final paragraphs reveal, the teleological end advocated in *Marly*— "the way" forward that the novel maps out for the plantation machine's future profitability and the enslaved workers' future liberation—is to affirm the rightness of Marly's enlightened "now":

> Now that he is seated at his ease, [Marly's] attention has been devoted to ameliorating the condition of his labourers, by every practicable means, without proving harmful to themselves or to his own interest . . . and to adopt every other mode of instructing and encouraging them, which may seem beneficial to all concerned. . . .
>
> Slavery will . . . gradually cease—an increase of free labourers will be the consequence—willing service will become less expensive than the present mode of forced work—and though black, a virtuous race of peasantry will

inhabit these islands, and happiness, contentment, and prosperity will be the blessings which will crown the whole.[31]

Drawing on the gradualist language used by Cynric Williams's fictional planter Mr. Mathews and the Antislavery Society's Thomas Fowell Buxton to emphasize the "natural," gradual end of slavery along with economic arguments about the inefficiency of slave labor over "free" labor, the novel closes with Marly ready to undertake the new work required of him as proprietor: improving his estate by reforming the way agricultural labor is (and will be) performed there, as well as the manners and condition of the laborers who perform (and will perform) it, both in the present as loyal slaves and in the future as virtuous peasants.

This, then, is the twin good celebrated via the machinery of this particular creole novel, the prospect of agrarian and labor reform as a unified and unifying goal, the attainment of which (according to the novel) serves the best interests of all. Of course, the fulfillment of this end depends absolutely on the presence of the laborer—a presence, as the novel implicitly acknowledges, that was guaranteed neither by coercion under slavery nor by the prospect of wages after slavery's end. Indeed, despite the certainty with which the novel's conclusion anticipates "free labourers" offering up their "willing service" on the estates, the recurring emphasis in writings on colonial labor testify to anxieties over maintaining adequate labor supplies: When (not if) enslaved workers are liberated, will they remain on the estates, or will they abandon estate work? Will they voluntarily become industrious participants in the plantation economy, or will they leave the estates en masse, to become "lost subjects" whose "natural" indolence is overcome only enough to grow food for their own subsistence?

The novel's engagement with such questions is more complex than its formulaic conclusion suggests. For embedded in *Marly*'s (successful) quest narrative—the story of Marly's arrival in Jamaica from Scotland, disguised and determined to recover his grandfather's estates, and the romance between him and Emily M'Fathom—is the crucial question of who performs the work of empire and how. Responding to this question requires the novel to perform a related but ultimately different kind of cultural work than that necessary to resolve the intertwined quest-romance plots. *Marly* must continuously negotiate between and around dialectical configurations of industry and idleness. Positioning workers along multiple axes—racially, of course, but even beyond the overriding "dialectic of [white] domination and [black] subordination"[32]—the novel and its hero attempt to distinguish between industrious and idle slaves, between those who work hard and reap the rewards, and those whose idle natures must be reformed.

Distinctions between industry and idleness appear throughout the regulatory discourse of the long eighteenth century, of course, featured in a wide range of texts, from sermons to court documents, from conduct books to Hogarth's iconic images of Francis Goodchild and Tom Idle.[33] In the Atlantic sugar colonies, however, the fact of institutionalized slavery complicates these categories. As the colonies grew increasingly reliant on the Atlantic slave trade to provide labor for the plantation machine, and as metropolitan antislavery sentiment increased proportionally, proslavery writers turned to any number of set arguments to defend slavery. One routinely invoked defense was to draw comparisons between the situation of West Indian slaves and that of the British laboring classes. Insisting that enslaved people in the colonies worked under conditions far more favorable than, say, Irish peasants or English seamen or Welsh and Scottish miners, planters and their allies—including *Marly*'s author—argued that West Indian slaves were better fed and clothed; they were better housed and received better medical care; and, unlike European miners "sequester'd from the day / . . . sunk far beneath / The earth's dark surface," the slaves performed their "pleasant . . . rural task[s]" under a kind master in a "blissful climate."[34]

Ironically, this particular strand of conventional proslavery argument becomes a source of anxiety for planters in the 1820s. For despite the "fact" that African and African Caribbean workers were necessary for the work of the Plantation, in such a "blissful climate" the reverse was not true. As the establishment of communities populated by self-liberated slaves and the Jamaican Maroons proved, the enslaved were well able to survive without assistance from the planter class. Contrary to planter rhetoric that constructed images of enslaved laborers as utterly dependent on the largesse and paternal care of proprietors like Marly ("the man upon whom they had a claim for every thing which they considered valuable in life, and who, in the present state of their society, was their natural protector") was another strand of creole discourse that bemoaned the ability of enslaved people to "satisfy the common wants of nature" with very little effort, "particularly in a Tropical climate."[35]

As *Marly*'s narrator observes, "[N]o created being from the frozen regions to the Equinoctial line desires or performs labour from a mere love of it."[36] This, the narrator states, is only natural in the tropics; furthermore, without incentives "strong enough to induce [black laborers] to toil in the same manner as the labouring class of mankind are compelled to do, in climates which are less fertile," they will remain in a state of barbarism.³⁷ So long as the enslaved (by nature "an indolent race") remain in such a primitive state, the narrator concludes, they are unfit "to be the judges of their own actions, or what may be called free men."³⁸

The novel's planter class, on the other hand, seems to have reached the developmental stage held out as the target for the enslaved, "that stage in society, where luxury, interest or ambition, stimulate men to exertions for the purpose of accumulating wealth or gaining celebrity."³⁹ Indeed, as I discuss in the following section, the attainment of such a "civilized" state of accumulated wealth produces the state of "ease" that gives Marly the authority to dictate the improvement of his enslaved laborers, to coax them along the path of progressive development by helping them acquire "artificial" or "fictitious wants."⁴⁰ These wants, of course, must be "of such a nature as to stimulate the mass of them to continued labour"—not the labor of subsistence agriculture mentioned above, but *continued* labor (i.e., postslavery) on the estates.

Enslaved and self-liberated people throughout the period of slavery resisted such notions of progress and civilization, but before turning to the forms that resistance assumes in *Marly*, it's useful to look again at Marly's place in this scheme of improvement, particularly as relates to the improvement of his (recovered) estate and of the agricultural practices employed on it. These improvements—ultimately tied to labor(er)'s reform—are, ironically, predicated on the planters' state of ease that allows Marly the leisure to undertake his civilizing mission.

Plotting the Estate/Improving the Plot

In the process of plotting out the intertwined work of the plantation machine and the machinery of his novel, *Marly*'s author, in effect, relies on a taxonomy of labor. The idealized planter class embodied by the Jamaica Marlys, of course, occupies the top of the hierarchical order, a position "earned" in the case of the Marlys, by the hard work of the family's founder, the first George Marly. His grandson and heir, the novel's hero, builds on this foundation, but his work is of a different sort. He is tasked, as mentioned above, with "improving the estate" left him by his grandfather, modernizing agricultural practices, instructing and ameliorating the labor conditions of the enslaved, and not least, helping them acquire fictitious wants so that they will be ready for liberation. In performing this critical agri/cultural labor, the younger Marly is offered up by the novelist as a "working" model for other planters concerned with the survival of the West India colonies.

The ascendance of young George Marly from the degrading labor of a bookkeeper on Water Melon Valley Estate to the state of leisure he enjoys as proprietor of Happy Fortune marks the novel's end, the close of the romance-quest narrative. But the two final paragraphs also project a forward trajectory: "*Now* that he is seated at his ease" Marly will become a model planter, a proprietor poised to usher in a new era of estate management as the acknowledged heir to the Marly fortune. This new era, however, would be impossible without the wealth accumulated by the first George Marly and the state of ease *he* attained through the acquisition of a large West Indian fortune. Such ease, of course, is clearly distinguished in the novel from idleness: the Marlys' ease represents the just reward of industry.

This interpretation of industry and ease as cause and consequence—as opposed to the more conventional binary opposition of industry and idleness—is borne out by the history of George Marly I. Encapsulated in one of the novel's early chapters, the elder Marly's story opens with his arrival in Jamaica, at a time when "the demand for white planters was great" (circa 1746).[41] Like many of his nonfictional counterparts in the mid-eighteenth century, the first Jamaica Marly arrives as a young man intent on making a fortune. And, like many narratives of colonial adventurers from the British Isles (including *Montgomery*), the novel recounts the process of his creolization through images of his hard work. First employed by an "industrious proprietor, who loved to reward the deserving," the elder Marly earns an "independency" through "diligence and good conduct," further secured through his frugality: "As soon as he was possessed of a year's salary, he laid it out in the purchase of a couple of negroes" whom he then hires out to his employer.[42] "In this system of strict economy, he persevered, and the negroes he purchased being healthy, they seasoned well; the consequence was, that in a number of years after his arrival, he found himself the master of a fine jobbing gang."[43]

Clearly, the elder Marly's rising prosperity, which coincides with the period of peak wealth generated from Jamaican sugar from the 1750s until the disrupted trade caused by the revolutionary last decades of the eighteenth century and the Napoleonic wars of the early nineteenth century, is predicated on the health and labor of those enslaved people initially purchased by him. Founding his fortune by selling the labor of "seasoned" Africans—that is, those enslaved people who survived the first year or two of their life under slavery in the Americas—he builds a network of financial creditors from among the already settled proprietors who hire his "gang" and secures the necessary capital to invest in land through a government grant. The initial outlays involved in clearing the land and erecting the sugar works put the new planter in considerable debt. But, we're assured, the first Marly's "self same good fortune" continued: within a few years "by a continued run of good crops, he was enabled to free himself of every incumbrance, so that he remained the undoubted proprietor of a free sugar estate, on which he bestowed the name of Happy Fortune, thereby denoting that his ambition as to property, was satisfied."[44]

In addition to deploying the rhetorical conventions and passive constructions that obscure the work of the enslaved in colonial texts like John Lunan's *Hortus Jamaicensis* and James Grainger's *The Sugar-Cane*,[45] the novel's description of the elder Marly's progress from unpropertied employee to master of a jobbing gang to slaveholding proprietor of a "free" sugar estate conforms to accounts of numerous real-life settlers. As Trevor Burnard observes in his study of Thomas Thistlewood's trajectory from bookkeeper to proprietor, white prosperity in Jamaica ultimately was predicated on the ownership of land, itself dependent on the ability to accumulate purchase money and, "more important, to buy slaves to work on the land."[46] In a journal entry of February 1751 Thistlewood describes the ways the colonial government encouraged such ambitions by proposing "to grant any person an Order for land" willing to "take the oath, [that] they have slaves and no land to work them on."[47] The novel's account of the elder Marly shows the fictional would-be planter taking advantage of such an opportunity, purchasing the slaves who would become "the key to [his] prosperity" by producing income despite his (temporary) landless status.[48] Like Thistlewood, the elder Marly's jobbing gang provides a guaranteed return on his initial investment due to the perennially high demand for well-seasoned, "healthy slaves" to cultivate sugar and other "staple" export produce.[49]

The descriptions of the elder Marly's sound economic principles and frugality also forestall any actual reckoning of the value of the labor of his enslaved workers. Glossing over the intensive manual labor required to clear the land and erect the sugar works, to cultivate and bring in the "run of good crops" during the estate's first years of operation (labor that frees the elder Marly of his debts), the account turns instead to the domestic economy associated with Happy Fortune estate, and the reproductive labor involved in founding a *legitimate* West Indian dynasty.

To this end, once the elder Marly has established himself and satisfied "his ambition as to property," he turns to the work of founding "a longtailed Creole family," whose name "would become as famed as the most celebrated names in the mother country."[50] In pursuit of this dream—and after a residence of thirty years in Jamaica—he marries a creole widow whose first husband has bequeathed her "a fine large property, adjoining one of old Marly's boundaries, called Conch Shell Penn," which is "well stocked with breeding cattle."[51] The cattle are not alone in performing reproductive labor on behalf of the Marly patriarch, for within a year of their marriage, Mrs. Marly produces a son, the eponymous hero's father.

The juxtaposition of the reproductive and productive labor—producing an heir, and planting and cutting sugar cane—illustrates the interdependence of endogamous marital arrangements and estate management. Such wedded activities clearly distinguish the desire of establishing a creole family, of building a *Jamaican* Marly dynasty, from more typical aspirations of colonial transplants, the majority of whom desired to return to Great Britain with a fortune—whether or not they were able to fulfill that desire. Even Montgomery and Maria, though creoles, leave Jamaica, uninterested in remaining in the land of their birth. *Marly*'s emphasis on rooting a family tree in Caribbean soil, on the other hand, becomes the driving force behind the clumsily plotted but ultimately resolved quest of the dispossessed hero.

But even as the transmission of the Marly property from grandfather to grandson guarantees the protagonist's place in creole society, it also marks a generational shift in conceptions of what comprises "a Planter's Life in Jamaica." In other words, the novel's resolution gestures toward a redefinition of the planter's labor, a movement away from the work of founding an estate to that of improving it. This shift, moreover, requires a reassessment of what improvement means in the 1820s, in light of a new era of export production marked by an international division of labor, the increasing mechanization of agriculture, and expanding networks of free trade arrangements. Whereas the first Marly arrives at a period in West Indian history during which the plantocracy was viewed as having opened a colonial frontier where boundless wealth could be amassed—at least by metropolitan commentators who wrote of West Indians returning to the metropolis to spend their money in ostentatious display[52]—by the time the younger George Marly arrives, he finds a different landscape from that cleared from the Jamaican bush by his grandfather's enslaved workers.

As Dale Tomich points out, the years between 1791 and 1815—a period roughly corresponding to the novel's chronology, which marks the elder Marly's death in 1796 and the younger Marly's arrival in 1816—saw the destruction of the mainstay of French colonial sugar production in St. Domingue brought about by the Haitian Revolution and the end of the Napoleonic Wars.[53] As early as 1805, William Playfair had noted the benefits of the French colony's collapse for British sugar producers: even as the Haitian Revolution raised fears of violent insurrection in the Anglo-Caribbean, it also diminished France's trading power in the region to such an extent that in his *Inquiry into the Permanent Causes of the Decline and Fall of Powerful and Wealthy Nations,* Playfair declared that "the superiority" of Britain's West India trade could be "set down as permanent." Without St. Domingue, which was "lost for ever," France would "never again be a formidable rival" in the Caribbean.[54] Although Playfair was right about France, he wasn't as prescient in regard to the permanence of West Indian dominance: even as these years saw a more rapid rise in British Caribbean sugar production than at any other time in its history, "the interplay of market forces and the anti-slavery movement" in England—not to mention the antislavery activities of the enslaved themselves—"pushed Britain toward a policy of free trade and undercut the competitive position of its West Indian colonies."[55]

In this sense, the differences between the temporal setting of *Marly*'s action (a point when West Indian sugar was enjoying a temporary resurgence) and the dates of its composition and publication in the late 1820s (when emancipation appeared imminent and market forces were dictating its decline) showcase the anxiety and tensions evident in planter discourse during the last years of slavery. On the one hand, the well-established properties the young Marly inherits and that he acquires with his new wife at the novel's conclusion are highly profitable enterprises worked by enslaved laborers; on the other hand, the novel's plot cannot help but be informed by its author's awareness of complex changes that "created new conditions for slave labor internationally. To the degree that Britain was able to exercise influence over world production through its control of the market," writes Tomich, "it was able to develop a flexible global economic and political strategy utilizing a variety of forms and sources of labor, ranging from slaves to tenants, sharecroppers, and peasants, and from indentured laborers to free wage laborers." In the end, Tomich points out, slave labor lost its privileged status for Britain: "the particular social form of labor became less important than its cheapness."[56]

The emerging contours of the global sugar market Tomich describes are sketched out in the lengthy speech of Mr. Broadcote, whose cautionary prognostics in *Marly*'s 1816 Jamaica are inflected by the author's sense of the changes that had taken hold by 1828 when the novel was published. Broadcote, we're told, had long been considered by his fellow white creoles as "one of their brightest stars," an "industrious opposer of the abolition of slavery."[57] After traveling abroad, however, his opinions became "less local than they had formerly been":

> In the course of his travels he had come into contact with intelligent gentlemen, who had seen many parts of the world, and whose mode of thinking, from the observations made on various countries, were very different from what he had entertained as correct notions of man when in the midst of a large slave population. His former opinions were first staggered, and the reflections upon what he heard and saw in the mode of raising colonial produce in Bengal and in Java, by means of free labour, dispelled the illusion of the necessity of slavery, and forced conviction on his mind that it was inexpedient even in an economical point of view.[58]

By turns reasonable and patronizing toward his fellow planters, Broadcote expresses himself in language that conforms to what Richard Drayton describes as the "third idiom of imperialism," "driven by those who understood themselves as cosmopolitans, and as the diffusers of universal progress.... We may call it the imperialism of the division of labour, to give credit to the proposition which best expressed its genius."[59] As *Marly* demonstrates, in the first decades of the nineteenth century, the place of slaves in this idiom was "complex and contradictory": on the one hand, as Drayton explains, "division-of-labour imperialism presumed a world of free labour, of contracts freely entered into, and indeed its allies supported the anti-slavery movement." Yet the soon-to-be ex-slaves of the British West Indies, like the "slaves of Brazil and Cuba, and the semi-slaves of the Dutch and British East Indies, were ... important producers and consumers well into the nineteenth century, as important for the factories of Lancashire as they were for the progress of 'free-labour' settlement" in the "new" frontiers of South America.[60]

Broadcote, whose speech suggests an appreciation of these complexities, including the importance of an emerging class of free black consumers, expresses frustration over what he perceives as his fellow planters' parochial and shortsighted views, taking them to task for their unwillingness to adapt to new global conditions. If they continue on such a path, he promises, there are those well positioned to take advantage of West Indian stubbornness—East Indian sugar producers:

> Gentlemen, slavery, or the compulsory labor of man, has been condemned by many intelligent people among ourselves, as being more expensive even than free labour. That this is the case at present is certain, if the truth is credited, for sugar produced by the labour of free people in Bengal and Java can be sold in

London cheaper than that grown in the West Indies. . . . It is quite evident . . . that if we could get quit of slavery without any violent commotion, and could induce the negroes to labour for hire after giving them freedom—a sugar estate could be managed cheaper than at this moment, and probably we might be enabled to undersell the Eastern growers.[61]

As Williamson points out, Broadcote's assessment of the threat posed to West Indian growers by those in the East Indies reflects issues raised in numerous pamphlets and parliamentary debates throughout the 1820s, particularly those that pushed for the repeal of longstanding protectionist policies favoring Caribbean planters.[62] The result of Broadcote's attempts to persuade his fellow planters that he has the West Indian cause at heart, that his arguments proceed from his "great desire for the improvement, the happiness, and the wealth of this and our other colonies in the West,"[63] is not revealed; the "lengthy harangue" of more than thirty pages ends with no indication of its success or failure. But given the concluding description of Marly's intended course of estate management, the major points of which conform to Broadcote's suggestions, it appears that the novel supports the notion that West Indian "prejudice (or the ignorance of vulgar minds) must give way to an improving mode" or the colonies' ruin is inevitable.[64]

The "improving mode" extends to all aspects of plantership, from the amelioration of the manners and morals of slaveholders (as in *Montgomery*) and the enslaved, to the most basic, material practices involved in West Indian sugar cultivation. Indeed, the perceived need for agrarian reform occupies a central place in the novel's didactic message, first conveyed by the description of Marly's observations on Water Melon Valley Estate during the early days of his residence. Much of what Marly observes conforms to the phrasing found throughout planter discourse—assurances to the reader that "what can be styled hard work, was not required from the negroes"; that, at day's end, "none of them seemed any way exhausted or fatigued with their day's toil"; that "[t]heir work could scarcely be said to be very laborious"—until, that is, the novel turns to the work performed during planting season.[65]

However disingenuous the narrator's account of daily toil performed by enslaved laborers for much of the agricultural calendar, descriptions of the planting season concede the laboriousness of putting land under cane. This, the narrator reveals, "is the season most abhorrent to the negroes" who, in the lead up to the actual planting must first clear the land in the case of uncultivated fields, or dig up the roots of old canes (ratoons)

Figure 10. "Holeing a Cane-Piece," which first appeared in William Clark's *Ten Views of the Island of Antigua* (1823), was republished accompanied by large-print text in a children's reader by the Ladies' Society for Promoting the Early Education of Negro Children [1833?]. (Courtesy of the John Carter Brown Library at Brown University)

that no longer yield cane juice "capable of being boiled into sugar" on established cane fields. Requiring the efforts of all estate workers, the process of "holeing the cane" is described in full detail (see fig. 10):

> On Monday morning, the whole negroes of both gangs commenced holing with the hoe, and the black tradesmen were on the ground, together with the overseer and the two book-keepers, to assist in carrying the lines, so that the holes might be regularly dug. . . . This process of excavation was performed with the hoe alone, two negroes being placed to one hole as nearly matched as possible, a strong negro having for his partner a weak one; but all had to perform the same quantity of work, and in the same time, in order to keep them in line; consequently a female or weak person had to dig nearly as much as the strongest. It was a stiff soil, and the work was more than ordinarily laborious; but though the people were not much hurried, as the day advanced they visibly became fatigued. After a week or five days of this kind of labour, very distressing to the people, few acres indeed were gone over, although there

were rather more than a hundred negroes employed, one day with another, digging only these holes in the ground.[66]

Lewis's *Journal* also notes the extreme working conditions that mark this season; as for Marly, he acknowledges that regardless of the hard work of Water Melon Valley's slaves, they are unable to put enough land under cane, requiring the overseer to hire a jobbing gang. "With the jobbing gang," the narrator interjects, "appeared another and a new view of slavery, for if slaves settled upon an estate can be said to be unhappy, those jobbers then must be miserable."[67] Indeed, the narrator confesses, the lot of these workers—whose life expectancy in the fields was a mere seven years—is so harsh that estate workers "pitied" them.[68] With no suggestion of irony, the narrator's sympathetic observation in relation to the jobbing gang reveals the dark foundation of the elder Marly's fortune, laid by his own jobbing gang of "well-seasoned Africans."

As sympathetic to enslaved workers as this description appears, the passage performs another function, one that assumes greater significance even than the acknowledgment of the hard labor performed during planting season. For *Marly*'s author, that is, bemoaning the arduous labor of the estate workers occasions one of the novel's multiple critiques of West Indian agricultural methods. Throughout Britain's Caribbean sugar islands, the narrator complains, as in all the European colonies "wrought with slaves"—agriculture remains unconscionably primitive. For despite the half-century of improvements introduced in British agriculture, West Indian planters have refused to incorporate new methods. In one of the most pointed of the novel's authorial interjections, the narrator denounces this backwardness as a disgrace: "No improvements in the mode have been adopted, since the first period of settling the sugar colonies. . . . [T]he self-same routine of ignorant and barbarous management is still continued; and it is probable, will continue, till absolute distress forces them to adopt improved plans."[69]

The narrator's frustration here—which Broadcote echoes in his speech—is palpable, one of several moments in the text when the author's proplanter sympathies appear strained by the perception of a plantocracy hostile to change, a class verging on self-destruction in the face of emergent global networks shaped by liberal trade policies favoring producers willing to increase efficiency and modernize production methods. Particularly galling, at least in the narrator's and Broadcote's opinion, is the refusal on the part of planters to incorporate what they see as the most easily adaptable improvements to the basic material conditions of agricultural production. Tools routinely employed in Great Britain—"the plough, the spade, the grape, the harrow, the rake, the scythe, the reaping-hook, and the wheelbarrow"—that would greatly reduce the inefficient use of human labor in planting are unknown, according to the novel, on West Indian estates.[70] Instead, planters and estate managers continue to rely on "the rudest of implements," the "hand-hoe, the bill-hook for cutting canes and brush-wood, the knife for cutting grass, and the basket."[71] With these, the entire farming work of the estate is performed, "under the direction," the narrator fumes, "of a civilized people, in the most civilized of ages, and in direct opposition to the well-known fact, that the unknown implements on a sugar plantation, could be beneficially employed in cultivating nine-tenths, at least, of the estates in the islands."[72]

Broadcote's assessment of the situation several chapters later repeats this theme, when he decries the absence of agricultural innovation in the West Indies, citing again the stubbornness of white creoles in condemning the enslaved to toil with such rude tools as the hand hoe, billhook, and basket. In this passage, Broadcote insists on the need for planters to modernize estate work, offering up one labor-saving implement that, he argues, could revolutionize West Indian sugar production: the plow.

Not only would replacing the hoe with the plow reduce "the labour of the people, and enabl[e] them to devote more attention" to the canes, Broadcote enthuses, but it also will allow them more time for "the cultivation of provisions for themselves, and food for the cattle upon the estates. In every point of view it would be beneficial."[73] This is a continuation of the sentiment expressed in the passage above describing the laboriousness of the planting season, and anticipates the novel's concluding paragraphs that lay out Marly's future course of estate improvement, the most specific detail of which is his determination to "abolish hoe-husbandry as much as possible, by the introduction of plough tillage to its fullest extent."[74]

The novel's emphasis on the plow is not unique in the literature of the period. Numerous accounts of West Indian practices—particularly those supporting East Indian over West Indian sugar—remarked on the West Indian planters' resistance to plow tillage so often that for many commentators it operates emblematically, standing in for the plantocracy's willful refusal to modernize their agricultural methods.[75] Such unwillingness, however, was not as universal as the commentaries—and passages in *Marly*—suggest. As discussed in chapter 1, local periodicals like the *Jamaica Magazine* routinely solicited and printed information about agricultural innovations, particularly those adapted to local conditions. In Jamaica as in the other Caribbean colonies, resident planters, overseers, and attorneys charged with the management of absentee-owned estates, formed agricultural societies whose mission was to assist individuals "desirous of enquiring into various branches of art or science, as well as to encourage all improvements in Agriculture and Horticulture."[76]

As for the plow itself, as Williamson points out, it had been in use in the West Indies since the mid-eighteenth century, incorporated along with various other improvements, though certain reforms were rejected as impracticable.[77] Even though plow tillage was rejected on the Grenada estate of absentee owner George Cornewall, for example, other improvements were adopted, including the installation of a steam engine in 1817 to power the estate's new sugar mill.[78] From self-taught botanists like John Lunan and Thomas Thistlewood to "Agricola," whose essays on cane cultivation were printed and circulated in the Caribbean, these creoles saw themselves as invaluable contributors to scientific knowledge, equals to their metropolitan counterparts in advancing the practice of agriculture and civilization through the agricultural and horticultural arts.[79]

But even as innovations were experimented with and adopted in ways that contradicted depictions of West Indian planters as stubbornly resistant to change, there was one area of estate management that commentators in the colonies and in Great Britain agreed was crucial: the absolute necessity of supervising estate laborers, whether enslaved or free, a necessity dictated by colonialist assumptions about the "natural indolence" of black agricultural workers. Without assurances that the enslaved would remain on the estates as free wage laborers, immediate emancipation would provoke a tragedy "similar to that which was performed in the neighboring island of Hayti": Jamaica, "the queen of the West Indies, with its finely cultivated fields, its elegant buildings and expensive works would become a waste—the houses would be burned—the works destroyed—and industry come to an end."[80] As in *Hamel* the specter of Haiti and the aftereffects of the Haitian Revolution loom large in the creole imaginary. And certainly the colonialist script narrating that event was predicated on representations of a thriving plantation culture destroyed by the savagery of the enslaved. The signs of civilization, the argument went, would be erased, supplanted by the rude and primitive; the culture built by the industry of the planter class would be destroyed through the untutored idleness of (too suddenly) liberated black people.

Industry or Idleness?

Depictions of enslaved people as naturally indolent are among the most common features of white creole writing, and *Marly* is no exception.

As discussed above, the novel has no problem declaring the exhausting and laborious work of white people within the context of the plantation machine, whether they are "self-made" proprietors like the elder George Marly, much put-upon but ambitious overseers or bookkeepers like P. L. Simmonds and Campbell and Marly himself during his time on Water Melon Valley Estate, or enlightened planters dedicated to improving the condition and morals of enslaved laborers like Broadcote and the newly acknowledged Marly heir. Nor, as discussed above, does the novel always neglect descriptions of the hard labor of field workers during planting season when emphasizing the need to improve estate efficiency.

However, descriptions of enslaved people as "industrious"—a word suggestive of the ability to labor dutifully, willingly, unsupervised, and unforced—are much rarer. Marly encounters one or two such individuals while employed on Water Melon Valley Estate, members of "reputable families" whose "private industry" enables them to make purchases of nonessential items that render them superior to the rest of the enslaved on the estate.[81] "[T]hese negroes," moreover, are ("comparatively speaking") in a "state of comfort and happiness" because they "did not know what liberty was. . . . They had no cares—they apparently had as few wants—the estate furnished them with herrings, and their grounds furnished them with provisions more than sufficient for their consumption, the overplus of which they carried to market."[82]

The contradictions here are striking in light of the gradualist tendencies of the novel, the foundation of which is laid in assertions of the need to defer emancipation until the enslaved exhibit signs of improvement—that is, industriousness and quiescence. Yet here, the very signs of meeting the prerequisites for liberty render these comfortable and happy slaves content with enslavement, specifically because their industry grants them purchasing power. There is no need to push for emancipation, either immediate or gradual, since they do not equate enslavement (according to *Marly*'s author) with the absence of liberty. Indeed, the novel insists, they do "not know what liberty is."[83]

But these "respectable negroes" (who "do not numerically amount to above the one-half of the slaves upon an estate") are not alone in their ignorance.[84] There is a far more numerous "body of idle, disorderly, and dissolute people," who—although "eager for their 'freedom'"—don't understand the real meaning of liberty any more than the industrious minority: "They think that freedom means a cessation from labour altogether—and that when they are allowed freedom, they are to work no more."[85] Here the novel's emphasis on the enslaved population's inability to comprehend what "true" liberty entails signals a lack of readiness for freedom, a common refrain throughout the colonialist history of Atlantic slavery and its construction of liberty as the "mastering capacity for freedom."[86]

As Laura Doyle describes this construction, "To be white is to be fit for freedom, and the white man's burden is to lead others by forging the institutions and modeling the subjectivities required to practice proper freedom, even if along the way this requires enslaving, invading, or exterminating those others who may not (yet) be fit for freedom."[87] In her study of the Anglo-Atlantic novel, Doyle suggests that claims about enslaved people's ill-preparedness for the "boon of freedom"[88] were not new to the emancipation debates of the 1820s. Rather, they formed an integral part of colonialist discourse from the beginnings of England's Caribbean expansion in the seventeenth century. Such assumptions were rife in the lead up to eventual parliamentary action on the question, a cornerstone of gradualist discourse, asserted by anti-immediasts of all political stripes and on both sides of the Atlantic.

In addition to participating in this rhetorical tradition, *Marly* also moves along the "coloniality/modernity border" described by Walter Mignolo, a border, Doyle writes, that is "not so much geographical as ontopolitical, inflecting language, sorting persons, and creating divergent bodily and social experiences through a racialized liberty discourse."[89] Thus, even as the novel unites "the whole of the negroes" by their supposed ignorance of what freedom and liberty mean, it also, at the same time, sorts and categorizes subgroups of individuals according to measures of industry and idleness, characteristics that define their social experiences.[90]

The fault lines at this border in the context of Atlantic slavery become obvious in *Marly*'s contradictory descriptions of industrious and idle slaves' provision grounds. Like the "reputable families" mentioned earlier, there are among the enslaved of Water Melon Valley Estate (where Marly is first employed) people who take advantage of "negro day" as the one day of the week that they are permitted to travel to tend their own crops. This temporary respite from coerced estate labor, however, cannot diminish the difficulties involved in such cultivation, beginning with the journey to and from the grounds themselves. For Marly and his fellow bookkeeper, who take the "delightfully romantic" trip by mule, the visit to the grounds comprises a "fatiguing day's work," despite the picturesque prospects found along the "sometimes fearfully dangerous" route.[91]

The enslaved, of course, undertake the journey on foot, through seemingly impenetrable Jamaican bush, up "steep hill and dale" to the estate's extensive mountain run, where "the axe had made very little havoc among the trees."[92] As for the individual plots cultivated by the enslaved, those "in the hands of the industrious well-behaved families, were in excellent condition"; but, "those held by the worst class of negroes, were in a deplorable condition," clearly showing that "they belonged to the sluggards."[93] Here provision grounds become proving grounds, a means of distinguishing between industrious and idle estate laborers. The clearest proof of industriousness this test provides is the calculable "overplus" cultivated by the individual or family, which signals their ability to participate in the island economy as producer of marketable goods and prospective consumer in the local cash economy. Those people who raise more provision than they require for their own sustenance and who sell the remainder on the internal domestic market of the island (unlike those idle individuals who fail to "work for their own behoof") have, in the novel's representation, acquired the "artificial" stimulus to industry.[94]

Yet in *Marly*, as in so many commentaries on the agricultural labor performed on marginal lands of estates where provision grounds were located, even the high yields of non-export crops grown by the enslaved for their own and local consumption generate contradictions. On the one hand, as Marly sees on his visit to the mountain grounds, even on small plots of less than half an acre, the industrious are "growing . . . plantains, bananas, yams, eddoes, sweet potatoes, melons, pine apples, Indian corn, and tobacco, besides many things of less moment," a profusion of what were referred to as nonstaple (i.e., nonexport) crops.[95] But even as such crops are cultivated by (exceptionally) industrious individuals, the value of their work is minimized through the description of the material conditions of provision ground labor. The very soil on which such crops are grown, we're told, is so fertile that "it is very seldom that . . . crops ever fail."[96] Indeed, the narrator insists, as "in all tropical climates where there is abundance of soil and moisture, the earth yields so spontaneously," "that the smallest exertion of labour produces far more than is requisite for the wants of man, in a semi-barbarous, or half civilized state."[97]

In this, the mountain grounds allocated to the enslaved on Water Melon Valley in *Marly* run counter to those described by Woodville Marshall, who discusses the problems encountered by enslaved agriculturalists that prevented "optimal cultivation."[98] In addition to the distance between slaves' housing and the mountain grounds, Marshall notes other "natural constraints on cultivation which such a location imposed." Such land was mainly forest and mountain, "difficult of access because of the steep slopes, difficult to clear because of virgin forests, difficult to cultivate because of boulders and stones, and impossible to protect against threats of land slippage and erosion."[99] These constraints, as scholars like Marshall, Sidney Mintz, Mary Turner, Jean Besson, Mimi Sheller, and others observe of provision ground cultivation, required the enslaved to go far beyond the "little effort" mentioned in *Marly*'s descriptions. Not only did those who worked mountain grounds undergo arduous physical labor, but they performed this labor with much greater efficiency than the novelist and other colonial writers claimed. Moreover, contributions that enslaved workers made to the Caribbean economy beyond their labor in export-crop production—Mr. Broadcote, for example, concedes the importance of this agricultural activity to the colony's ability to feed itself—make it clear that such efforts were crucial not only to the colonies' internal economies, but to the very survival of their inhabitants.

Despite this clear contribution to colonial self-sufficiency and well-being, the resistance to acknowledging this level of industry on the part of enslaved workers—the people who, at the same time, are represented as the foundation of the post-Emancipation plantation workforce—remain, in the colonialist view, semicivilized, semibarbarous agriculturalists whose crops flourish due to spontaneously yielding tropical soil rather than the growers' agrarian knowledge.

More worrisome than the rude agricultural practices of the enslaved, however, is a "fact" Mr. Broadcote decries in his critique of West Indian planting. From the beginnings of the Caribbean colonization project white planters, he claims, have relied on those same "primitive" agricultural methods for the cultivation of the colonies' export crops. "Our present system is deplorably bad," he complains to his fellow planters, for West Indian sugar producers have "borrowed" their system, "not from a race superior or equal" to them, but from "those objects of our contempt, and of our dread—the negroes."[100] The visual evidence supplied by watching enslaved field laborers leads Brodcote to the inevitable conclusion that "the mode of our agriculture is of the most unscientific, and the least improved description than it is possible for the mind of man to conceive."[101] Despite the prevalence of such attitudes—which continued to be held toward the West Indian peasantry long after Emancipation—as the people engaging in such practices understood, and as more recent historians and agronomists recognize(d), this was clearly not the case. The productivity and agro-diversity visible on small plots, mountain grounds, and houseyard spots—as remarked even in a work like *Marly*—testify that the methods used by the proto-peasant farmers were both sophisticated and flexible.

Of course, acknowledgment of the perseverance, knowledge, and skill involved in provision cultivation is missing from the novel and from most colonialist writing, incompatible with the construction of a benevolent master class taking care of its "people" and preparing them for the boon of freedom. But this imagined relationship between planters and slaves is undermined by the persistent anxiety that enslaved workers will abandon the estates if emancipation takes place before the (ex)slaves have acquired those "artificial wants" that will inculcate the desire to work for wages to buy the goods they lack. In other words, according to the novel's logic, the plenty that can be produced on the provision grounds visited by Marly and described by Mr. Broadcote lies within easy reach of industrious *and* idle slaves. The latter, according to the novel, make up the vast majority of enslaved people; they will abandon the estates, forego all possibility to improve themselves under the supervision of their enslavers, and in so doing, ruin the colonies. By engaging fully in subsistence-level (or, more properly, cash-and-subsistence level) production, the argument continues, they will retrograde completely to the primitive state of their ancestors and thus become "lost subjects" of British rule.[102]

Plot and Plantation

To understand more fully the significance of the anxieties swirling around notions of "free" West Indian labor(ers) and their "retrogradation" to "semibarbaric" agricultural practices—that is, their possible (probable?) disengagement from plantation economics—it's helpful to turn to Sylvia Wynter's groundbreaking analysis of the relationship described by her essay's title, between "Novel and History, Plot and Plantation." Wynter's essay traces the intersections between fictional form and the cultural work performed in the Caribbean context, acknowledging crucial differences between the kind of (agri)cultural work carried out on the plantation and on the plots and provision grounds of the enslaved. Reading the "plot system" of provision growing as "the focus of resistance to the market system and market values" driving colonial/imperial plantation economics, she examines the implications for the twentieth-century West Indian novel. Since 1971 when Wynter published her essay in one of the early issues of *Savacou*, subsequent scholars have analyzed the patterns of resistance arising from provision ground cultivation, and contemporary Caribbean novelists have woven such plots of resistance into their narratives.[103]

But Wynter also notes the ambivalence arising from the relation between plantation and plot for agricultural laborers. If, writes Wynter, "the history of Caribbean society is that of a dual relation between plantation and plot, the two poles which originate in a single historical process, the ambivalence between the two has been and is the distinguishing characteristic of the Caribbean response."[104] Explaining this ambivalence more fully, Wynter argues that even though the enslaved were able to create "on the plot a folk culture" that privileged traditional use value over the plantation economy's system of exchange value—becoming in effect "a source of cultural guerilla resistance to the plantation system"—they remained tied to the estates. Since the enslaved laborer "worked on the plantation and was in fact the Labour, land and capital, he was ambivalent between the two."[105] After Emancipation, the previously enslaved peasantry grew crops for food and to sell, but the plantation structure that remained in place after 1838 required mass labor and the planter class used their ownership of the land to compel the "slave-turned-peasant . . . back to [estate] work; and to his role in the structure of exchange value."[106]

As my reading of *Marly* suggests, the laborer's ambivalence between plantation and plot was shared—though for vastly different reasons—by the planters and their affiliates. Wynter's essay, in other words, has much to offer to an analysis of *Marly,* particularly in terms of the novel's vexed representations of industrious and idle slaves and of the prospective autonomy offered to them by the provision and mountain grounds.

The heightened anxiety over the agricultural labor of enslaved and self-liberated people at and outside the margins of the plantation complex is crystallized in the novel's constructions of the Jamaican Maroons. As discussed in relation to *Montgomery,* the Maroons occupy a liminal position both in colonial narrative tradition and in the lived experience of the enslaved. Given the terms of the treaties of 1739/40 that ended the First Maroon War, the Maroons were acknowledged by the colonial authorities as a free people, with rights of self-governance and title to extensive mountain lands. It's the relationship to these lands that *Marly*'s author is most concerned with—suggesting that the "free blacks of the mountains" offer indisputable proof of the disastrous consequences of immediate emancipation. There is no need to guess what path the enslaved will follow once freed, no need, the narrator insists, to look any further than to the Maroons:

> That [suddenly emancipated slaves] would be of no use . . . in an agricultural point of view, we have not to learn. The maroons . . . have been a free people for some generations, yet they have not improved either as an intellectual race, or as industrious subjects. In fact, they have not made the slightest advances towards improvement. . . . Their manners and their mode of life are those of

an indolent people, and yet they have had before their eyes for nearly two centuries the comforts of civilized life, and the improvements of civilized men. Of these views of life, they have taken no advantage; they are still the same slothful, improvident race which they were when in a state of slavery. . . . They have made no attempt to better their condition by means of agriculture or any other species of industry or labour. . . . These are a race of free blacks, and . . . the present negroes, if loosened from their bondage, would [not] act otherwise than them.[107]

The insistence with which the text repeats charges of uselessness (for plantation agriculture), improvidence, slothfulness; and the frustration over the (perceived) lack of industry, of desire for improvement or "comforts" of civilization—all reveals the colonialist perturbation over the Maroons' self-determined rejection of the plantation economy. This passage ironically also reveals the "fiction" of that economy as mutually beneficial to masters and slaves by emphasizing the power of the Maroon counter-model—that is, the attraction of living, like the Maroons, as "free blacks of the mountains" outside the estate's domain.[108]

As Lalla writes, for white creoles Maroons were "the ultimate outcasts," their presence provoking the kind of "frustration and hostility" exhibited in *Marly*'s descriptions.[109] For the Jamaican planter class embroiled in the debates of the 1820s and facing increasing pressures to move toward the free labor model, the Maroons represented not a military threat, but a cultural threat, one that reemphasizes the divide between plantation and plot, between the kinds of agriculture performed on and off the estates. Relying on the example of the Maroons to embody the most visible and extreme example of the "natural" indolence of Africans and their African Caribbean descendants, the novel pointedly ignores the agricultural practices on display in Maroon villages and settlements. But the novel's glossing over of Maroon cultivation, paired with its emphasis on the most commonly cited characteristics of the Maroons—their intimacy with Jamaica's mountainous cockpit country, their skill as hunters, their formidability as bush fighters—present a grossly oversimplified picture even for proplanter rhetoric.

The planter-historian Robert C. Dallas, on the other hand, provides a more nuanced image of Maroon culture, particularly in respect to agriculture. In his account of the Trelawney Town Maroons before the Second Maroon War of 1795–96, Dallas describes their agriculture practices as "a very simple science." But even in observing the simplicity of Maroon cultivation, Dallas neither ignores nor dismisses the labor involved.

FIGURE 11. "Trelawney Town, the Chief Residence of the Maroons," engraving by James Sargant Storer from a drawing by Edward Dayes, 1800. The engraving appeared as a fold-out plate in volume 1 of Bryan Edwards's *The History, Civil and Commercial, of the British Colonies in the West Indies*, 1801. (Courtesy of the John Carter Brown Library at Brown University)

Despite the Maroons' reliance on hunting for much of their food supply, he writes, they do not "neglect the cultivation of land"; moreover, they are "by no means so averse to the toil it demands, as they have been represented. Many of them were negligent of the more certain modes of labour," Dallas concludes, "but none could be said to be indolent"[110] (see fig. 11).

Dallas's defense of the Maroons' agricultural practices, lukewarm as it is, explicitly repudiates charges of slothfulness and improvidence stressed so heavily in *Marly* and other colonialist accounts. More to the point, his description of their provision grounds emphasizes a superabundance of produce, not just for the Maroons, but for nearby white settlements as well:

> Plantain, Indian corn or maize, yams, cocoas, toyaus, and in short all the nutritious roots that thrive in tropical soils, were cultivated in their grounds. In

their gardens grew most of the culinary vegetables, and they were not without some fine fruits . . . the Avocado, or Alligator-pear, . . . Mammees, and other wild but delicious fruits, were at their hand, and pine-apples grew in their hedges. They bred cattle and hogs, and raised a great quantity of fowls. When to this domestic provision of good and wholesome food, we add the luxuries afforded by the woods, the wild boar, ring-tail pigeons, and other wild birds, and the land-crab, which some esteem the greatest dainty in the West Indies, we may doubt whether the palate of Apicius would not have received higher gratification in Trelawney Town than at Rome.[111]

Dallas's description of Maroon plenty, of agricultural practices perfectly adapted to the site of production, perfectly suited to the needs of the Maroon community, presents evidence of an industriousness that *Marly*'s author refuses to acknowledge. And even though Dallas designates it as a "simple science," Maroon agriculture, coupled with related food production activities, yields not only "good and wholesome food," but luxuries and dainties as well. Dallas's emphasis on such surplus production—like *Marly*'s account of the provision grounds cultivated by industrious enslaved laborers—speaks to the capacity of black agriculturalists to grow for self-sufficiency as well as for a wider domestic market. Whether or not these farming communities *choose* to engage more fully with that market is an altogether different question—and a different source of tension between plot and plantation.

Too, both of these colonialist depictions of Afro-Caribbean farming obscure the realities of food production by enslaved and self-liberated people. Just as Marshall points to the difficulties and hard work involved in cultivating mountain grounds, Maroon historians emphasize the high costs of pretreaty resistance to the British in the early eighteenth century, when starvation was an ever-present threat. As Richard Price observes of Maroon communities throughout the Americas, "the maroon viewpoint . . . suggests . . . that the harsh natural environments of early communities at first presented terrifying obstacles, and that it was only with a great deal of suffering, and by bringing to bear the full range of their collective cultural experience and creativity" that the people adapted and survived.[112]

Against such evidence of hard-won self-sufficiency and determined autonomy, *Marly*'s account of "unimproved" Maroons appears outrageous, though not surprising. For underlying these more typical depictions of a semibarbaric people—incapable of following the model of civilization presented by the planter class—is the very material concern over the future of West Indian sugar production: Who will labor on the estates "if such a revolution as manumitting the whole slave population at once took place"? In the end, then, it becomes not a question of industry or idleness, of primitive or civilized, but of a particular kind of industry tied to a particular site of agriculture. And—despite the evidence that both Maroons and enslaved people are more than capable of managing their own time—the planter class to which *Marly*'s author is affiliated insists on the need for a gradualist approach to emancipation measured by an undeterminable-interminable length of time necessary to teach West Indian laborers those fictitious wants that, according to the logic of free market capitalism, will tie them to the estate and bind them to the path of "civilization."

The progressive direction of this path, acknowledged by the likes of Broadcote and repeated in the descriptions of Marly's plans to improve the estate, is presented as both desired future end and fait accompli. Certainly the ability of the West Indian lobby, despite its diminishing influence in the metropole, to delay emancipation and to institute the Apprenticeship period, prevented many previously enslaved people from leaving the estates to establish autonomous communities beyond the reach of the plantation. Not that resistance to the plantation ended with the termination of slavery—the free village movements, the communities of freed people and their descendants who refused to work on the estates; the estate workers who organized and agitated for better working conditions and land reform all speak to continued challenges to plantation economics.

Marly, however, despite its acknowledgment that the institution of slavery will end, maintains the fiction of a plantocratic dynasty able to order time and place, at its own pace. The transition from slave to wage labor anticipated in the novelist's closing pages suggests a refusal to acknowledge even the possibility of industrious ex-slaves' willingness to divorce themselves from the plantation machine, to construct a time-place of their own. In the decade between *Marly* and E. L. Joseph's *Warner Arundell*, however, that willingness finds expression not through the gradualist discourse of *Marly*, but through the self-emancipatory ethos manifested in Sam Sharpe's Baptist War of 1831, the eloquence of Mary Prince in her *History* published in 1831, and Afro-Caribbean political thought circulated in newspapers like *The Watchman and Jamaica Free Press*, founded in 1829 by Edward Jordan and Robert Osborn.

As an editorial from an 1830 issue of *The Watchman* proclaimed, "the streets of Paris have recently flowed with blood, and it may not be long before the streets of Kingston may witness a similar sight.... Now ... we will give a pull, a long pull, a strong pull, and a pull all together, bring the whole fabric down with a run, strike the chains from the captive, and let the oppressed go free."[113] For the white planter class the intensity of such revolutionary fervor called for a reassessment of white creole history, a reaffirmation of the rightness of white creole rule that *Marly*'s author so readily assumes. As the following chapter demonstrates, *Warner Arundell* takes up this challenge—on the very eve of full freedom in the anglophone Caribbean.

4 Recentering the Caribbean
Revolution and the Creole Cosmopolis in *Warner Arundell*

LIKE *Montgomery, Hamel*, and *Marly*, Edward Lanza Joseph's *Warner Arundell, The Adventures of a Creole* documents the various historiographic impulses exhibited by early white creole writers anxious to validate their version of Anglo-Caribbean culture and creole identity. For Joseph, as with the creole novelists discussed in previous chapters, "history" is a construct, a shifting, ongoing revisioning and rewriting of events clearly tied to the past, but also very much alive in these writers' present and prescient of their future. This perception of history, which reveals at once the hermeneutical and epistemological concerns undergirding the production of early creole culture, recalls Baucom's observation that the fatal "Atlantic 'beginning' of the modern . . . is more properly understood as an ending without end"; that "time does not pass but accumulates."[1] In the first decades of the nineteenth century, acknowledging such a process of accumulation meant looking back to a period of violent revolution and the "paradigm-shift of the Haitian Revolution,"[2] and forward to a period of uncertainty, as discussed in relation to *Montgomery, Hamel*, and *Marly*.

Unlike these three pre-Emancipation novels, however, Joseph's *Warner Arundell* appears at the starting point of a "free" British Atlantic, at the end of the Apprenticeship period and during the first year of full Emancipation in 1838. Although neither a planter nor a bookkeeper, the Anglo-Jewish Joseph—who arrived in Trinidad in 1817 and spent the rest of his life there working primarily as a writer and journalist—clearly was invested in the fortunes of the Caribbean planter class. Despite that interest, the novel (published the same year Joseph died) does not reflect the sense of "loss and foreboding" that Watson identifies in a work like *Hamel*, and that operates in much creole writing as a de facto defense of slave-holding colonial societies. The absence of this sense is possibly explained by the fact that Joseph was not explicitly tied to institutional slavery and by his own marginalized position as an Anglo-Jewish colonial subject. But it is somewhat surprising given that his hero *is* a member of the Anglo-Caribbean plantocracy, up to the moment of emancipation a slaveholding creole like Henry Montgomery, Oliver Fairfax, and George Marly. Moreover, the eponymous hero of *Warner Arundell*, whose "memoirs" constitute the bulk of the novel, is closely tied to the earliest days of Anglo-Caribbean slavery, with Joseph's first-person narrator endowed with a genealogy reaching two centuries back into England's Caribbean history.[3] Despite his family's West Indian bona fides, however, the novel's protagonist displays little if any nostalgic yearning for a romanticized pre-Emancipation past. Instead, Joseph's adventurous creole looks ahead from a position of "native" authority, emphasizing throughout his memoirs a confidence in the emancipated Caribbean's centrality in world affairs, particularly in light of opportunities presented by the opening of a newly independent South America as a space for a new generation of West Indian adventurers.

In this chapter, I explore the implications of such a forward-looking perspective, particularly as it relates to Caribbean historiography and the construction of the post-Emancipation white creole subject and culture. This subject, as discussed in chapter 3, is anticipated in the figure of George Marly, who, from his construction as an enlightened ameliorist planter, looks ahead to slavery's (gradual) dissolution, the emergence of a free black peasantry, and increased profits from his improved Jamaican estates. Of course, in the decades between Marly's arrival in Jamaica in 1816, the novel's publication in 1828, and the appearance of *Warner Arundell* in 1838, full Emancipation—at least in legal terms—had been declared. This new Caribbean reality called for a "new" creole hero, one who appears ready to leave the past (though not his Caribbean home), behind. Joseph's hero, in other words, is a novel kind of West Indian adventurer, one unfettered by any overriding sense of the cultural and moral superiority of Great Britain, or by any need to prove himself according to metropolitan ideals. The text acknowledges as a matter of course that Great Britain is necessary, for example, to the political and economic well-being of the Caribbean colonies (and vice versa); that, relative to European states like Spain and France, Great Britain is superior to other imperial powers. More importantly for my reading, the novel complicates models of subjectivity in the metropole and in the Caribbean colonies. As discussed in my introduction, Anglo-Caribbean creoles were crucial to the formulation of British identity in the pre-Emancipation period—the colonial "other" that operated as a foil for enlightened Britons. But, with

Emancipation legislation realized rather than imminent, there is no need for Joseph to contend with slavery's immorality, no imperative to insert his novel in the antislavery debates as a "party work." With the narrative's moral and political burden lifted, *Warner Arundell* turns to other cultural labor, most notably to the imaging of a new plantocratic order, one no longer dependent on institutionalized slavery.

Of course, the end of slavery did not end the reign of the plantation machine. Rather, as Nicholas Draper and others have pointed out, planter interests assumed new forms, established new sets of relationships, built up commercial and financial networks of commodities, credit, and capital, expanding and regulating global "zones of flow" that continued to shape societies and individuals in the Atlantic world well into the nineteenth century. Not least of those were the newly emancipated slaves who remained tied to estates performing the same labor they had performed under slavery—the vision anticipated by *Marly*'s author. Shifts away from colonial slavery to wage labor, from the unrivaled power of Jamaican planters in the mid- and late eighteenth century to the growing influence of those whose wealth was generated in the "new" New World—in colonies like Guyana and Trinidad (Joseph's and Warner Arundell's place of settlement) and in the vast continent of South America, whose recent independence from Spain offered new arenas for investment and settlement—all speaks not to the end of an order but to its transformation and regeneration.

At the same time that Joseph's novel points enthusiastically to the possibilities inherent in such a transformative moment, it also remains tied to (mired in?) Caribbean history. Like the other early creole novels examined in *Crossing the Line*, *Warner Arundell* (re)produces a distinctly white creole version of the past, presented in novel form in order to "make a difference to how the [slave-holding] past was understood."[4] The family history Joseph concocts for his hero tracks a colonial past filled with swashbuckling outlaws, provincial planters, and island governors and assemblymen riding out the booms and busts of West Indian economies over a two-hundred-year span, a legacy that firmly establishes Arundell's Caribbean roots. Paradoxically, this sense of rootedness is deepened by the peripatetic adventures he embarks on after the death of his father and that last until his marriage to a South American creole heiress: at ten, the boy Arundell leaves his birthplace of Grenada for Trinidad, then for Antigua to attend school; a few years later he returns to Trinidad under the protection of a "worthy creole Spaniard," who sends him to Caracas to study law; after the earthquake of 1812 levels that city, he crosses the Atlantic to study medicine in London, but—not feeling at home in England—leaves after four years to make his way back to the Caribbean; sailing as a recruit in Simón Bolívar's army of independence, he arrives on the Spanish Main, is captured by royalists, and escapes to Trinidad, to Antigua, and again to Trinidad, where he marries the South American criolla who had saved him during the Bolívarian wars. Married life in Trinidad ends his adventures—but the Caribbean roots of the Arundell dynasty have been deepened.

Remarking on the range of Arundell's inter-island travels and the novel's clear turn from the metropole toward a Caribbean center, the editors of the 2001 critical edition of *Warner Arundell* note "the ways in which the peripatetic culture of the Caribbean basin continually repositions its inhabitants within a broader Atlantic tradition. . . . Although he still identifies with British values," Brereton and her coauthors write, Arundell's loyalties are "to the New World rather than the Old."[5] These New World loyalties are attended by a (re)invigorated sense of the creole's worldliness, an assertion of transnational, transcolonial, at times transracial cosmopolitanism privileging Caribbean rather than metropolitan frames of reference. This perspective generates the novel's celebratory representation of a more independent creole identity as personified by Warner Arundell, whose "life, adventures, and opinions"[6] transcend the kind of frontier parochialism satirized in earlier works featuring West Indians and produced on both sides of the Atlantic: *Hamel*'s Solomon Guthrie, for example, refuses on principle to leave his native Jamaica because everything he needs is on the island; similarly, Warner Arundell's father, Bearwell Arundell, is best remembered by his son as literally "planted" in a chair by the seaside, drinking rum, and shooting wild doves while attended by his devoted slaves.[7]

This kind of fixity—whether brought on by smug parochialism as in Guthrie's case, or by depressed indolence as in Bearwell Arundell's case—provides a sharp contrast to the easy mobility of Joseph's hero. On one level this contrast represents a generational difference between "old school" planters like those who frustrate *Marly*'s Mr. Broadcote and like the older Arundell who is unable (or unwilling) to adapt to change, and adventurous creoles like his son. And even though Warner's sense of self (as represented in the novel) is absolutely founded on a localized, experiential, and quotidian knowledge of the Caribbean, he is much more worldly than his parent, more able to actively participate in its future.

A Stranger Nowhere in the (Caribbean) World: The Creole Cosmopolite

In some respects, Arundell's position in this world recalls Srinivas Aravamudan's "tropicopolitan": that is, as a colonized subject positioned as "other" in a British metropolitan framework, he "exists both as fictive construct of colonial tropology and actual resident of tropical space, object of representation and agent of resistance."[8] Like the tropicopolitan, Warner Arundell challenges "the developing privilege of Enlightenment cosmopolitans," but whereas the tropicopolitan operates, as Aravamudan describes it, as a shadow image, Joseph's creole protagonist explicitly engages with and complicates center/margin binaries that privilege European constructions of "worldliness." As a creole cosmopolite, shaped by active participation in the globalized circuitries of pan-Caribbean colonialism, Arundell's worldview departs in significant ways from European conceptions of the cosmopolitan, particularly those attendant on passive acts of consumption.

Configurations of the latter are seen throughout metropolitan literature of the long eighteenth century, from the prophetic lines of John Dryden's *Annus Mirabilis,* which celebrates London as a phoenix rising from the ashes of the Great Fire to become the center of world commerce, a "fam'd Emporium" ready to receive goods from around the globe, to Joseph Addison's famous *Spectator* essay No. 69, which describes the Royal Exchange as the nerve center of a grand universe, an urban space where the promised returns of speculative trade generates a spirit of tolerance and well-being. These early iterations of metropolitan cosmopolitanism are clearly bound up with the workings of empire, colonialism, capitalism, and the fictions of "progress" and "civilization" that those interrelated systems simultaneously rely on and (re)produce, as discussed in previous chapters. But, in Mr. Spectator's exuberant descriptions of the Royal Exchange, these systems' operations attain value only insofar as they serve the interests of the metropolitan center: "There is no place in the town," Mr. Spectator exults, "which I so much love to frequent as the Royal Exchange. It gives me a secret satisfaction, and in some measure gratifies my vanity, as I am an Englishman, to see so rich an assembly of countrymen and foreigners consulting together upon the private business of mankind, and making this metropolis a kind of emporium for the whole earth."[9] Here, geospatial differences are introduced from Mr. Spectator's urbane perspective, offered up to readers through his textual meanderings, and then effectively erased as he describes how "wealthy Societies of Men that are divided from one another by Seas and Oceans" are brought together in the various "Walks" of the Exchange—the Turkey Walk, the Barbadoes Walk, the Jamaica Walk, the Jews Walk.

The cultural work performed by Mr. Spectator's appreciative gaze as he strolls among the "ministers of commerce" populating the E/exchange, anticipates that of Walter Benjamin's flâneur in the Parisian Arcades: "Sometimes I am jostled among a body of Armenians; sometimes I am lost in a crowd of Jews; and sometimes make one in a group of Dutchmen. I am a Dane, Swede, or Frenchman at different times; or rather, fancy myself like the old philosopher, who, upon being asked what countryman he was, replied that he was a citizen of the World."[10] Prefiguring the cosmopolitan flâneur's fetishization of commodities available in the "safe" and clean interiority of the arcades, Addison's Mr. Spectator fetishizes the physical and ideological space—the Royal Exchange as site and emblem of speculative finance capitalism—where the groundwork is laid for the flows and exchanges that facilitate subsequent commodity fetishism.[11]

One hundred years after Addison and contemporary with the European arcades Benjamin describes, Joseph presents a different, reoriented version of cosmopolitanism. This version is generated an ocean away but nevertheless is situated at modernity's center, the physical, geographic site that makes Mr. Spectator's and the flâneur's leisurely stroll possible: the Caribbean. As part of the Caribbean world that Joseph Roach describes as circum-Atlantic, Joseph's New World is a vibrant place located "at the heart of an oceanic interculture."[12] Nowhere in the novel is its vibrancy more precisely rendered than in Warner Arundell's childhood impressions of Trinidad's Port of Spain, a description that recalls Addison's essay:

> The bustle of this place astonished me; as did also the mixed hue and costume of the population, and Babylonish variety of tongues. Here strutted the gaudy officer of militia. . . . There lounged . . . an officer of the line; here and there rolled along a naval officer; the gaily dressed Spaniard shewed his laced frill and gold buttons; and the plainly dressed Englishman . . . stood beside the smart Frenchman . . . Sometimes a Chinese or two would appear; . . . groups of the mixed race between Indians, negroes, and Europeans, called *Peons*, . . . Crowds of negroes, chattering, jesting, and laughing, . . . while here and there were numbers of . . . women, of the classes called mulattoes, mestees, and quadroons, who were the most beautiful of those classes which I, at that time, had ever seen.[13]

As Brereton and her coauthors observe, Warner's enthusiasm here typifies his responses to other Caribbean sites/sights, as he revels in the region's "racial and cultural hybridity," acknowledging the crucial role of mixing in the Caribbean cosmopolis.[14] Unlike Mr. Spectator's sense of consciously "losing himself" in the crowd of the Exchange—an act dependent on the exertion of his powers of fancy—Arundell's place in the Caribbean center is not predicated on any sense of self-abdication, dislocation, or displacement; it reflects instead his sense of "native" identity, of his at-homeness in the world he describes. The immediacy of his world(ly) experience, in fact, constitutes a striking difference between the novel's creole cosmopolitanism and its European counterpart.

Of the latter, John K. Noyes observes that over the course of the eighteenth and nineteenth centuries, "everyday life" in Europe was opened up to the "new found knowledge of a cosmopolitan identity, of what it meant to be a citizen of the world" by the movement of goods into metropolitan centers. To the "exotic" goods from the West Indies and other colonial sites refined and sold in Europe, Noyes adds another commodity: the knowledge and stories brought back by European travelers, observers, merchants, and colonizers. Various narrative forms, in particular the novel, Noyes argues, were instrumental in "imagining cosmopolitan identities," largely because the novel "created the kind of virtual community that could allow the individual to take possession of the world, so to speak, without having experienced this world first-hand."[15] On one level, Joseph's novel, like *Montgomery*, *Hamel*, and *Marly*, contributes to this virtual community. As Arundell says, he doesn't "write these memoirs merely for the West Indian reader," but for British audiences as well.[16] But Noyes's assumption of a metropolitan readership, of a sense of cosmopolitanism nurtured in the metropole by the consumption of "foreign" material, highlights the degree to which Joseph's novel departs from early nineteenth-century ideas of enlightenment cosmopolitanism, a departure that stresses the vicariousness of worldliness attained through passive consumption.

The fragility of such a second-hand construct is conveyed through Warner Arundell's descriptions of the time he spends in London pursuing his medical studies. The three chapters devoted to this four-year period of his life include a satiric essay addressed to those of his creole readers who "have never crossed the Atlantic," entitled "A Creole's Notion of 'Home.'" Poking fun at the tradition of histories and commentaries that claimed to describe the manners and customs of the inhabitants of the West India islands, Arundell announces his novel stance by offsetting the word "home" in quotation marks. This typographic convention, of course, points up Joseph's awareness of the ironies of the colonial subject's relationship to the metropole, crystallized by the tendency of many colonials to sentimentalize England as "Home"—however distant they are geographically from the "mother country." Unlike the editors of the *Jamaica Quarterly Journal, and Literary Gazette* discussed in chapter 1, Joseph's protagonist feels no compulsion to declare unity with the metropole. Indeed, the playful turn on "Home"—the distinctions between what Arundell finds "homely" and "unhomely"—throughout this section of the novel clearly emphasizes the disruptive uncanniness of London for the creole, which in turn points back to the Caribbean as the source of Arundell's at-homeness.

Although Selwyn Cudjoe reads this section of the novel as Joseph's celebration of England as the "country in which [Arundell] feels at home and that has provided him with all his virtues and the means by which to value his achievements,"[17] I suggest that Arundell's London commentary challenges rather than upholds notions of metropolitan superiority. Even though Arundell finds some things worth praising (paintings, the theater, the cleanliness of the poor), the metropole is described not so much as "a place to be adored and admired" than as a site of absence and lack.[18] From the moment of his arrival, Arundell feels himself "in a new world": "the climate; the lofty houses, with glass windows, and chimneys; the immense population; the total absence of black, coloured, and Indian people; . . . the dissimilarity of the feathered tribe; the absence of the palms of a tropical climate, and the total difference of all vegetable nature—for not a tree, shrub, fruit, legume, leaf, flower, nor even blade of grass, was exactly like aught I ever before beheld,—all, all I saw made me feel as though I was transported into another planet."[19]

The culture shock Arundell experiences in the face of all this différance is most intense when he encounters what he comes to see as a defining characteristic of the English: "the coldness of Englishmen respecting the concerns of their neighbours."[20] Growing up in the West Indies, he had often read, he says, of "Old English hospitality: I suppose this term meant the hospitality of England in the days of old, for the English of the present time do not seem to understand the meaning of the word. I certainly did meet with some hospitality in London, but it was in the apartments of retired West Indians."[21] The "want of charity in the people of England often shocked me," he continues, emphasizing the stark difference between creoles and Britons.[22] Charity in the Caribbean, he asserts, operates across lines of class, race, and gender, exercised by the wealthiest planter and the poorest slave, both of whom stand ready to extend compassion to individuals of whatever rank or color:

> Often I have witnessed acts of benevolence from persons in the colonies, who have a multitude of sins for their charity to cover. Many a wretched white man, when attacked at one and the same time by poverty and the yellow fever, has been succoured by poor mulatto women of the most unfortunate and degraded description; .... In the Antilles, even the poor slave allows no child of want to solicit in vain, while he has the power of relieving him. ... Having witnessed the above general benevolence of the Caribbean Islands, I was frequently shocked in England at beholding the indigent solicit in vain the cold hand of charity.[23]

Documenting his London experience from the position of an outsider—a position that, despite its implications of dislocation, he revels in throughout these chapters—Arundell repeatedly condemns Londoners for their lack of compassion. Despite its place at the "heart" of empire, he suggests, London is heartless, a shocking revelation to the creole.

On the one hand, Joseph's strategic overturning of metropolitan assertions of white creole depravity and incivility points to the role West Indian benevolence and hospitality played in the planter response to abolitionist charges of cruelty from the 1780s through the 1830s. As Christopher Petley points out, prior to the intensification of abolitionists' efforts to forward the antislavery cause in the last decades of the eighteenth century, Britons in the metropole were willing to overlook the foibles and shortcomings of West Indian planters, to offset their distaste for colonial boorishness with tolerance due to their good-hearted, generous natures. From the 1780s, however, metropolitan subjects—themselves subject to shifting conceptions of "Britishness and nationhood" in the wake of the American Revolution—were "less accommodating of the sorts of divergences from the metropolitan norm indulged in by colonial Caribbean slaveholders."[24] And although those in Britain who defended the plantocracy in the abolition debates "saw the famous generosity of white colonists as a valuable weapon in their armory," evocations of the eminently hospitable and "nobly generous" nature of the West Indian planter class did little to overturn metropolitan criticisms.[25]

But even as Joseph's novel works to perpetuate ideas of West Indian benevolence, it is not concerned in 1838 with defending *slave*holders per se, but in promoting a creole identity rooted in compassionate generosity that crosses lines of race and class. Of course, this is not to suggest that Arundell's examples do not romanticize the kindness of black slaves and brown women toward white men who arouse their pity; they do. But the passage also reveals Joseph's construction of an expanded form of West Indian hospitality, one not limited to the planter elite—the group most widely identified throughout the long eighteenth century with the "cult of [West Indian] hospitality," to use Trevor Burnard's phrase—but to creoles of all colors and castes. As Cudjoe writes, one consequence of this construction is Joseph's acknowledgment that "in spite of the condition of slavery, enslaved persons fashioned a culture that consisted of both sharing and giving."[26] As importantly, the emphasis on the generosity of those creole subjects of "the most unfortunate and degraded description"— poor slaves and mulatto women—presents cross-racial relationships that are based neither in that of master and slave nor in the sexually exploitive relationships involved in concubinage.[27]

By invoking West Indian generosity as a "native" characteristic— defining the creole subject against the ungenerous metropolitan—Joseph contributes to "the invention, not simply the discovery of tradition," an act integral to those questions of identity that are at the heart of cultural production.[28] In other words, shared traditional practice revolving around the exercise of humanity and tolerance, Joseph's novel suggests, constitutes the familiar for his creole subjects and, by extension, nurtures the communal and familial bonds that shape creole identity. Its absence, in contrast, engenders the sense of dislocation and strangeness the (fictionalized) creole experiences living in London at a particular historical moment, 1813 to 1817, when the "war of representation" waged between white creoles and their allies and emancipationists—a war, Petley argues, the planters ultimately lost—was at its height.[29]

In addition to inserting a kind of corrective footnote to "historical," that is, past images of creole depravity like those discussed in the introduction and chapter 1, *Warner Arundell*'s London scenes also anticipate and complicate the role of the "stranger" in the metropole as it takes shape in various urban writings. That is, the repeated shock and astonishment Joseph's hero experiences in England, the place historically defined as "home" for *all* British subjects, contributes to the tensions implicit in representations of European urban space as "the site of strangeness."[30] However, the experience of strangeness in later writings, like the examples discussed by Noyes above, is limited to the experience of the metropolitan cosmopolitan subject. The (masculine) resident of the metropole, as Richard Sennett writes, is introduced by an influx of "foreigners" to "a world of people he could not classify," and thus he finds himself open to "the possibility of the unknown other."[31] For European intellectuals, Sennett continues, the European city represents "both a puzzle that cannot be deduced and something that is compellingly attractive. Thus," he concludes, "the quality of cosmopolitanism for these urbanists at that time had to do with the notion of being engaged by the unknown. That is what cosmopolitanism meant." For the European cosmopolitan, in other words, "the stranger is a bearer of a new kind of freedom."[32] In this sense, the liberating, pleasurable act of "experiencing the stranger"—like Mr. Spectator's consuming gaze on the London Exchange—becomes yet another form of metropolitan consumption, emphasizing the European city as privileged site. This privileging, moreover, is found not only in eighteenth- and nineteenth-century literature, but also persists in more recent theoretical writings.

Given the ready assumptions underlying these Eurocentric formulations, Joseph's novel appears all the more striking, particularly in its anticipation of later postcolonial Caribbean writers and their focus on the conditions of exile that shape the Caribbean subjects' experience of the European metropolis. As Brereton and her coauthors rightly observe, to read Arundell's London adventures alongside twentieth-century works by George Lamming, Jean Rhys, Erna Brodber, and V. S. Naipaul (all of whom write their own versions of "A Creole's Notions of Home") highlights the shared experience of "the mother country as place of displacement, loss of privilege and an absence of nurturing": England is a cold place in which Caribbean transplants suffer, just as transplanted Englishmen suffered in the heat of the Torrid Zones.[33]

In this, moreover, the critiques of metropolitan culture contained in all these narratives indicate a longstanding attempt by Caribbean writers to reconfigure a sense of worldliness derived not from the absorption of the anonymous other into the metropolitan center but from a "truer," lived experience of the global that extends far beyond the island of England. Such reconfigurations ultimately depend on mobility and fluidity. Certainly Joseph's novel, as Brereton and her coauthors observe, shares with later Caribbean literature "the pervasive presence of the sea," which becomes, as in the poetry of Derek Walcott, an "ennobling medium, a location beyond the constraints of an oppressive social order in which a man's true worth can be measured."[34] Arundell's fluid movements between Caribbean islands and across the Atlantic are also empowering, bestowing on him a narrative authority rooted in his knowledge of the world's geography. This, too, is part of Joseph's critique of European cosmopolitanism, crystallized in the novel by Arundell's impatience with the "want of geographical information" exhibited by Londoners, a lack that "pervade[s] all ranks of society." Despite the "world" power that Great

Britain represents, he complains, the "national" ignorance of that world is as "astonishing" as English cold-heartedness:

> Great Britain rules one-fourth of the globe in all parts of the world; she possesses colonies; her merchandise and manufactories supply every mart; her ships crowd every sea; her travelers penetrate every inhabited and uninhabited country: and yet the English, in general, know as much of geography as a mole knows of longitude.... Repeatedly, in the House of Commons, the most finished orators have talked of "the island of Demarara;" and I myself heard a senator of some celebrity say, "he hoped for the day when the negroes in the West Indies would peaceably *enjoy their own firesides!*" Talk of a people enjoying their firesides in a climate where, in the month of January, the mercury stands at 92 in the shade! There is fever in the very thought.[35]

Here Joseph tackles head on the question of metropolitan authority, juxtaposing the Londoner's solipsistic world view against his own knowledge of how the world works, not just of things West Indian, but of global relations facilitated by geographical knowledge.

Behind the satire, the underlying seriousness of Arundell's criticism is central to the novel's recentering of the Caribbean and its creole subjects, an attempt to undo the long process of marginalization and othering imposed by Britons "at home" onto colonial residents. Evidence of this attempt can be seen in Arundell's repeated frustration over the many "geographical blunders" accepted as "true" by metropolitan cartographers who, Arundell observes, content "themselves with merely copying" the maps of others and thus perpetuating ignorance about the region.[36] Such is the case with maps of Trinidad, an island that, though a British colony, had never been surveyed by the English, forcing them to rely on Spanish maps, themselves marked by errors due to "the characteristic indolence" of that nation.[37] Even the map produced on behalf of the British Royal Geographer, "from which all the rest are copied, although it impudently pretended to be taken from actual survey, was a mere blundering transcript; for the ... most ludicrous mistakes appear in it."[38]

Of these mistakes, Arundell takes particular umbrage at certain markings that appear on the British cartographer's image of the Gulf of Paria. "In about one hundred places" the map includes "such notices as these, '14 breakers, 13 breakers, 12 breakers,' &c. Now, as any one, who has ever been in the gulf, knows you may as well look for icebergs there as breakers, they are puzzled to understand it: the fact is, the Spanish hydrographers put down all over the gulf 14, 13, 12, not breakers, but *brazos*— *Anglice,* fathoms."[39]

Once again Arundell pits familiarity with place, in this case the Trinidad coast and the Gulf of Paria, against second-hand repetition, "real," local knowledge against metropolitan arrogance and ignorance. But Arundell's cartography lesson reveals another facet of his worldliness, more proof of the integral role fluidity and mobility play in shaping the creole protagonist's identity—that is, the linguistic fluency that enables Arundell to move adroitly from English to Spanish to "Anglice" for the edification of (metropolitan) readers.

Highly suggestive of the flows of ocean currents and people, this fluency reflects and facilitates Arundell's physical movements in and around the circum- and cis-Atlantic world, gesturing toward the new structures of cultural exchange discussed by recent scholars working in Atlantic Studies. As Christopher Iannini observes, these new structures are marked by the "shift from national 'roots' to transnational 'routes,' with the latter term posed by cultural theorists such as Paul Gilroy as a challenge to forms of nationalist essentialism long entrenched in the disciplines of history and literary criticism."[40] *Warner Arundell* illustrates that not only are forms of nationalist essentialism long entrenched, but challenges to it as well. Certainly, as Joseph's novel suggests, nothing threatens assertions of national hegemony more than a celebration of the polyglot.

The most remarkable feature of Warner Arndell's character, evident from childhood, he confides, is "his surprising aptitude in mastering both living and dead languages."[41] This skill is absolutely central to his protagonism and to Joseph's construction of creole cosmopolitanism. At key points of his adventures, Arundell's sense of self as a cosmopolite is affirmed by his ability to engage verbally when others cannot, as when he acts as translator on board an English ship that has captured a French privateer prior to landing the ten-year-old Arundell on the island of Antigua. When no one else responds to the captain's call for "any one . . . who can *parley vouze Francais,*" the young Warner steps up. "The fact is," he confesses, that

> I spoke the jargon called in these islands, "creole French," a lingo principally made up of corrupt French, but mixed with African, Spanish, and English words. However, this *patois* is the mother tongue of about a million and a half of people in this part of the world. Fortunately for my credit as a linguist, most of the privateer's men had been long enough amongst the islands to learn the lingo alluded to, so that I did duty as a good interpreter. I pleased the commander, and the crew, and myself, by shewing I was of use on board. To use a creole expression, "I looked on myself as somebody."[42]

The explicit connection here between the validity of "creole French," its hybrid composition, and Arundell's choice of a "creolism" to express his sense of self-worth is important—an early instance of the novel's celebratory embrace of creole identity independent of European validation.

The emphasis on linguistic hybridity, moreover, serves as a reminder of racial, ethnic, and cultural mixtures of the Caribbean, visible even to the young Arundell in Port of Spain's thrilling bustle. "The dialects of the people of Port of Spain," he tells readers, are "as mixed as their complexions and dresses": "Chinese, corrupt Arabic . . . . a hundred different vernaculars from Guinea; English, with its proper accent, and then with its creole drawl; Spanish, with its true Castilian pronunciation, as well as with the slight corruption with which the South Americans speak it; creole French, European French, Corsican, various kinds of *patois*, German, and Italian, were all spoken in this town."[43] Moving seamlessly between multiple languages, whether European or the "various kinds of *patois*," Joseph's hero "belongs" everywhere in his Caribbean world. Whether his fluency advances his fortunes—as when he learns the location of buried treasure from Spanish-speaking robbers—or whether it protects him from danger—as when he overhears two would-be murderers plotting his death in creole French—it illustrates the superiority of what the novel presents as a democratized, creolized, pan-Caribbean multilingualism over nationalistic monolingualism.[44]

These multilingual exchanges—often privileging patois and creolisms—demonstrate Arundell's liberation from nationalistic boundaries, a seemingly willful erasure of difference (something shared with European cosmopolitanism) but one that allows him to move freely within the various creole communities he flows into and out of. Many Caribbeanists identify such fluidity as a hallmark of Caribbean identity and culture, including Stuart Hall in his germinal essay "Negotiating Caribbean Identity." Nearly two hundred years after Joseph pens his description of Port of Spain and remarks on England's surprising and "total absence of black, coloured, and Indian people," Hall describes a journey back to the Caribbean in preparation for a BBC series on the region, another "creole" writing about the Caribbean for consumption in the metropole. After visiting a number of islands, some for the first time, Hall reports being "staggered by the ethnic and cultural diversity" he encounters. "Not a single Caribbean island looks like any other in terms of its ethnic composition," Hall writes, "including the different genetic and physical features and characteristics of the people. And that is before you touch the question of different languages and different cultural traditions that reflect the different colonizing cultures."[45] *Warner Arundell,* as the quotation above illustrates, *does* touch on such questions, exploring a range of languages and cultural traditions through the vehicle of Arundell's memoirs. Like the military, financial, and romantic successes Arundell enjoys throughout his "adventures," the sense of self Joseph endows his hero with is intimately tied to the ability to navigate different cultural and linguistic modes.

Warner Arundell's Creole Embrace

For all that Joseph's novel celebrates what I've been calling a creole cosmopolitanism, the fluidity and admixtures of Caribbean cultures; for all that the novel presents a seemingly benign construction of "free" Caribbean subjects, *Warner Arundell* remains a troubling text. For the post-Emancipation plantocratic model that it imagines—ironically through the recuperation of the hero's pre-Emancipation escapades—continues to assert the "rightness" of racialized social and cultural hierarchies as a way to maintain the power of the plantation machine—even as that machine remains well in the background of the novel's action. As Brathwaite writes of *Hamel,* despite that novel's ability to explore beyond the system's superficies, *Warner Arundell* also remains a deeply color-conscious work, clearly supportive of an oppressive system predicated on notions of white superiority. In other words, despite Joseph's attempts to move past questions of slavery, despite distancing his hero from "creole gentlemen of the old school" like his father, who "had high notions with regard to the absolute authority of an owner over his slaves,"[46] Joseph remains enmeshed in plantocratic power structures that, in the end, operate more insidiously even than those of old school plantocrats who "lost" the Emancipation debate.

One way to interrogate the text's role in promoting this novel plantocratic order is to examine the ways its seeming embrace of creole hybridity controls the rewriting of Caribbean history. As mentioned above, the novel celebrates racial, ethnic, and linguistic diversity, indeed, points to such "mixtures" as a means of asserting the creole cosmopolis as central rather than peripheral to worldly affairs. But even as Arundell (like George Marly) damns the "abominable prejudice of the West Indies," the racial "purity" with which Joseph invests his hero, his un-mixed status as a white man, ensures his authority over the novel's other African and African-descended "mixed" characters and their histories as related in Arundell's memoirs. Hence, when Joseph's hero learns that he has siblings—seven brothers and sisters fathered by Bearwell Arundell and anonymous enslaved women on his Antiguan estate—he rejects the "accursed distinction which existed between members of the same family, whose complexions differed," embracing these newfound relations without reserve.[47] Indeed, at their first meeting, Arundell was so eager to demonstrate his affection for his family that, instead of waiting on shipboard for the small boat bringing them to meet him, he threw "off [his] jacket, waistcoat, and shoes; and, regardless of sharks, plunged into the water, swam alongside, . . . caught a rope, jumped into the main chains, thence on deck, and rushed, dripping as I was, into the arms of my brothers and sisters."[48] The eagerness of Arundell's embrace and the powerful emotions on display at this meeting do not result, of course, in a renunciation of his privileges as a white man. Rather, these privileges are "naturalized" by the "natural brothers and sisters" who validate his authority: despite the fact that he is their youngest brother, they assure him, "you are the head of the family, because you are a white man."[49]

The novel's "owning" of mixed-race characters, part of its push to privilege a free and expansive (white) creole experience as regenerative rather than degenerative, plays a central role in its historiographic work. In this, I would argue, Joseph presents his protagonist as a liberated "revolutionary," turning over old ways and past prejudices. But the novel's engagement with revolution is not limited to that of customs and manners; it also includes the protagonist's involvement in the political revolutions that preceded Emancipation in the anglophone Caribbean.

As a historical register, *Warner Arundell* incorporates numerous events and people from the Caribbean's revolutionary history, at times blurring generic lines, as noted in my introduction. This tendency clearly impressed the reviewer of the *Literary Gazette,* who acknowledged that even as the narrative is heightened "by the pen of the author, it is evidently founded on a basis of fact." The ultimate result, the reviewer writes, is that some parts of *Warner Arundell* "look like fiction, some like truth, some like novel, some like history."[50] The blurred lines between "fiction" and "truth," "novel" and "history," are characteristic of historical fiction in general, and resonate in peculiar ways in Emancipation-era creole novels. For my reading of Joseph's novel, I focus on a specific moment in Caribbean history, rewritten by Joseph and woven so intricately into his protagonist's memoirs that without this foundational event, there would be no "adventures of a creole": the Grenadian rebellion led by Julien Fédon, a creole planter of French and African descent who joined forces with Grenada's enslaved people to overturn the British plantocracy in 1795–96.

In (re)presenting the revolt and its leader, reworking colonial histories to "flesh out" the figure of Fédon, Joseph literally gives birth to his creole adventurer, who is delivered in the rebel leader's camp and, after the death of his mother, returned safely to his father in the closing moments of the fifteen-month-long revolt. Reading the novel's version of Fédon's (ultimately unsuccessful) revolution, we can see that Joseph's reworking constitutes a different kind of embrace than the conciliatory gesture dramatized in Arundell's family greeting, although it, too, contributes to the constitution of white creole order.

Most importantly for my argument, the novel's (ambivalent) embrace of revolution and revolutionaries constitutes an attempt to acknowledge and contain "the diasporic and genocidal histories of Africa and the Americas" that persisted after Emancipation in the "circum-Atlantic world."[51] As Roach describes it, this Caribbean-centered world (as opposed, he says, to a transatlantic one), "locates the peoples of the Caribbean rim at the heart of an oceanic interculture embodied through performance" and shouldering the weight of a "circum-Atlantic memory" imbued with "unspeakable violence."[52] Within this context we can read Fédon's revolt and its aftermath as part of this circum-Atlantic performance, and Joseph's protagonist as its documentarian.

As MENTIONED ABOVE, the opening pages of Joseph's novel informs readers of Warner Arundell's descent "from one of the most ancient English families in the West Indies"; after an introductory first chapter filled with anecdotes about his illustrious family, the novel turns to Arundell's personal history, beginning with his birth on the island of Grenada in 1795, a year, he explains, when "the West Indian colonies were convulsed in an awful manner, from one end to another." From the revolution in San Domingo, to the Second Maroon War of Jamaica, to insurrections on Martinique, Guadeloupe, and St. Vincent, the colonies were "infected" with the spirit of French republicanism under the leadership of "that barbarous agent of the convention," Victor Hugues.[53] As the imperial military historian J. W. Fortescue would describe it a century later, 1795 was "the most terrible" of "all the years in the history of the West Indies, since the Spanish Furies of the first conquerors," a year of "massacre, plunder, and ruin; of war not only of French and English, but of the subject against the dominant race, of the black man against the white. Kindled first in San Domingo by the sparks that flew from the central conflagration at Paris, the flames spread swiftly from island to island, until there was hardly one that was not ablaze."[54] In choosing such a specific moment for his hero's birth, Joseph inextricably links Arundell to the revolutionary history of the Atlantic world that he inhabits.

Joseph's choice of Grenada and Fédon—from all the other sites of rebellion and rebel leaders—isn't surprising given that colony's physical and ideological "place" in the British West Indies and Caribbean affairs in the last years of British Atlantic slavery. Like Joseph's adopted home of Trinidad, Grenada was a relatively "new" British colony, the latter ceded to Britain from France at the end of the Seven Years' War in 1764 (Trinidad became a British colony in 1797). Both islands, moreover, are located in close proximity to the Spanish Main. At the time of the fictional Arundell's birth, Grenada still retained a large French- and French-creole speaking population, many of whom were Catholic.[55] Since Britain first took possession of the island in 1764, tensions had run high between British planters and Britain's new francophone subjects; fifteen years later French forces retook Grenada for a brief period (1779–83), and when the colony was recaptured by the British, colonial administrators passed a succession of arguably punitive legislative acts designed to assert control over the island's French creoles. According to Grenadian historian and former prime minister Sir George Brizan, between 1783 and the outbreak of Fédon's Rebellion in March 1795, the governing council imposed a number of oppressive laws leveled against French proprietors and Catholic subjects. The resentment of Grenada's francophone planter class, especially the free colored population—including the family of Julien Fédon—was given an outlet by events in France and in Haiti.

In terms of its chronology, Grenada's late eighteenth-century history can be read alongside the more familiar historiographic narrative recounting the impact of the French Revolution in Haiti. Joseph himself was intimately aware of the connections and parallels between events in Haiti and throughout the Windward islands, as his account of the conflicts in Dominica, St. Lucia, and St. Vincent in his *History of Trinidad* makes clear. But even as Joseph links the multiple insurrections of 1795–96 to Republican fervor among Atlantic "citizens" in the eastern Caribbean, he also distinguishes the fifteen-month uprising in Grenada from the rest: "In Grenada," he writes, "scenes were acted similar to those which took place in St. Vincent, but with this difference—the war there commenced with one of the most atrocious massacres known in modern history; the governor and thirty-eight of his friends, when on a peaceful mission, were seized and butchered, before war was declared. After a long and ill-managed war . . . the island was finally in possession of the British."[56]

Following these few sentences, which comprise the whole of Joseph's account of the Grenada Revolution in his *History*, he adds a footnote: "I have heard from authority which I cannot doubt, that the infamous

Fédon, the chief of the Grenada insurrection, escaped to this island [Trinidad], and was here at the time of its capture [i.e., 1797]. The story of his having been drowned, coming from Grenada, was a mere fabrication."[57]

The atrocity Joseph refers to is the execution on April 7 of Grenada's lieutenant governor, Ninian Home, and forty-seven (not thirty-eight) other prisoners who had been captured by Fédon's forces on March 3, the day after the insurrection broke out. But as most contemporary accounts reveal—shocking though the executions were—they were neither as sudden nor as unanticipated as Joseph's encapsulated history suggests.[58] According to Gordon Turnbull's "eye-witness" *Narrative of the Revolt and Insurrection of the French Inhabitants in Grenada,* on March 4, Fédon, who had been appointed by Victor Hugues as commander of the republican forces on the island, sent two emissaries—both, like Fédon, propertied men of color—with a demand for the immediate surrender of the island. Fédon's "Declaration," accompanied by a copy of a proclamation by Hugues addressed to the British commanders-in-chief in the region, makes clear that the insurrection in Grenada was part of Hugues's wider plan to recapture French colonies lost earlier in the century, and perceived by his recruits as a battle in the war against Britain.

"In case of your not submitting," Fédon's message warned the council,

> you shall be liable to all the scourges of a disastrous war; and that all persons whomsoever that shall be taken in arms, or who shall not have joined the National Flag in such time as we shall judge fit (but without the smallest delay), shall be punished with death, and their estates burnt, and the land confiscated to the use of the Republic. We farther give you notice, that by the success which has already attended our arms in this colony, the tyrant Home, lately Governor of the island, Alexander Campbell, and a great number of English, having been made our prisoners, that their heads, and the heads of all others, shall answer for the conduct of those in authority, and this without delay.[59]

The council rejected Fédon's demands out of hand, circulated their own addresses in English and French to the island's francophone residents promising pardons and leniency for all who "returned to their duty" as the subjects of King George III, began organizing resident British troops and the colonial militia, and soliciting military aid from Spanish Trinidad, British-held Martinique, and elsewhere. On April 6–7, realizing the need to act militarily sooner rather than later, the council's president, Francis Mackenzie, ordered an attack on Fédon's camp, located on his plantation Belvidere in the mountainous interior of the island. In quick response, Fédon executed Home and all the other prisoners, save for three men.

What followed was more than a year of battles and skirmishes during which both sides failed to attain a clear victory, with the British holding only the capital of St. George's while most of the island's interior was held by Fédon's army. According to a member of Grenada's colonial militia writing in May 1795, Fédon's forces, which occupied "the range of the inland Country," comprised a diverse array of the island's inhabitants. The French creole planters, Samuel Cary wrote to his father in Massachusetts, "have been joined by a number of negroes from English estates and they now consist of the white French of the Country, the coloured race of free people of the Country, all the French negroes, and many English negroes."[60]

Despite British colonialists' insistence that all subjects on the island were well treated, contemporary documents reveal that the French and Catholic people of Grenada had a long list of grievances against the colonial government, particularly under Home. More importantly, for people of color like Fédon, Jacobin ideals of liberty and equality assumed a far greater urgency in the Atlantic world than in the metropole, a fact that Hugues and, writing after the fact, Joseph understood. The animosity of contemporaneous anglophone accounts of Fédon—reviled as a bloodthirsty archfiend—suggests that Hugues's strategy throughout the contested eastern Caribbean, like unfolding events in Haiti, was "a waking nightmare" for the British planters. As H. J. K. Jenkins points out, the direct military threat posed by Hugues and his forces was serious enough, "but what chiefly perturbed them was the spectre of hated 'Jacobinism' stalking the Caribbean, deliberately and systematically fomenting revolt among the slave population, hitherto viewed more as cattle than as men. The dread of slave rebellion was a longstanding one in the British West Indies, and for it to stem from the policy of the French Government made it appear doubly dreadful."[61] Cast in these terms, the lines of conflict appear starkly drawn: British slavery versus French emancipation. And—despite the novel's apparent rejection of nationalism in favor of creole cosmopolitanism—*Warner Arundell* demonstrates the push and pull of competing articulations of creole identity in plantocratic post-Emancipation historiography.

Joseph's acknowledgment of such tensions, as well as their root sources, is illustrated in the *History of Trinidad,* which appeared the same year as *Warner Arundell.* Following his cursory description of the "chief of the Grenada insurrection" and brief overview of the rebellion, Joseph turns to the pan-Caribbean implications of revolutionary ardor and Jacobin idealism:

It may be asked, how it happened that the French possessed the power of arming the coloured population of several islands against their enemies. It may be answered, that they promised them liberty and equality: that they ever intended to give them these boons may be doubted, considering the deep-rooted prejudice entertained against the mixed European and African races, called Mulattoes. But these people had been for ages treated little worse than slaves; they were looked upon as a suspicious and degraded race; hence the promise of liberty and equality made them rush to arms. They fought desperately against the English: they were taught to look on the English as the enemies of their rising liberty.[62]

As numerous scholars have pointed out, the question of mulatto rights was an increasingly significant issue in the anglophone Caribbean, particularly after the role played by the *gens de couleur* over the course of the Haitian Revolution. As Gad Heumann, Sara Salih, and others have noted, the push for greater civil rights for free people of color—many of them slaveholders—assumed a new urgency in the last years of slavery, and certainly Joseph's depictions of the historical Fédon and the fictional Arundell family—all the "natural" half-siblings Warner discovers in Antigua along with nieces, nephews, cousins, aunts, and uncles—suggest a recalibration of white anglophone creole attitudes toward mixed-race creole subjects: in laying claim to his family Arundell alludes to and repudiates the "abominable prejudice of the West Indies," not confining it to French colonialists as suggested by the language of the *History*, but attributing it to a wider, transnational residue of unenlightened, backward thinking.

But even as Joseph presents Arundell's tolerance as a sign of his liberal (and liberated) cosmopolitan embrace of difference, the figure of the Afro-French creole Fédon troubles Joseph's rewriting of revolutionary history, generating an undeniable ambivalence in the text. The initial assessment of Fédon presented in Arundell's memoirs, for example, presents a man "not destitute of courage and ordinary abilities"; he was, however, not the best leader among the "rich coloured proprietors" of the island.[63] But even though Arundell's description stresses Fédon's failings as a commander—belied by the historical fact that Fédon's forces held the island for fifteen months—it by no means dismisses his motivations for initiating the rebellion.

Whereas Selwyn Cudjoe sees Joseph's memoirist as "intent on maligning the motives and activities of anyone—for example, Julien Fédon, a colored person, or Victor Hughes, a colored official of the French Revolutionary Government, who proclaims the abolition of slavery in

Guadeloupe—who challenges British rule in the Caribbean," I would argue that the impulses with which Joseph imbues his protagonist and Fédon are much more complicated.[64] Certainly Joseph (via the fiction of Arundell's memoirs) does not depict Fédon's motivation as "absurd," nor does the novel's representation of his impassioned plea against the race-based oppression of Grenada's *gens de couleur* serve to minimize Fédon's "actions and abilities" as "outlandish."[65] This is not to suggest that Joseph's depictions of Africans and of African-creole subjects are not unproblematic—they are very problematic, indeed, and reflect his easy acceptance of widespread attitudes about the "natural" inferiority of African and Afro-Caribbean people even as he appears to dismiss "abominable" prejudices.

But the problems that inhere in the novelist's depiction of Fédon demonstrate the difficulties involved in rewriting Caribbean history, particularly that history's revolutionary moments, and in (re)producing those moments as the basis for an enlightened, post-Emancipation future that no longer needs the violence of coerced labor or of armed resistance to slavery. Reading Joseph's Fédon against contemporary histories that simply vilify him as a "brutal assassin," as in Turnbull and Joseph's own brief account of "the infamous Fédon" in the *History*, the novel's portrait appears unquestioningly sympathetic. Indeed, the first words put in Fédon's mouth make sense of the revolution and provide the rationale for preserving the infant Warner's life: because Bearwell Arundell had once defended the rebel leader from racial slurs. Bearwell responds by accusing Fédon of stirring rebellion in order to satisfy his own selfish ambitions, of placing himself "at the head of an insurrection which has deluged this lovely island with blood" in order to "revenge the disgrace of being affronted."[66] Fédon defends himself from accusations of such mean-spiritedness in a lengthy speech, the novel granting, as it were, the historical Fédon a voice silenced in other accounts:

> No; not merely for revenge, and certainly not for ambition, did I consent to become the leader of this war: my object was more noble. I fought for liberty and equality—not as these words are, I find, understood by the hollow-hearted French, but I aimed at emancipating the slaves, although I myself possessed a valuable gang. I wished to make the negro respected despite his inky skin, to induce the mulatto to consider himself a man, although his brown complexion told him he was the son of the tyrannical white man. This archipelago . . . once possessed a numerous and happy progeny; the white man came, and the red children of the Antilles were exterminated. Millions after millions of the dark

tribes of Guinea have been brought hither by white men: where are they? They have perished, except a miserable few, who live to give birth to offspring whose inheritance is bondage, whose complexion is reproach.[67]

Fédon's speech here appears straightforward enough, an impassioned plea for equality and justice for all colonial subjects regardless of race, and a succinct recounting of the evils and injustices perpetuated by the so-called civilized European race. Joseph's Fédon makes clear, moreover, that although he may have been influenced by the French Revolution, his revolutionary aims are far nobler than those of his French counterparts, for in the West Indies, he sees clearly the role that race plays in determining who rules whom, even in a republic.[68]

Given the "truth" of Fédon's recriminations, Arundell's father has no response. Not that Fédon leaves much time for debate, for he "rushed into his frail canoe, which, in an instant, was propelled out of sight" by some of his fellow rebels. "Scarcely had it disappeared, ere the face of the sea assumed a frowning aspect," leaving Bearwell to offer up "a sincere prayer for the safety of the preserver of his child, amid the storm, which raged with awful violence."[69] Bearwell's prayers, however, go unanswered. A few days after Fédon's escape, the canoe is found at sea, "upside down, with a compass nailed to its bows, . . . which seemed to indicate the fate" of Fédon's party. The novel's introductory account of Fédon's Rebellion comes to an abrupt end, as we're told in suitably dramatic fashion that "The infant, preserved by the humanity or gratitude of Fédon, is the writer of these pages"—who repays the deed by "immortalizing" the lost Fédon in his memoirs.

With this deliberate entwining of Fédon's and Warner Arundell's histories, Joseph introduces a doomed revolutionary figure, whose ghostly presence haunts key moments of Arundell's adventures, including that of the protagonist's own exile from Grenada. A decade after the death of his wife in Fédon's camp, Arundell's father succumbs to the despair and lethargy provoked by grief and the destruction of his property during the rebellion. His ten-year-old son leaves Grenada, a departure that marks the beginning of his circum-Atlantic career. Despite his orphaned status, Arundell travels the archipelago with ease, performing his fluid identity as the creole cosmopolite discussed above.

As it turns out, Joseph's Fédon also has been wandering the Caribbean—not at his ease, however. Rather, Fédon's movements provide the antithesis to Arundell's adventures. Whereas the white creole's mobility, his ability to converse and converge with multiple Caribbean communities, signals a freedom denied to the "preserver of [his] life," Fédon's wanderings are represented as the forced exile of a criminal. Working against the grain of most colonial histories of the 1795–96 rebellion, which repeat the discovery of the overturned canoe as evidence that Fédon drowned, Joseph brings Fédon back to life. Not happily so, however, for the fiery revolutionary is haunted by the memories of his lost homeland and his failure as would-be liberator. Joseph creates in Fédon the ultimate outcast, tormented by guilt for the crimes he committed in the early days of the revolution.

This uneasy resurrection offers a dramatic accompaniment to Joseph's footnote in the *History of Trinidad*, which goes only so far as dismissing as "mere fabrication" the story of Fédon's drowning. But in *Warner Arundell*, Joseph adds other chapters to Fédon's history, fabricating details of his exile in order to understand (from a colonialist perspective) not only the Grenadian revolution, but the wider revolutionary Caribbean as well. Making sense of that revolutionary history, in other words, performs the cultural work necessary to shore up white colonial order in the post-Emancipation Caribbean—by minimizing the significance of the self-liberation ethos of Afro-Caribbean subjects visible in historical events like the Haitian Revolution and its Grenadian counterpart; by diminishing the potency of such a history for African Caribbean subjects in the future; and, finally, by maintaining a model of white historiography that lays the past to rest in order to embrace future possibilities offered by a new New World. In short, a "living," defeated Fédon is worth more to Joseph than a dead revolutionary hero.

My reading of Fédon's rewritten history and its significance for the post-Emancipation plantocracy differs from Sally Everson's argument that Joseph's novel "rewrites the failed Grenadian Revolution as a success, such as that of Haiti, rejecting a racist basis for modern Creole society."[70] Arundell, in fact, describes the Haitian Revolution as leading to "the worst form of government known—a military tyranny." And even though *Warner Arundell*'s Fédon eloquently justifies his revolutionary activity in the speech described above, the counter-narrative that Joseph provides through his fiction emphasizes Fédon's failures.

Fédon's failed revolution and his subsequent exile, moreover, is linked to that part of his history that—according to the narrative's indemnification of race-based prejudice—should not matter: his ancestral ties to Africa. One of the most striking proofs of this contradiction—and of the failed revolt's place in Caribbean history—is the fictional relationship Joseph constructs between the rebel leader and "Old Julie Sanois, the celebrated sibyl of St. Domingo," once advisor to Toussaint L'Ouverture and later companion to Fédon during his twenty-five-year exile.[71] In Joseph's rewriting, Fédon has been reduced over the course of his wanderings from dangerous rebel to a ghostlike presence, from passionate advocate of racial justice to a racially ambiguous figure: his skin, Arundell recalls, "had such a pallid hue, and his visage seemed so cadaverous, that it was not easy to decide from what race or races he was descended."[72] Old Julie, by contrast, is described as having "skin of glossy blackness, and her eye clear enough to belong to a person who had only attained middle age"—despite being nearly one hundred years old.[73] Whereas Fédon is a walking skeleton, a "spectral mulatto" on the brink of death—in fact, desirous of death—Old Julie is described in terms that emphasize her aliveness and her African-ness (as constructed by white writers of the period). Like Hamel Old Julie appears ageless, possessed of occult powers, and strongly distrustful of "white cockroaches."[74]

When these three individuals—Arundell (the white creole), Fédon (the African French creole), and Old Julie (the African)—meet accidentally on a boat traveling from Cayenne to Trinidad, they do not recognize one another. Shortly after, though, Fédon rescues Arundell once again, this time when the latter nearly drowns in a "lake of pitch" in Trinidad where he intends to settle after serving in Bolívar's army.[75] During the night Arundell overhears Old Julie insisting that Fédon kill the young man, learning from their conversation Fédon's true identity. Fédon grumbles at Old Julie's advice, chafing under the African's influence; as for Arundell, while biding his time to make an escape, he witnesses the sleeping Fédon's suffering as "the ghastly somnambulist" addresses a priest-confessor in his dreams:[76] "'No, no! neither hair shirt, flagellation, prayers, nor fasting, though I have continued them twenty-five years, can plead at the throne of mercy for pardon; after these murders it cannot be. . . . It cannot be. . . . If I were forgiven, they would not visit me as they do. I tell you that often, amid the darkness of the night, and sometimes in the glare of the sun, the forty-eight murdered men glide before me in middle air—they come even now—do you not see them?—there they are, marked with blood and soil.'"[77]

Despairing of mercy, Joseph's Fédon agonizes over acts that God cannot forgive, but that apparently Arundell can. In his view the crimes appear part of a buried history, a closed chapter that doesn't merit reopening. Despite Arundell's admission that Fédon's execution of the prisoners-of-war was an atrocity "scarcely to be paralleled in the annals of the crimes of civil war," Arundell nevertheless declares to himself (and his readers) that Fédon's "death on the gibbet at this time could have answered no good purpose"; moreover, "the local government would not have thanked any one who should have forced them to punish a man for crimes committed a quarter of a century ago."[78] More important to Arundell than punishing Fédon for twenty-five-year-old murders, it turns out, is reassessing the rebel leader's importance to his own history: Fédon, he declares, "possessed one virtue: he was grateful, and to his gratitude I owed my life."[79]

Of course, Arundell learns (though the novel does not expand on the revelation) that he also owes his life to Old Julie, who, Fédon reveals, had performed the office of midwife and wet nurse to him when he was an infant. As John Gilmore points out, the anxiety provoked by the intimate proximity of black women and white children during nursing was typically expressed in the language of disease and corruption, as illustrated in John Singleton's *A General Description of the West-Indian Islands* (1767).[80] Anticipating Edward Long's warnings in *History of Jamaica* (1772) against the common practice of white women employing black wet nurses, Singleton articulates the shock provoked by such highly visible "physical intimacy across racial boundaries" in blank verse:

> [R]ather use all art the babes to rear,
> Than e'er condemn them to the sable pap's
> Infectious juice! for, with the milky draught
> The num'rous vices of the fost'ring slave
> Deep they imbibe, and, with their life's support,
> Draw in the latent principles of ill;
> Which, brooking no controul, in riper years,
> Grow with their growth and strenghten with their strength.[81]

Such anxiety is allayed in *Warner Arundell* by Bearwell's difficult but ultimately successful search for a white woman to perform the office of nurse for his son. Not that Old Julie appears to harbor maternal feelings for Arundell. In fact, unlike the Irish foster mother who sacrifices her life to protect Arundell, Old Julie pushes Fédon to kill him, trying to persuade the tortured exile that his secret will be revealed to the authorities if Arundell lives.

The conflict between Fédon—the grateful penitent and preserver of "the son of the good white man ... my dearest friend" Bearwell Arundell[82]—and Old Julie—past companion to Toussaint L'Ouverture and the white creole's would-be murderer—reveals a fascinating complex of ideas, not least of which is the demonizing of Old Julie's African-ness. Not only does

Fédon come off as a gullible dupe of Jacobin radicalism in this reunion scene, but as a hostage to African conceptions of liberty and self-rule embodied by Old Julie. The death of the old prophetess, however, breaks her hold over Fédon and over the revolutionary history Joseph attempts to rewrite: after the confrontation with Arundell, both Fédon and Old Julie leave Trinidad for Martinique, a sea crossing that ends with Old Julie drowning. Fédon, surviving yet again, lives long enough to return to Grenada in secret to search for a treasure he had buried before leaving that island twenty-five years earlier. Although the treasure has already been unearthed and stolen, Fédon does find various legal papers related to Bearwell Arundell's estates. He dies soon after and, in his final confession, reveals to a priest the significance of the papers, eliciting a promise to deliver them to Arundell.

With the African threat embodied by the spirited and unrepentant Old Julie Sanois contained and supplanted by the more reassuring (second) death of Fédon—whose final act of expiation restores Arundell to his father's properties on Grenada and Antigua—the longevity of white privilege in the Caribbean seems assured. Erasing Old Julie's African presence and reducing Fédon to an object of Arundell's pity, Joseph assigns the Grenadian revolt and its leader to a place conformable to colonialist history. Unlike Hamel's failed revolution, which marks the end of the obeah man's interventions in a universalizing linear history, Fédon's failure to conquer Grenada in the name of Afro-French republicanism assists in that same history's unfolding. By building on the historical fact of Fédon, Joseph revives the mulatto long enough to receive the sympathetic embrace of the revolutionary white creole Arundell, whose forgiveness of the mixed-race subject facilitates the historiographic aims of a newly "emancipated" planter class. This class, to which Arundell indisputably belongs thanks to the restoration Fédon makes possible, is free to move forward—with the same racial hierarchies of the old order firmly in place.[83]

As MENTIONED in the opening pages of this chapter, Warner Arundell—the representative of a new plantocracy relieved of the moral burden of slavery and fears of slave revolt—looks not to the metropole, but to the Caribbean and the newly independent Spanish Main for affirmation. The continent that falls under Arundell's westward gaze has emerged from its own revolutionary moment, the South American wars of independence led by another creole: Simón Bolívar. Like Fédon's attempted revolution, the Bolivarian wars act as a regenerative force in Joseph's novel, providing the occasion for Arundell's homecoming from the metropole and the wedding celebration that "ends" the creole's adventures and begins his life of creole domesticity.

In this sense, Arundell's engagement with the South American patriots is represented as a means to an end; in his attempt to leave London and return home, the penniless Arundell is persuaded to enlist in Bolívar's army as a medical officer in order to secure passage to the Caribbean. But as with Fédon's rebellion, the Bolivarian wars constitute much more than historical color for Joseph's novel. Acknowledging the iconic place of Bolívar in Latin American and Caribbean history as the "liberator of South America," Joseph forges his protagonist's history to converge with that of El Libertador. Significant as are Bolívar's attempts to throw off the yoke of Spanish colonialism, Arundell's increasing appreciation for the patriots' cause—including a righteous indignation at Spain's persistent privileging of Spanish-born colonials over creoles—opens space in the novel for the romance plot. It is during one of Arundell's military adventures that he meets the "angel of mercy," the beautiful and wealthy criolla Maria Josefa Ximenes. Initially wedded to the royalist cause, Maria Josefa changes allegiances soon after helping Arundell escape imprisonment at a royalist camp; the two are separated for a time, but ultimately reunited in Trinidad, where Maria Josefa Ximenes "adds Arundell" to her impressive list of family names. Like the romantic plots of earlier creole novels, Arundell's marriage consolidates wealth and property for a ruling-class elite. But unlike the marriages of Henry Montgomery, Oliver Fairfax, and George Marly, Warner's nuptials to a South American–born creole heiress establishes a distinctly pan-Caribbean alliance, a reaffirmation of the novel's Caribbean orientation. Warner Arundell's marriage, in other words, is presented as an end to his adventures but also a return to the roots of "creole" discussed in my introduction: a designation drawn from the Ibero-American *criadillo* and its associations of creole domesticity. With this return, the novel's conclusion gestures toward a revolutionary creole identity, privileging a Caribbean cosmopolitan perspective that (re) presents its history and sees its future in the New World.

Conclusion
The Unfinished Business of Early Creole Novels

I CLOSE my study of early creole novels with a consideration of several works published not long after the end of the Apprenticeship period and the enactment of full emancipation in the British Caribbean colonies in 1838: Samuel Gray's *Old Port-Royal; or, The Buccaneer's Home*, published in Kingston in 1841; J. W. Orderson's *Creoleana; or, Social and Domestic Scenes and Incidents in Barbados in Days of Yore*, which appeared in 1842 and featured a dedicatory signature line from Bridge Town dated 1841; and Trinidadian Michel Maxwell Philip's *Emmanuel Appadocca; or, Blighted Life. A Tale of the Boucaneers*, published in London in 1854. Each of these novels deals with the pre-Emancipation past and each reengages earlier novels' depictions of white creole culture and creolized subjectivities from a post-Emancipation moment of fashioning.

The self-consciousness with which these novelists engage in creole historiography appears on their respective title pages: Gray identifies his narrative of seventeenth-century Jamaica as "An Historical Novel," and Orderson situates his nostalgic view of pre-Emancipation Barbados in "Days of Yore." Philip's three-part title doesn't reference history or the past per se, but in the novel's preface he declares that "the machinery of the story is based on truth—the known history of the Boucaneers."[1] Each of the novels, then, is as firmly grounded in the (re)production of Caribbean history and historiography as the pre-Emancipation works discussed in previous chapters. As importantly, *Old Port-Royal*, *Creoleana*, and *Emmanuel Appadocca* rewrite a history shaped by the epistemological labor performed by the novels that preceded them, texts that had become part of the anglophone Caribbean's "received past on offer."[2]

As I discuss below, the instabilities of an accretive Caribbean history that makes up that received past, the precarious piling up of nows and thens, are illustrated by the novels' self-conscious cultural labor as historical fiction. In placing their narrative action in "an age when . . . cultures are in conflict" and introducing "fictional personages who participate in actual events and move among actual personages" (as Walter Scott describes the historical novel), Gray, Orderson, and Philip navigate the uncertainty and promise of a new Caribbean history and of the creole subject's place in it. Gray, a Jamaican planter writing to teach fellow creoles about their island's history, speaks to a past moment that encompasses the heyday of Anglo-Caribbean piracy, when Henry Morgan commanded his infamous fleet out of Port Royal before the 1692 earthquake destroyed that city. Orderson does not reach as far back into West Indian history, but presents instead a nostalgic image of idealized planter life in late eighteenth-century Barbados. *Emmanuel Appadocca*—the only one of the novels written by a creole of African and European descent, the first such novel in English—is set in Philip's contemporary post-Emancipation present, confronting the slaveholding past through the mixed-race hero's quest for vengeance against the white planter father who abandoned him as a child.[3] Each of these novels, despite their different temporal and geographic settings, confronts and perpetuates a conflicted sense of Caribbean history, particularly when depicting the violence on which that history was founded.

The push and pull of the violent past and contested present in the Anglo-Caribbean colonial world raises particular questions about the shape historical fiction assumes in the immediate post-Emancipation era. Using José de Piérola's "working definition" of the historical novel, we can explore such questions, beginning with those arising from the ambiguities surrounding historical fiction as a genre. Writing about the Latin American literary context, Piérola points out that despite the explosion of historical novels published in the late twentieth and early twenty-first centuries, despite the form's lengthy genealogy, and despite the scholarship that followed, a clear theorization of the historical novel remains elusive. In large part, he argues, this is because no satisfactory definition of the form has been articulated. "The historical novel," he writes, "is a special case in literature. It seems to combine 'facts' taken from the historical record with freely invented fictional elements." This combination, he continues, "is done in a way that makes it difficult, if not impossible, to differentiate which is which: it seems to be a hybrid of two genres, but refuses to be read as either."[4] For Piérola the seemingly oppositional relationship inherent in the form offers the basis for his working definition: "The historical novel is not a genre," as previously described, "but a 'mode of writing' that creates and sustains an unresolved tension between history and fiction."[5]

By emphasizing this meta- and intratextual tension, we can put historical novels like *Old Port-Royal, Creoleana,* and *Emmanuel Appadocca* in productive conversation with one another, with the creole novels that preceded them, with subsequent West Indian literature, and with the historical fiction produced by Caribbean novelists of the late twentieth and twenty-first centuries. Across periods the novels engage a shared past marked by the experiences borne of Atlantic slavery and its legacies, while the authors' different presents inform their role as historical novelists and actors.

The works that I focus on in closing emerged in the immediate aftermath of E/emancipation—legislative, political, and cultural—and provide a clear revisioning and rereading of colonial plantocratic history. But the recovery of lost histories is only one part of the cultural work these novels perform. In choosing to write historical novels, Gray, Orderson, and Philip are also engaged in a hermeneutical enterprise, relying on the reader's recognition that "history" and historiography are integral components of their "fictions." In this sense, as Piérola observes, historical novels like *Old Port-Royal, Creoleana,* and *Emmanuel Appadocca* not only invite readers to recognize the tensions between "facts" and "fictions," but to ask how that tension is created and sustained and—given its irresolvability—why?[6]

My conclusion is not, then, about "fixing" Caribbean (literary) history so much as "unfixing" it. It illustrates how creole novelists of the first half of the nineteenth century engage in literary acts by writing stories about history and in doing so write the history that subsequent generations of Caribbean authors grapple with. In this each novelist demonstrates how their mode of writing—the terms of their engagement with the historical novel—reflects the particularity of their own moment and that moment's relationship to past, present, and future.

One Volume at a Time: *Old Port-Royal*'s Missing Piece

Before beginning my reading of Gray's *Old Port-Royal*, I must acknowledge an obvious challenge: only one of the novel's two volumes is accessible and available for reading at the National Library of Jamaica. According to Frank Cundall's annotation in *Bibliografia Jamaicensis*, compiled near the turn of the twentieth century, the Institute of Jamaica (now the National Library) holds "vol. I only" of *Old Port-Royal*. The complete novel, apparently, consisted of two volumes (rather than say, three or four), a bit of information included in the novel's bibliographic entry in the 1885 *Transactions of the Institute of Jamaica,* which suggests that at some point during the fifteen years or so between the compilation of the *Transactions*'s bibliography and Cundall's *Bibliografia Jamaicensis,* the second volume of Gray's historical novel was lost or destroyed. I hope, of course, that a more exhaustive search will turn up the missing volume. In the meantime, I want to focus on what Gray's volume 1 says about the development of Caribbean historical fiction.

As I have argued throughout *Crossing the Line,* one of the most visible tendencies in early creole novels is the turn to Caribbean settings, characters, and history as fitting topics for a work of fiction. This is true of Gray, whose brief preface speaks to the significance he attaches to such cultural work: "To edit and publish a Work of Fiction in Jamaica," he writes, "may be considered by some, the height of folly"; but, having "long contemplated such a step, and calculated the chances of success," Gray sets out to undertake the task. Like *Montgomery*'s author thirty years earlier, Gray introduces his work as pointedly didactic—not as in the case of *Montgomery* to teach morals and manners, but to give (white) Jamaican readers a lesson in history, addressing them in the authorial third person: "To those [readers] who are creoles by birth, he would say, patronise the undertaking with your accustomed generosity—the object is to illustrate the early history of your native country. To those who, like the author, are . . . [creoles], by adoption, he would urge, that while he admits they must yearn towards the land of their nativity, as he does, he deems it impossible that they will not exhibit some interest in what relates to the one they live and thrive in."[7] Gray's opening remarks suggest an understanding of the role fiction played in shaping (and reshaping) Caribbean colonial identity, in particular the role of historical novels in the first decades of the nineteenth century, a period that saw the abolition of slavery, the end of the Apprenticeship period, and the emergence of a planter class whose members—like Gray—were attempting to (re)assert their authority over colonial life, and who appear all the more anxious to construct a stable history with which to counter the instabilities of the liberated British Atlantic.

The confidence with which Gray assumes his creole readers will appreciate his literary production, his representation of them as generous cultural patrons and thriving participants in creole culture is buoyed by the certainty that historical fiction rooted in the West Indian past is the fittest medium for his work. Drawing on his understanding that "the method of teaching history, manners, and morals by means of the novel" was perceived by his reading audience as one of the most important "inventions of modern times,"[8] Gray calculates his chances of success, assumes the risk of writing a novel, and sets out to perform the cultural work of inculcating an appreciation for the island's history.

Such work requires Gray to engage Caribbean history in numerous ways, not least of which is through the poetic license he takes with the various historical characters and events that fill his narrative. The novel's first volume, for example, begins and ends with the narrator's commentary on the great earthquake of 1692 that destroyed Port Royal. His first chapter opens with a rhetorical question posed in Gray's present moment of 1841: will Port Royal be engulfed by another cataclysmic earthquake, or will the city "be permitted to remain as a memento of that awful convulsion, which for magnitude and disastrous effects stands unrivalled in the pages of history"?[9] The apocalyptic language here is typical of the moralistic reading of the earthquake as punishment visited on the wickedest city in the New World. And certainly in the "pages of history" that Gray himself contributes to, he seems intent on reveling in the decadent excesses of pre-quake Port Royal, metaphorically digging through the rubble of the razed city to unearth its earlier history. Setting the present action of the novel in 1668, when Port Royal "was in its glory . . . the home or the resort of the most powerful, sanguinary, and detestable band of pirates that ever hoisted the black flag, and proclaimed war against the whole world,"[10] Gray paints a city reviled and celebrated for its fabulous but ill-gotten wealth.

The second allusion to the earthquake, which closes volume 1 of *Old Port-Royal,* is different in tone, less moralistic and more self-consciously engaged in literary archaeology of the kind discussed in my introduction—a process more typically associated with twentieth- and twenty-first-century historical novels by writers like Toni Morrison. Winding down the action—and the volume is action-packed—Gray's narrator provides some suggestive hints about the contents of volume 2, including a continuation of the ill-fated romance between Henry Morgan and Ellen Mansvelt, the beautiful, "half-caste" daughter of the pirate-king Mansvelt, whom Morgan succeeds as admiral of the buccaneer fleet. Morgan is, of course, an actual person, as is Mansvelt, while Ellen—the daughter of "a half-caste mahometan woman" her father had met "near the Island of Madagascar"—is entirely the product of Gray's imagination.[11] Gray assures his reader that volume 2 will contain other noteworthy material as well, not least of which is a description of the attempts and ultimate success of "the Hebrew race" in overcoming the "jealousy and prejudice of the early colonists," and establishing themselves in Jamaica, the "Queen of the Antilles."[12]

These hints about the main plot's trajectory are followed by a self-conscious description of the challenges faced by the historical novelist, which constitutes the last paragraph of volume 1, and the (unintended) end of *Port-Royal*—at least until a copy of the second volume is located. This passage, I suggest, operates both as an admission of the fragility of documented history and as an implicit vindication of historical fiction as a method of making up and making up *for* its incomplete nature. "It has long been a matter of regret," the narrator observes,

> that the public records and documents connected with the early period of English occupation were unfortunately lost or destroyed by that awful visitation of Providence, which engulphed the city of Port-Royal in 1692, yet we find the Hon. House of Assembly, nine years after that event, at issue with the then Governor, Sir William Baston, and declining to proceed to business on account of his refusing to give account of large sums of money, books, and writings found after the earthquake, and we are satisfied, that even now, if strict search were made in the libraries of Europe, many valuable and rare manuscripts might be discovered, highly interesting to the historian and the antiquarian, and throwing considerable light on this imperfect portion of history.[13]

Presenting the Jamaican archive as a treasure trove, a buried cache of valuable and rare knowledge, the narrator suggests loss, but not necessarily an irrecoverable one. Until the rare and valuable manuscripts are discovered and interpreted by the historian and antiquarian, novels like Gray's will provide a proper sense of history. Our situation as readers in this instance is analogous to that of the novel's heroine, Ellen Mansvelt, who, betrayed by Morgan, discovers the location of her father's fabled treasure but is unable to do anything with it until she can unfold a plot and take possession of it.

The allusions to the historical fact of the 1692 earthquake, as mentioned above, bookend the first volume's attempt to throw light on the "imperfect portion" of Jamaica's history prior to 1692. Many pages, for example, are devoted to Morgan's exploits as a pirate during the time he was headquartered in Port Royal: the sacking of Cuba, Panama, Maracaybo, and Portobello. In describing these events, Gray's novel seems to follow the general outline of Morgan's career offered up in works like Exquemelin's *History of the Bucaniers*. Gray depicts Morgan's cruelty with relish, attempting to qualify the sensationalist tone of his descriptions with repeated assertions of truthfulness. When relating Morgan's treatment of the inhabitants of Maracaybo after learning the city's riches have been taken away and hidden, for example, the narrator assures those readers who may "consider the picture overcharged," that he does not exaggerate. Morgan is so enraged in this instance of Gray's reimagining, that the pirate "surpasse[s] the most savage of his band": "Such a compound of refinement and savage inhumanity," the narrator insists, "never before or since existed to shame the name of man."[14]

In recounting and condemning Morgan and his band of pirates as bloodthirsty and barbaric, Gray participates in a fairly longstanding tradition in the print culture of the early Americas, a "literature of piracy" that, as Richard Frohock points out, is filled "with some of the most exaggerated and blood-soaked rhetoric in all of Euro-American print culture."[15] These descriptions, Frohock notes, are at odds with more recent scholarship that suggests a less sanguine, more democratic society, as in the work of Marcus Rediker and Peter Linebaugh. Rather than attempt to read *Old Port-Royal* as fitting either one or the other of these two models, Gray's Morgan can be viewed as a transformed and transformative figure.

The trajectory of Morgan's history as told in the history books and in Gray's historical novel points toward the pirate's transformation from bloodthirsty buccaneer to plantocrat and colonial administrator. Morgan's progress along this path of improvement depends ultimately on the outcome of Morgan's courtship of the daughter of a Royalist planter and one of Charles II's favorites, William Beckford, who arrives in Jamaica not long after England takes the island from the Spanish in 1655 and establishes an estate on the island. After noting that Jamaica from the time of its English occupation under Cromwell was perceived by early colonists as neutral ground on which both Royalists and Cromwellians planted themselves, Gray engages in more poetic license to sing the praises of the Royalist camp. "For although," the narrator explains, "they brought with them but little wealth, most of them having cheerfully placed their all at the disposal of their thoughtless master [Charles II], they possessed rank, intelligence, and high and polished bearing which could not fail to produce a sensible effect on the tone of society, which much needed such an infusion."[16] Here the narrator forbears describing in any detail "the labours and difficulties [Beckford] had to contend against" because they would be superfluous to his readers. Those white creoles by birth or adoption that Gray addresses in his preface are well schooled in the discursive privileging of the labor and suffering of white settlers over that of black subjects—a privilege upheld in works like *Montgomery* and *Marly* but challenged in later works by writers of color, like Philip's *Emmanuel*

Appadocca, which I return to below. Creole readers' imaginations may easily supply the details that Gray's account of Beckford omits; and it is only necessary to add that Beckford, at the moment of his introduction in *Old Port-Royal,* has become a "flourishing and prosperous planter."[17]

The "polished bearing" Gray attributes to his version of the paternal patriarch who founded the Beckford fortunes in Jamaica is a stark contrast to the man described by William May, rector of Kingston in the early eighteenth century. Writing peevishly to the Bishop of London about the "estated Creolians" that he must contend with, he points out that the father of the famous Peter Beckford who died one of the wealthiest men in the world in 1710, came to the island soon after the English occupation "with 2 or 3 Negroes . . . &. being a hunter, he & his Negroes catch'd horses and sold them again, for some years, by which he made a beginning of his fortune here."[18] This image—and May's complaints about the unruly and decidedly *un*polished planter class—conforms to the depictions of white creoles more commonly found in writings describing the West Indies, particularly those produced in the metropole, and intensifying over the course of the eighteenth century as the slavery and abolition debates began to heat up.

What, then, is Gray doing in his rewriting of this chapter of Jamaican history? On the one hand, his historical novel is similar to other narratives produced by white creoles during the pre-Emancipation period, in which they routinely defend themselves and their proslavery position, and insist that one can be a planter and a humane, civilized subject. This is clearly the case in *Montgomery,* as discussed in chapter 1, a novel troubled by the question of West Indian depravity and corruption but also filled with numerous examples of benign planters whose virtue and generous treatment of enslaved workers contribute to their success. But Gray's novel—written in 1841—isn't concerned with writing about planters as *slaveholders,* even kind-hearted ones. Rather, he is working, like the author of *Marly* and Joseph in *Warner Arundell,* to provide a respectable genealogy for the planter class, skipping over, as it were, the ugly business of slavery, and writing instead about bloodthirsty pirates and *their* relationship to the planting class during the earliest days of Jamaica's English history.

That relationship as depicted in *Old Port-Royal* is complex and sometimes contradictory, as we see in the last pages of volume 1, when Gray describes Henry Morgan as "the founder of Jamaica's prosperity." Through him, the narrator assures us, "the island became the most brilliant jewel in England's crown. The wealth poured in by his sanguinary band enabled the planters to construct works that otherwise would have been a matter of impossibility, whilst the terror of his name protected the fleets that bore homeward the riches of the virgin soil of the teeming tropical isle."[19] Here, Jamaica's wealth is traced to pirate booty, the rise of the plantation machine made possible by an early infusion of ill-gotten plunder and the (at-times) state-sanctioned privateering of Morgan and his contemporaries. In a sense, this explanation of West Indian wealth performs the same kind of obfuscation of the actualities of slavery and slave labor that is suggested in the earlier elision of Beckford's labors and difficulties, and in fictions like *Montgomery* and *Marly*.

But although the novel's first volume routinely engages in such obfuscation, it doesn't entirely ignore slavery—or resistance to it. There is a cameo appearance by Juan de Bolas, one of the famed leaders of the early Maroons who fought with the Spanish against the English at mid-century. Described as "a gigantic negro of herculean proportions," Bolas (spelled Bola by Gray) is "elegantly, even splendidly attired in the spanish costume. His arms were bare, the sleeves of his embroidered tunic being rolled up nearly to the shoulders, and displayed a muscle worthy of a Roman gladiator."[20] This depiction follows conventions of colonial writing about Maroons, most notably its fascination with physical strength and ambivalence toward self-liberated and self-reliant fighters who posed a distinct military threat to the English. Bolas, the narrator explains, is not just "the Captain of the Cimarones," but one of the progenitors of "the race of Maroons, who, for one hundred and forty years, infested the interior of the island, defying all the military skill and determined valor that could be opposed to them."[21]

A second treatment of slavery occurs much later in volume 1, and brings us back to the notion of novelistic archaeology. This particular passage contains a description of the fabled Spanish Jamaican city of Sevilla Nueva, "the most splendid city that ever flourished in Jamaica," "founded by Don Juan d'Esquimel *A.D.* 1510." Begging the reader's patience, the narrator provides a brief history of its "rapid rise and fall" and "its premature decay," which are now, the narrator observes, "matters of history":

> little does the passing traveller as he rides along the sea shore and bends his admiring gaze on the luxuriant canefields . . . think that on that very spot where vegetation and the planter's art now reign triumphant, was once the busy scene of a populous and wealthy community. . . . [T]he negro digs his cane holes, and little dreams, that beneath that tough soil which tries his sinews, are vaults filled with golden ingots—that in the vicinity is a mine of the precious metal, to work which sixty thousand Indian lives were sacrificed . . .

[B]ut the fame of the enormous wealth contained in this precious city caused its ruin. The Caribbean Sea was then infested with French Corsairs who sacked it repeatedly, and at length, the few inhabitants who had escaped with their lives, removed into the interior, where they imagined themselves more secure, and founded St. Jago de la Vega, or St. Jago of the Plains; but many of those who perished in these terrible conflicts, deposited their wealth, for security, in vaults constructed beneath their dwellings, and even now, in the archives of the Havannah, are to be seen the drawings and descriptions of these places of concealment.[22]

Once more, Gray constructs an idealized, romanticized historical archive that will set "history to rights," as it were. But until that archive can be mined, we have to rely on the historical novel to catch glimpses of West Indian history, always unfolding and always under construction in the early literature of the Caribbean.

Constructing the historical archive as a buried treasure waiting to be unearthed provides a tantalizing close to Gray's volume 1, but the figurative language operating here also recalls the buried treasure located by Morgan's abandoned lover, Ellen Mansvelt, and the promise she makes herself to thwart his romance with Rosaline Beckford, the wealthy planter's daughter. The vengeful creole woman of color appears as a stock character in later Caribbean historical fiction—from H. G. De Lisser's Annie Palmer in *White Witch of Rosehall* and Ellen Morgan in *Morgan's Daughter* to Isobel in Marlon James's *Book of Night Women*. But as my reading of Orderson's *Creoleana* demonstrates, the figure of the mixed-race antiheroine is necessary not only to disrupt the creole romance, but as importantly, to maintain the creole fiction of racialized Caribbean hierarchies and histories.

A Little Matter of Difference: J. W. Orderson's *Creoleana*

Unlike Gray's fictionalized depiction of Jamaica's piratical history, Orderson's *Creoleana* performs its cultural work through nostalgic representations of the plantation machine. In this narrative, the creole marriage plot and constructions of domesticity, similar to those found in *Montgomery, Hamel, Marly,* and *Warner Arundell,* uphold ideas about creole endogamy and white creole culture, as I discuss elsewhere at length.[23] But in *Old Port-Royal* and *Creoleana* creole domesticity is threatened in ways not seen in the earlier novels, disrupted by the figure of the brown woman whose very presence gives the lie to assertions of racial and moral "purity" privileged in celebrations of white endogamy.

Rejecting the notion of racial reconciliation presented in, say, *Warner Arundell*—carefully crafted and troubling as that is—*Creoleana* instead focuses on and then tries to override the dangers of interracial "romance." The most obvious embodiment of this danger appears through the character of Lucy, the mixed-race daughter of the planter-merchant Fairfield and one of his nameless slaves. Convinced of his duty toward his illegitimate child, Fairfield "saves" Lucy by taking her away from her mother and into his household as a maid/companion to Caroline Fairfield, the legitimate heiress of his wealth. The threat posed by Lucy is defused only when she dies in childbirth, she and her stillborn daughter effectively written out of Orderson's plot. Rid of the "tragic mulatta," whose presence constitutes undeniable evidence of what the novel calls an "unhallowed" (because interracial) relationship with Lucy's anonymous mother, *Creoleana* moves steadily toward its resolution: the proper marriage between Lucy's "pure" and uncorrupted half-sister Caroline, and Johnny Goldacre, son of a neighboring planter.

Although *Creoleana* is more heavy-handed than *Hamel, Marly*, and *Warner Arundell* in its treatment of mixed-race subjects, all of the early creole novels illustrate white West Indian novelists' attempts to allay anxieties about race by reordering creole domestic desires. These attempts in *Creoleana*, however, are not as tightly bound to the private creole household of Fairfield—the domestic scenes from Days of Yore—as initially appears. Rather, they expand through Orderson's engagement with the conventions of historical novels, specifically in *Creoleana*'s depiction of "actual personages" moving about in Orderson's fictionalized Barbados.

Two such people are Rachel Pringle and Prince William Henry of Britain, future king. Both of these figures contribute to the novel's representations of the historical place of mixed-race sexual relationships in early creole culture. In the case of Rachel Pringle, however, Orderson appropriates her plot to display and patronize the African Caribbean tradition of the trickster figure[24] (see fig. 12). The owner of a Bridge Town inn (and reputed brothel), Orderson's Pringle is an astute businessperson whose history includes several roguish attempts to dissemble and deceive—and to profit. As John Gilmore points out, Pringle's escapades recall those of Ananci, the popular African Caribbean trickster who "plays fool fuh catch wise." In Pringle's case, the supposed "wise" person she catches by playing the fool is none other than Prince William Henry, who gained a reputation for interracial sexual liaisons during his naval tour of the Caribbean in the 1780s. During one of his two visits to Barbados (in 1786

FIGURE 12. "Rachel Pringle of Barbadoes," hand-colored print by Thomas Rowlandson, after "E.D.," 1796. This high-quality (and high-priced) portrait, sold by the London print seller William Holland, was not, like much of Rowlandson's work, designed as a caricature. (Courtesy of the Royal Collection Trust/© Her Majesty Queen Elizabeth II 2016)

and 1789), the prince encounters Pringle, their meeting incorporated into Orderson's novel as a piece of local history.

But this historical encounter also invites comparison between the actual personage of Pringle and the fictional Lucy, two mixed-race women whose actions pose direct challenges to white masculine order in *Creoleana*. In teasing out the wider significance of these two plots, it is useful to engage Wilson Harris's discussion of Caribbean artists and activists who attempt to transform "the antagonistic energies" of the colonial past "into a creative syncretism" in their present moment. A novel like *Creoleana*, of course, is part of the "destructive imperialism" that those artists respond to. But it is also true that the early creole historical novel contains the "persisting regenerative seed" that will undermine its epistemological and historiographic work. This seed, contained in the representations of women like Lucy and Pringle, fractures the text's surface realism "by the intrusive irrational, by dream and madness."[25]

In both *Old Port-Royal* and *Creoleana*, Ellen Mansvelt and Lucy (and, in a different way, Rachel Pringle) embody the intrusive irrational. Certainly, *Creoleana* presents multiple scenes of madness and irrationality, and in doing so provides a counter-narrative to accepted colonial and colonialist histories. Thus, even as Pringle—who directly challenges the future monarch of the colonizing power—is "taken from the life," borrowed from "history," while the figure of Lucy—"the madwoman in the hut" (to borrow Wyrick's phrase)—is the fictional corrective to the subversive elements contained in Pringle's story, both women push at the boundaries of race and gender that Orderson's novel attempts to uphold. Even as Lucy appears to be written out and Pringle reduced to caricature, the presence/absence of both women continues to resonate, their depictions becoming part of the history Orderson (re)constructs. In short, Lucy as tragic mulatta and Pringle as trickster-survivor—though seemingly contrasting constructions of brown women's identity and place within white creole cultural (re)production—embody those disruptive elements of Caribbean culture that many of the early creole historical novels sought to contain. The success, or rather, failure, of this endeavor can be read in *Emmanuel Appadocca*.

"A Mixture of Blood"

Crossing the Line opens with a consideration of *Montgomery; or, The West-Indian Adventurer*, the first anglophone novel published in the Caribbean; it closes with a brief reading of another first, Michel Maxwell Philip's *Emmanuel Appadocca*, the first anglophone Caribbean novel written by a person of color. In this sense, Philip's novel allows my study to come full circle, as it were, but in such a way that marks that circle's widening circumference. Connected to the earlier works by its representation of "Creole society and Creole sentiment," Philip's novel takes on the work of rewriting Caribbean history and subjectivity just as *Montgomery, Hamel, Marly,* and *Warner Arundell* do in the pre-Emancipation period and that *Old Port-Royal* and *Creoleana* do in the decade after slavery's end. There are other connections as well. As in *Warner Arundell,* the action in *Emmanuel Appadocca* is set on ships sailing the Caribbean Sea, oriented toward Trinidad. Like Joseph's novel, *Hamel,* and *Marly,* Philip's narrative involves a quest, though in the case of Appadocca the hero seeks revenge rather than a lost estate.

The construction of Philip's hero as a young man educated in the values of Enlightenment sensibility provides another important link to *Montgomery,* signaling the refined morality of the pirate hero in ways that are absent in Gray's Henry Morgan. But whereas Henry Montgomery exhibits sensibility through the sighs and tears associated with a passive man of feeling, Emmanuel Appadocca displays his by the "conduct, which a high-spirited and sensitive person would probably follow" when confronted with social injustice.[26]

Appadocca's more politicized sensibility recalls the Jacobin ardor that fueled fiction of the 1790s such as Wollstonecraft's *Maria; or, the Wrongs of Woman,* Godwin's *Caleb Williams,* and Mary Hays's *Victim of Prejudice.* Unlike the injustices encountered by English heroines and heroes in the metropole, however, the wrongs suffered by Philip's Appadocca—son of a free woman of color and a white planter—spring from the transformative violence of Atlantic slavery and its aftereffects, specifically the "abominable prejudice" against creoles of African ancestry.[27]

As Philip specifies in his brief preface, the immediate occasion for his midcentury novel is passionate indignation over "the cruel manner in which the slave holders of America deal with their slave-children," and the "hideousness of begetting children for the purpose of turning them out into the fields to labour at the lash's sting."[28] This declaration ties *Emmanuel Appadocca* to the debate over slavery in the United States in the decade preceding the American Civil War, his own ancestry making the denunciation of the mistreatment of mixed-race children a personal matter. However, as William Cain observes, *Emmanuel Appadocca* "does and does not derive and develop its meanings from slavery and abolition"; although Philip's novel "is forthrightly antislavery in its implications, . . .

its potent critique would be missed if today's readers were unaware of its historical contexts.... *Emmanuel Appadocca* is everywhere 'about' slavery, yet is at the same time distanced from it."[29]

I would argue further that Philip's decision to situate his novel in the Caribbean (rather than, say, the southern United States) reveals its engagement with questions of West Indian historiography and literary form in the post-Emancipation period. Grappling with such questions calls for a mode of writing akin to that described by Piérola and discussed above, one that "creates and sustains an unresolved tension between history and fiction."[30] Although Philip's plot does not incorporate actual historical events or people as do *Warner Arundell, Old Port-Royal,* and *Creoleana,* the Tale of the Boucaneers certainly generates and perpetuates unresolved tensions by positing a Caribbean history different from that constructed in earlier creole novels, thereby challenging colonialist history's propagation of white privilege.

These unresolved tensions generate *Emmanuel Appadocca*'s textual ambivalence, most notably the ambivalence surrounding the creole subject's place in past and present. The sense of anger that drives the first of the preface's three paragraphs, for example, places the novel in 1854. The closing paragraph, however, describes "the Author's native isle" of Trinidad—its "green woods, smiling sky, beautiful flowers and romantic gulf"—in nostalgic strains that not only introduce the picturesque imagery used to describe the novel's Caribbean scenes, but also to convey the power of past events on present actions. Philip closes his prefatory remarks—written during the period he studied law in London—with the hope that one day he will return to Trinidad, to be interred "on the rising ground that looks over the sea" near his mother's grave.

Here the pull of the *pays natal* recalls Hamel's desire to return to the "land of my birth—my mother's country,"[31] and anticipates the return to Africa that figures so prominently in the work of later Caribbean writers and activists like Aimé Césaire and Marcus Garvey. But Philip and his protagonist—like Joseph's Warner Arundell and Julien Fédon—identify the Caribbean as their ancestral homeland rather than Africa. The novelistic expression of this desire, the story of Appadocca's journey from Paris to London to his birthplace in Trinidad, where he is eventually buried beside his mother's grave, can be read as the literary fulfilment of Philip's wishes, of course, even though the future attorney general of Trinidad follows a course quite unlike that pursued by the pirate hero Appadocca.[32] But the parallels between the author's life and his hero's reveal a strand in the novel absolutely crucial to the production and reproduction of creole histories and creole subjects: the place of the mixed-race mother in Emancipation-era historical fiction.

Much like the novel's treatment of slavery, the woman of mixed race is both central to and marginalized in Philip's text. The only such person depicted in *Emmanuel Appadocca* is the hero's mother, an unnamed Trinidadian woman abandoned by Appadocca's white planter father, James Willmington. Unlike the mixed-race women depicted in *Crossing the Line*'s other novels—Michal in *Hamel,* Warner Arundell's half-sisters, Ellen Mansvelt in *Old Port-Royal,* Lucy in *Creoleana,* and the only other woman of color in Philip's novel, the obeah woman Celeste—Appadocca's mother is a memory rather than an actual character.[33] She is described only briefly, when Appadocca explains how he "found [him]self a pirate, cruising in the Caribbean Sea."[34] This inset history, shared with his university friend Charles Hamilton, an officer aboard the naval vessel where Appadocca is imprisoned while awaiting trial, opens with an account of his mother's death, news of which he receives while studying in Paris. The news has an "overwhelming effect" on Appadocca. Unable to bear his grief—mother and son entertained a "more than ordinary fondness" for each other—Appadocca languishes under the effects of a fever. He recovers slowly to find that with the loss of his mother, he is penniless. Despite their closeness, his mother has hidden from him the sacrifices she has made on his behalf: "all her little fortune," he tells Hamilton, "had been devoted to my education, and had been expended for the purpose of keeping me . . . on a level with the station which her ancestors had occupied."[35]

The ancestors Philip's Appadocca alludes to—likely based on the author's own family history—would have been free creoles of color, belonging to a network of affiliated families in the Eastern Caribbean, many of whom were large landowners and planters. The Philip family, for example, was descended from a French Grenadian planter, Honore Philip, his wife Jeanette, and their nine mixed-race children, some of whom migrated to Trinidad in the 1790s. On Honore's death Jeanette inherited a 160-acre plantation on the island of Carriacou, just off the coast of Grenada, along with 89 enslaved people who cultivated cotton there. By the time of Fédon's Rebellion in 1795—in which at least two of Jeanette's sons served as Fédon's officers—Jeanette's daughter Judith had assumed the role of family matriarch. At the time of her death in 1849, she owned three large plantations and more than 150 slaves, as well as a fashionable house in London.[36]

Conclusion

This pattern of strong matriarchs is disrupted by Philip's writing of Appadocca's mother in absentia, her life told only through the son's reading of a posthumously delivered letter. The letter reveals not only the young man's loss of fortune, but also the truth of his parentage—that contrary to what he has been told, his father is not dead, but living the prosperous life of a Trinidadian planter. Despite his mother's written injunction "to cherish and respect him who was pointed out to me as my sire," Appadocca is convinced "that my good mother had been treated with injustice" by his white father. "[V]engeance," he tells Hamilton, "was my first impulse."[37] Appadocca's immediate interpretation of his mother's letter, based on the power of his feelings rather than the words themselves, casts his mother in the role of victim of injustice and himself as her avenger. With this particular interpretation, Appadocca's mother, though rarely mentioned again, is enshrined in the Tale of the Boucaneers, the pirate's (re)constructed memory of her abandonment the driving impulse of his quest.

The relegation of his mother to victimhood is in keeping with Appadocca's Romantic idealization of women, which he represents to his friend as "peculiar." Of the two sexes, he declares to Hamilton, he always considered woman not only superior to man, but

> as the embodiment of goodness, that sweetened existence with its smiles, and made sorrow shrink into insignificance by its sympathy; as a being in whom intellect and propensities were happily not made to preponderate over the loftiest attributes of human nature—the sentiments. Holding this belief, I had worshipped her in whatever condition I found her;—in gorgeous magnificence, or in sordid rags, as pure and spotless as the lily, or polluted or stained with the foulest crimes. To me she ever was woman, and that was sufficient.[38]

Here Appadocca makes a virtue of his peculiarity, emphasizing that—unlike contemporaries willing to designate only "pure and spotless" women angels—all women, regardless of their reputation for sexual chastity, are worthy of veneration. On the one hand, Appadocca's belief that a woman's sexual history should not disbar her from being considered virtuous allies him with feminist writers of the Enlightenment like Wollstonecraft and her friend Mary Hays, women whose political novels insist that no woman should be condemned for coerced or voluntary sexual relationships outside marriage. On the other hand, the pirate's peculiar attitude toward women—the objectification of the entire sex as "the ultimate link" between the spiritual realm and "a higher and more refined humanity"—omits any possibility of individuation or of agency in navigating the material conditions under which women labored during the time period—particularly women of color.

Appadocca's view does, however, suggest the novel's engagement with the dominant stereotypes of women of color in West Indian texts. Like the counter-image of the brown woman who sets out to ensnare white men, the abandoned woman of color has a long history in colonial texts, from the story of Inkle and Yarico found in Ligon's *History of Barbadoes,* to John Stedman's story of Joanna in his *Narrative of a Five Years' Expedition . . . to Surinam,* to Orderson's Lucy. Philip perpetuates this trope, despite the evidence of female agency embodied by his own maternal ancestors, free women of color who wielded social and economic power. As Kit Candlin points out, numerous families were founded in the Eastern Caribbean through marriages between French planters and women of color, but as many or more were headed by unmarried, propertied women of color, like Philip's relative Judith:

> many of the free coloured women born of this time were not simply concubines and bit players in a European colonial drama but were creditors, partners, mothers and fellow planters participating on much the same level as their white counterparts, taking advantage of the new flexibility of political developments in the last half of the eighteenth century. . . . [Women] like Judith Philip . . . used effective strategies to circumvent a social milieu that seriously impeded free coloured advancement.[39]

The strategies and courage necessary to achieve such status are worth acknowledging, but it is also important to note that, during the pre-Emancipation period, the wealth accumulated by families like Philip's depended on owning land and slaves, placing a number of creoles of color in an ambivalent position regarding slavery. Although a generation's worth of Caribbean history separates Philip's hero from his mother's slaveholding forebears, the "little fortune" that remains to her—that pays for his European education and maintains the social footing he shares with her ancestors and white men like Charles Hamilton—ties the pirate to Atlantic slavery as surely as his paternal connections.

The key difference between Appadocca's maternal and paternal antecedents, however, constitutes one of Philip's clearest critiques of white colonial subjects' claims to superiority over other subjects. It is through his maternal line that Appadocca traces his civilized heritage, that provides for the Enlightenment sensibility and refinement that distinguishes the pirate from his white father, James Willmington. The text emphasizes repeatedly the avarice, cowardice, and insensitivity that marks the white planter's character, making for a sharp contrast to Appadocca's noble bearing and the sense of justice that drives him. This contrast, I would argue, is presented as proof against all the negative stereotypes of mixed-race creoles—the "mongrels" denigrated in West Indian texts like Edward Long's *History* and Moreton's *Customs and Manners*—and their incapacity for self-rule and the persistent belief among ruling class whites in the corrosive influence of African blood. Philip counters these attitudes through the representation of Appadocca's exceptional character, brought to the fore in the philosophical disquisitions that reflect his "mastery of European values" and Enlightenment accomplishments. Unlike his white contemporaries, as Appadocca reminds Hamilton, those ideals were founded on "the wisdom of the race which you affect to despise," the genius of his achievements in mathematics and astronomy traced to African civilization.[40]

But, despite such heroic reconfigurations of creole identity, the tragedy of *Emmanuel Appadocca*—his suicide following closely on the fulfillment to avenge himself and his mother through his father's death—can be traced to the inability to completely divorce himself from his ties to slavery, and the various accommodations made by an African European planter class attempting to maintain their standing of relative privilege in the plantation economy before and after Emancipation. This unease is embodied in the relationship between Philip's Appadocca and Jack Jimmy, described by Alexandra Ganser as "the coon-figure . . . frequently compared to a monkey . . . whose physiognomy is repeatedly designed as the grounds for his typologically fixed role of a figure of comic relief."[41] Like James Willmington, Jack Jimmy functions as a foil to the noble and handsome, pale-skinned Appadocca. And—just as the pirate's biological father points to his paternal ties to slavery—Jack Jimmy serves as a reminder of Appadocca's African ancestry, which includes both slaves and slaveholders through the maternal line. This latter connection cannot be obscured, despite the narrative's cursory treatment, for Philip endows Jack Jimmy with a voice that identifies Appadocca as his "young massa."

As with Appadocca's confrontation with his white father, the reunion with his former slave takes place on board the pirate's ship, *The Black Schooner*. The significance of this particular site has been noted by a number of critics, including William Cain, Ganser, and Sarah H. Ficke, all of whom discuss the ship as an extranational space where Appadocca rules according to the (relatively) democratic ideals that recent scholars have attributed to pirate communities. This attribution comes with a caveat, however; as most readers note, the inequities that remain entrenched even on Appadocca's ship are exemplified by the presence of Jack Jimmy. But the authority that maintains order on the *Black Schooner* and that allows the crew to accept Appadocca as jury and judge of his father's crime of abandoning his son, violating one of nature's most sacred laws, is temporarily shaken when Philip's hero is faced with Jack Jimmy:

> [H]e threw himself at the foot of the captain, . . . clasped his knees frantically [*sic*] in his arms, and yelled out,—"Garamighty! da ee—da ee—da me young massa."
>
> Jack Jimmy sobbed aloud, as he the more tightly clasped the knees of the captain. The latter looked down calmly and cooly on the little man, seemed to recognize him, but said not a word to him.
>
> Pained by the apparent forgetfulness of his young master, . . . Jack Jimmy cried out, piteously:
>
> "You no know me—you no know me, massa—you no know Jack Jimmy—you no 'member Jack Jimmy in de mule-pen—you—"
>
> "Yes, I do recollect you Jack Jimmy," interrupted the captain, "but you must neither make such a noise here, nor continue where you are." He made a sign with his hand, and two men stepped forward and led away the affectionate Jack Jimmy.
>
> "Ah! my young massa," continued the affectionate negro as he was taken away, "ee bin da gie me cake—ee bin da gie me grog—and when dey bin want foo beat me ee bin da beg foo me."[42]

The effect on Appadocca of Jack Jimmy's speech—representing, according to Cudjoe, an accurate transcription of Afro-Trinidadian speech rather than the racist caricature read by some scholars—offers a provocative glimpse into the complexities of intraracial dynamics in Trinidad's post-Emancipation nineteenth century, as Ficke points out.[43] The calm, cool silence that meets Jack Jimmy's initial outburst, the pirate's subsequent acknowledgment of their relationship, the dismissal, and the reassertion of the master–slave dynamic cement the racialized hierarchy of their shared history.

The awareness of this shared history, moreover, persists beneath the surface of the novel's plot, just as the social, political, and economic tensions between white, black, and brown creole subjects persisted in the post-Emancipation period. This is not to suggest that Appadocca's treatment of Jack Jimmy invalidates his condemnation of his father's betrayal—indeed, it's possible to see Appadocca's recognition of his paternalistic relationship to Jack Jimmy as a correction of Willmington's refusal to acknowledge his biological son. But reading Philip's novel as a work of creole historical fiction, we can see the relationship between Appadocca, Appadocca's mother, and Jack Jimmy—the three characters who share African ancestry—as an expression of the need to confront the residual impact of Atlantic slavery on creole subjectivity. Whether or not Philip succeeds in this is a matter of debate: Jack Jimmy, reunited with his master, steps back into the role of happy, devoted slave, a regression worthy of the white creole novels discussed throughout my study, and despite his legal status as a free man in the novel's 1850s present. Appadocca's mother similarly is relegated to a role familiar to readers of the early creole novel, despite the evidence of empowered brown women whose unmarried status did not necessarily impinge on their agency, as Candlin points out. As for Appadocca, his suicide follows the familiar story of the tragic mulatto who, despite having fulfilled his quest for vengeance through the death of the (white) father, nevertheless has no future beyond that goal. In the end, the only character to survive of these three is Jack Jimmy, though his previous "excitability . . . yielded to a melancholy and dull somberness" once he buries Appadocca under the sea-grape tree that marks his mother's burial place.[44] Once the object of laughter, Jack Jimmy attains a gravitas defined by grief, his smile "never seen more . . . ; and when the winds howled more loudly than usual, the drops calmly fell from his now aged eyes."[45]

Ultimately, the history of Appadocca's "blighted life" ends ambivalently, with the pirate's abdication of his natural rights—symbolized, as Ganser observes, by the sinking of *The Black Schooner* in a tremendous hurricane. The ship—itself a sign of Appadocca's modernity, fitted out with technology so advanced it outstrips any ship in Britain's imperial navy—becomes the tomb of Appadocca's white father. And although the manner of Willmington's death accords with the natural justice Appadocca seeks—the ignorant and cruel father avenged by the machinery built by his son's superior intelligence—Appadocca's death immediately after makes his a pyrrhic victory. Too, Appadocca's story does not end, as Ganser suggests, with his union with the oceanic element that represents the ultimate emancipation, but with his burial on dry land, specifically the Trinidadian ground where his mother is buried, along with the familial associations with slavery. This gravesite isn't neglected, however. Feliciana—the South American woman who falls in love with Appadocca only to be left behind when the hero opts to continue the pursuit of his father instead of making a new life with her—makes an annual pilgrimage from the convent she entered after Appadocca's death, tending to the son's and the mother's graves. But, as with the other events of Appadocca's history, even this act of piety carries a note of tragedy. There is no conclusion to the romance between the would-be lovers; his death and the ironically named Feliciana's celibacy make it clear that Appadocca is the last of his line.

The lack of regeneration suggested by the unconsummated romance stands in stark contrast to the white romances celebrated in the earlier creole novels, suggesting that *Emmanuel Appadocca*'s work of reclaiming Caribbean history through the novel form is unfinished at best. Instead, it re-presents the paradox of fluidity and groundedness of Caribbean novels whose authors must navigate the possibilities of multiple literary and material histories opened by Emancipation. These are the histories—competing versions of a past that is never really finished—that converge to shape succeeding generations of Caribbean writers.

IDEAS OF generation and regeneration, as Erna Brodber suggests in her novel *The Rainmaker's Mistake,* are central to the ongoing project of engaging multiple histories in novel form. As her protagonist Queenie describes her wishes for the unborn child she carries, her hopes for regeneration arise despite what she knows of slavery's history and its legacies: she wishes to "make a healthy child who, poor little rich child, will continue to search and to reproduce and to cultivate."[46] That child will "have to," she continues, "for it is in the search that the other positive comes: happiness.... We have no choice.... We really have no choice.... See you there. In the free."

For Brodber as for many contemporary Caribbean novelists, the act of searching is mandatory; the denial of history—in whatever form that history takes—is not an option. Paradoxically, only through the compulsory labor of seeking and uncovering the past can a future "in the free" be realized. *Crossing the Line,* I hope, will contribute to this search, opening further critical conversations about the early creole novel, its place in Caribbean literary history, and, most importantly, its contributions to the long reach of the history it helps to construct—and of the history it seeks to silence. Throughout the study I have offered what I see as the possibilities inherent in such conversations. More work is necessary, for example, to fully elaborate on the early creole novels' connections to novels studies in general and to more recent Caribbean fictions in particular—to bring together the early novels and works like *The Rainmaker's Mistake* and Brodber's earlier *Myal,* with its recognition that "if the half has never been told, you must know what *has* been told and have some wind of what has not been told."[47] Marlon James's neo-slave narrative, *Book of Night Women*, also deals with told and untold histories, giving an unflinching depiction of plantation violence and resistance, rewriting the counter-histories erased, obscured, or defused in the early creole novel. These and many, many other contemporary works provide the opportunity to critically engage the dialectical relationships between the narratives that make up the history of the anglophone Caribbean novel—and the history of the novel in its broadest sense.

Moving further ahead, I hope such conversations extend beyond the anglophone Caribbean, to explore multiple Caribbean histories and fictions, bringing in early novels like Cuban creole Gertrudis Gomez de Avellaneda's *Sab* (1841) and the work of contemporary writers from the wider African Caribbean diaspora like Edwidge Danticat, Maryse Condé, Julia Alvarez, Junot Díaz, and so many others. Ultimately, I believe such conversations will reveal that the plantocratic histories contained, produced, and reproduced in novels like *Montgomery, Hamel, Marly, Warner Arundell, Old Port-Royal, Creoleana,* and *Emmanuel Appadocca* can be seen as cultural artifacts not just of particular historical places and spaces, but also of an unending and unended moment of global modernity. The novels in *Crossing the Line,* in other words, constitute unfinished business for readers, writers, and scholars desirous of making sense of the "Caribbean" world we live in.

Notes

Introduction

1. Kamau Brathwaite discusses a number of these novels in his germinal article "Creative Literature." Brathwaite offers "'Creole' . . . [as] perhaps the most satisfactory criterion to apply to a consideration of this literature, since not all the writing of native West Indians concerned the West Indies," and that authors were "creole to the extent that they had intimate knowledge of and were in some way committed by experience and/or attachment to the West Indies" (129). NB: All citations from Brathwaite's article are from the reprint.

2. Holt, *Problem of Freedom*, 93.

3. Nadi Edwards, back cover blurb for C. Williams, *Hamel*. This latter move, I argue, facilitates a more nuanced and complex reading of recent Caribbean and diasporic literature. For groundbreaking work in early anglophone literary history, see Jean D'Costa and Barbara Lalla, eds., *Voices in Exile: Jamaican Texts of the 18th and 19th Centuries* (Tuscaloosa: University of Alabama Press, 1989); and Thomas Krise's anthology *Caribbeana: An Anthology of English Literature of the West Indies, 1657—1777* (Chicago: University of Chicago Press, 1999).

4. Dillon, "Original American Novel," 241.

5. Ibid., 236.

6. See James Cheshire, "Mapped: British, Spanish and Dutch Shipping 1750–1800," Spatial.ly: Visualisation, Analysis and Resources," http://spatial.ly/2012/03/mapped-british-shipping-1750–1800/ (accessed 4 January 2017). "The creation of this dataset," explains Cheshire, "was completed as part of the Climatological Database for the World's Oceans, 1750–1850 (CLIWOC) project. The routes are plotted from the lat/long positions derived from the ships' logs," of voyages between 1750 and 1800.

7. Equiano continues his description of the cruelty he experienced and witnessed on board the slave trader: "One white man in particular I saw, when we were permitted to be on deck, flogged so unmercifully with a large rope near the foremast, that he died in consequence of it; and they tossed him over the side as they would have done a brute" (Equiano, *Interesting Narrative*, 55).

8. Behrendt, Eltis, and Richardson, "Costs of Coercion," 456. See also Berry, *Path in the Mighty Waters*, 74–76.

9. Emma Christopher cites the example of a revolt on the slave ship *Amity*, which involved two enslaved men (Will and Dick), a man identified as a mulatto (Stuart), two Irishmen (John Mathew and Alexander Evans), an Englishman (Richard Squire), and a free black man (John Boadman) (*Slave Ship Sailors*, 51–54).

10. Ibid., 52.

11. Smallwood, *Saltwater Slavery*, 120.

12. Rediker, *Slave Ship*, 272–74.

13. Joseph, *Warner Arundell* (2001), 200–201.

14. FitzRoy, *Narrative*, 2.57–58. On February 17, 1832, Charles Darwin underwent the ceremony: "We have crossed the Equator, & I have undergone the disagreeable operation of being shaved. About 9 oclock this morning we poor 'griffins', two & thirty in number, were put altogether on the lower deck.—The hatchways were battened down, so we were in the dark & very hot.—Presently four of Neptunes constables came to us, & one by one led us up on deck.—I was the first & escaped easily: I nevertheless found this watery ordeal sufficiently disagreeable.—Before coming up, the constable blindfolded me & thus lead along, buckets of water were thundered all around; I was then placed on a plank, which could be easily tilted up into a large bath of water.—They then lathered my face & mouth with pitch and paint, & scraped some of it off with a piece of roughened iron hoop.—a signal being given I was tilted head over heels into the water, where two men received me & ducked me.—at last, glad enough, I escaped.—most of the others were treated much worse, dirty mixtures being put in their mouths & rubbed on their faces.—The whole ship was a shower bath: & water was flying about in every direction: of course not one person, even the Captain, got clear of being wet through" (*Charles Darwin's* Beagle *Diary*, 37).

15. Joseph, *Warner Arundell*, 200. For more on the ceremony see Marcus Rediker, *Between the Devil and the Deep Blue Sea* (Cambridge: Cambridge University Press, 1988), 179–89.

16. Anonymous, *Marly*, 1. Here the young George Marly abbreviates the quotation from Tobias Smollett's *The Adventures of Roderick Random*, whose title character describes Jamaica as "that fatal island, which has been the grave of so many Europeans" (*The Adventures of Roderick Random*, [1748; Oxford: Oxford University Press, 1999], 207).

17. As Ward and Watson point out, the Caribbean region was constructed as a "kind of special non-space" whose "perceived tropical excess—meteorological, mercantile, and sexual—was in direct proportion to its imagined cultural poverty" ("Introduction," 11).

18. See, e.g., Mintz, *Three Ancient Colonies*, esp. chap. 5, "Creolization, Culture, and Social Institutions," 182–214.

19. Carolyn Allen, qtd. in Bolland, "Creolisation," 16.

20. Qtd. in Allen, "Creole Then and Now," 49. Citing the early seventeenth-century Spanish Incan chronicler Garcilaso de la Vega (El Inca), Allen observes that the use of "creole" as applied to New World offspring by enslaved Africans was also derogatory. According to de la Vega, the latter group "consider themselves more honourable and of higher status for being born in their homeland, and not their children who were born abroad, and the parents are very offended if they are called Creoles" (49). For a further in-depth discussion, see Bauer and Mazzotti, "Introduction," 1–57.

21. Bauer and Mazzotti, "Introduction," 6.
22. Allen, "Creole Then and Now," 50.
23. Brathwaite, *Development of Creole Society*, 296.
24. Bolland, "Creolisation," 18–19.
25. O'Callaghan, "'Unhomely Moment,'" 96.
26. Morrison, "Site of Memory," 192; J. Sharpe, *Ghosts of Slavery*, xi–xiii.
27. Holt, *Problem of Freedom*; C. Hall, *Civilising Subjects*; Lambert, *White Creole Culture*. In *Creole America*, Sean Goudie emphasizes the connections between North American and West Indian "creoles." Despite these connections, Goudie argues, an emerging nationalistic discourse reveals that Anglo North American colonists ultimately rejected their "creole" identity in favor of an American identity.
28. S. Hall, "Cultural Identity," 234.
29. Ibid. The "contact zone" here refers to Mary Louise Pratt's construction of the term in *Imperial Eyes*, 6.
30. Qtd. in Bauer and Mazzotti, "Introduction," 2, citing Kupperman, ed., *America in European Consciousness, 1493–1750* (Chapel Hill: University of North Carolina Press, 1992), 23.
31. Qtd. in Sypher, "West Indian," 503.
32. Lambert, *White Creole Culture*, 12. This demarcation, as Lambert reminds us, was not only imaginary but codified by the state, as with Lord Chief Justice Mansfield's 1772 ruling that established Britain as "free" and the West Indian colonies as "slave."
33. As chapter 3 demonstrates, by the 1820s metropolitan abolitionists (among them supporters of East Indian sugar) argued that the West Indian colonies were a drain on the national coffers and that preferential monopolies as well as slavery should be abolished.
34. Grainger, *Sugar-Cane*, I.17. Keith Sandiford argues that colonial texts like Grainger's poem (and, I would add, the early creole novels examined in *Crossing the Line*) reveal the centrality of the "West Indian Creole" to the "search for legitimacy and ... anxiety over ... cultural dilution," finding "the dynamic tension" of creole texts arising from "the formation of Creole identity," particularly in those instances when the author's identity and interests merge with those of the narrative voice (*Cultural Politics*, 4).
35. A number of Johnny Newcome prints circulated in London and sold in

printsellers' shops like that of William Holland. For more on Johnny Newcome, see Ward, *Desire and Disorder,* 185–201; and Buckley, *British Army* and "Frontier," 152–62. Lady Nugent's journal repeats many assertions about creole life found in works like Edward Long's *History of Jamaica* and J. B. Moreton's *West India Customs and Manners.*

36. The nature of long-term relationships between white men and black and brown women is not easy to determine. As Jenny Sharpe notes, "there is a third way of explaining sexual relations between master and slave other than the proslavery narrative of seduction and the antislavery one of rape" (*Ghosts of Slavery,* 64). For example, she reads in Phibba's relationship with Thistlewood "signs of a domestic arrangement that cannot be explained as either black women's seduction of white men or white men's rape of slave women. Rather they show a struggle for power that extended over a period of time" (64). This reading does not ignore, Sharpe insists, the imbalance of systemic power, or the precariousness of the black or brown woman's position in Atlantic slave culture. For more on Thomas Thistlewood, see D. Hall, *In Miserable Slavery;* and Burnard, *Mastery, Tyranny, and Desire.*

37. Schaw, *Journal,* 112. For Edward Long's discussion of the perceived threat of a propertied mulatto class to the white creole ruling class, see *History of Jamaica,* 2.327.

38. Brathwaite, "Creative Literature," 160.

39. Wylie Sypher's germinal work on eighteenth-century antislavery literature is useful here, particularly his enumeration of the volume of print matter devoted to the abolition (and emancipation) debates (*Guinea's Captive Kings*).

40. Rev. of *Creoleana, Tait's Edinburgh,* 405. The *Westminster Review* went so far as to credit *Hamel*'s author with memorializing and preserving "the manners of the present creole inhabitants, which another half century will probably see materially changed" (Ward and Watson, "Appendix A," 430).

41. Anonymous, *Marly,* 4.

42. Rajan, "Wollstonecraft and Godwin," 222.

43. In other words, the creole novelists I examine were able to play on reactionary responses to political unrest in Great Britain and Europe, to paint West Indian rebellions as worthy of a similar response, and thus to take advantage of the situation to educate metropolitan readers "primed" by the French Revolution, Jacobin activity in England, the reign of terror, and the Napoleonic Wars, and assure readers that remedying the West India Question demanded a knowledgeable, firsthand reading of the local situation.

44. Advertisement for *Montgomery* in *Morning Chronicle* (11 July 1817 and 16 July 1818).

45. Reeve, *Progress of Romance,* 1. 110, 111.

46. Sandiford, *Cultural Politics,* 3.

47. Baucom, *Specters of the Atlantic,* 216.

48. Sandiford, *Cultural Politics,* 3.

49. C. Williams, *Hamel*, 421. The ability to understand and speak creole, a language shared at least partly by creoles of all racial backgrounds, signaled a membership in the creole community that was closed to metropolitan outsiders.

50. Anonymous, *Marly*, 2.

51. *Hamel, Warner Arundell,* and *Creoleana* were published in London; *Marly* in Glasgow.

52. Although the documentary evidence of a Caribbean readership is more difficult to trace, the Kingston publication of *Montgomery* and its inclusion in a list of novels for sale at Frank Treadway's Kingston bookshop, along with evidence uncovered by Tim Watson of *Hamel*'s sale to a Kingston bookseller attests to those novels' circulation (though limited) in the region (see Ward and Watson, "Introduction," 14, and 14–15n2). In terms of British circulation *Marly* was popular enough to be reprinted; *Hamel* was listed in the catalogs of a number of circulating libraries in London, Belfast, Dublin, Manchester (subscription library), and Newcastle-upon-Tyne through 1838, according to the British Fiction database.

53. E.g., although the Whiggish *Morning Chronicle* advertised *Montgomery* as a work containing "a just picture of the manners and customs of all classes" in Jamaica, the reviewer for the *Monthly Review*—after dismissing the novel on aesthetic grounds—irritably pointed out the contradictions generated by the novel's recycling of "the old argument in favour of the slave-trade which has been so often answered" (Rev. of *Montgomery*).

54. Stephen, *Slavery*, 2.106n.

55. Ibid. Also qtd. in Williamson, "Introduction," xx.

56. Stephen, *Slavery*, 2.106n, 2.145n.

57. Watson, *Caribbean Culture*, 2.

58. Ibid., 17, 18.

59. Ibid., 18.

60. As Watson observes, "Romance and realism are never far apart in the transatlantic circuits that joined Britain and the Caribbean in the nineteenth century" (*Caribbean Culture*, 6).

61. Anonymous, "Preface," 326; my emphasis.

62. For example, Lyndon Dominique traces the influence of Bryan Edwards in Maria Edgeworth's *Belinda* (*Imoinda's Shade: Marriage and the African Woman in Eighteenth-Century British Literature, 1759–1808* [Columbus: Ohio State University Press, 2012]). Creole and metropolitan writings on obeah, which Edwards also addresses in his history of the West Indies (*History, Civil and Commercial*), are also "scripted," as is discussed in chapter 2. For an in-depth discussion of the influence of Long, Edwards, and "settler historians" like Robert C. Dallas of Jamaica, see Gordon Lewis, "Pro-Slavery Ideology," in *Main Currents in Caribbean Thought* (Baltimore: Johns Hopkins University Press, 1983), 94–136.

63. Ward and Watson, Appendix A, 437–38.

64. Dalleo, *Caribbean Literature*, 5.

65. Baucom, *Specters of the Atlantic*, 19.

66. Ibid., 333.
67. Ibid., 16.
68. Ibid.
69. Ibid.
70. Dillon, "Original American Novel," 241.
71. Ibid., 241, 236.
72. Baucom, *Specters of the Atlantic,* 218. In many ways, we can say that the abolitionists and the supporters of West Indian slavery occupy the same "problem-space." This term, as David Scott defines it, "is meant first of all to demarcate a discursive context, a context of language. But it is more than a cognitively intelligible arrangement of concepts, ideas, images, meanings, and so on—though it is certainly this. It is a context of argument, and, therefore, one of *intervention*. A problem-space, in other words, is an ensemble of questions and answers around which a horizon of identifiable stakes (conceptual as well as ideological-political stakes) hangs" (*Conscripts of Modernity,* 4).
73. Lears, "We Came, We Saw"; D. Scott, *Conscripts of Modernity,* 2.
74. Draper, "Rise of a New Planter Class," 66. Caribbean economists like George Beckford and Kari Levitt have articulated theories of plantation economics that describe the persistence of the plantation model of development, clearly visible in the tourism model, with all-inclusive resorts serviced by poor people living on the margins of those properties, and the imposition of export agribusiness models dictated by western trade agreements.
75. Draper, "Helping To Make Britain Great," 79.
76. McClelland, "Redefining the West India Interest," 127.
77. C. Hall, "Reconfiguring Race," 163.
78. See, e.g., *Woman of Colour* (1800), which although it depicts the title character sympathetically, lacks the sense of immediate and intimate familiarity with colonial life depicted in the novels examined in *Crossing the Line*.
79. C. Williams, *Hamel,* 175.
80. Anonymous, *Montgomery,* 2.278.
81. Lamming, *Pleasures of Exile,* 38.

1. Hortus Creolensis

Thanks to Elaine Treharne for pointing out the productive semi-tautology at play in the chapter title's use of "creolensis," from the Latin "creare" ("to create") and its simultaneous evocation of "creole."

1. The author's twenty-five-year residence is stated in the *Morning Chronicle*'s advertisement for the novel, which ran in the Friday 11 July 1817 issue and again in the Thursday 16 July 1818 issue (British Fiction Database, accessed 23 May 2012).

2. Cundall, "Press and Printers," 343. Cundall's bibliography of newspapers, journals, books, and ephemera published on the island prior to 1820 remains an invaluable resource ("Press and Printers," 355–412).

3. Ibid. In Jamaican parlance, a "pen" or "penn" is a property devoted to livestock, though in the later eighteenth century it was used more broadly to indicate a property or estate *not* devoted to large-scale export crop production, and sometimes in the sense of "a gentleman's estate or park" (Cassidy and Le Page, *Dictionary of Jamaican English*, 345).

4. Brathwaite, "Creative Literature," 160.

5. Sandiford, *Cultural Politics*, 2.

6. Anonymous, *Montgomery*, ix.

7. R. Williams, *Marxism and Literature*, 13.

8. Ibid.

9. Benítez-Rojo, *Repeating Island*, 9. As Benítez-Rojo argues, "We can speak . . . of a Caribbean machine as important or more so than the fleet machine. This machine, this extraordinary machine, exists today, that is, it repeats itself continuously. It's called: the plantation. Its prototypes were born in the Near East, just after the time of the Crusades, and moved toward the West. In the fifteenth century the Portuguese installed their own model in the Cape Verde Islands and on Medira, with astonishing success. . . . [T]he venture was too big for any single man. It turned out that an entire kingdom, a mercantilist monarchy, would be needed to get the big machine going with its gears, its wheels, its mills. I want to insist that Europeans finally controlled the construction, maintenance, technology, and proliferation of the plantation machines, especially those that produced sugar" (8–9). See also Mintz, *Sweetness and Power*, 32–73.

10. According to Roderick Cave, the Lunan family "had a long connection with the [Jamaican] printing and book trade." Through his study of wills and inventories of the island, he suggests the beginnings of a family tree: John Lunan Sr., a "land surveyor of the parish of St. George" had died in 1776, leaving various bequests to three sons: James, John (1770–1839), and Andrew (d. 1831). James, a "gentleman of Jamaica," died in 1794, leaving their widowed mother Catherine (living in Scotland at the time the will was written) an annuity of £25 sterling, to his brother Andrew (identified in James's will as a "bookbinder in the City of London") £500 currency, and to his other brother John, "printer of Kingston," the residue of his estate. Cundall suggests that Andrew was active in the Kingston print business in 1792—suggesting that James's will was composed earlier than the year it was proved, 1794, though it's unclear how many years passed between its composition and Andrew's arrival in Kingston (Cave, *Printing and the Book Trade*, 151). John served for many years as "Printer to the Honourable Council" of the Jamaica House of Assembly, and his burial tablet in Spanish Town refers to his service as a Member of the Assembly of Jamaica as well as his forty-four-year residence in St. Catherine's parish, where Spanish Town is located (*Monumental Inscriptions of Jamaica*, ed. Philip Wright [London: Society of Genealogists, 1966], 98). According to the *Jamaica Almanac* of 1816, John was also proprietor of Armistead's Pen, worked by forty slaves, and of Hampstead, worked by another forty slaves. In the almanac of 1828, John is still listed as the proprietor of

Hampstead, with the number of enslaved people attached to that estate listed at forty-nine; Armistead's Pen is no longer listed as his property, but Congreve Park is, with forty-eight enslaved workers listed with that property.

11. Codell, *Imperial Co-histories*, 21.

12. The problem-space, as David Scott defines it, is "a discursive context, a context of language . . . a context of argument. . . . A problem-space is very much a context of dispute, a context of rival views, a context, if you like of knowledge and power" (*Conscripts of Modernity*, 4).

13. *Montgomery*'s publication date of 1812–13 comes nearly a quarter-century after the appearance of what is considered the first North American novel, *The Power of Sympathy: or, The Triumph of Nature* (1789), a sentimental epistolary work written by William Hill Brown and printed in Boston.

14. The *Kingston Chronicle* ran from 1805 to 1820; Andrew Lunan was likely the founding editor—at least he is identified as its editor in 1806, when he was brought before the Jamaica Assembly, charged with "a breach of the privileges" of the House for publishing in the newspaper "certain resolutions highly reflecting upon the House" (Cundall, "Press and Printers," 366). For more on Andrew Lunan and the *Kingston Chronicle*, see Cundall, *History of Printing*. For an extensive contemporary account of the 1806 charges against Lunan and several other Kingston printers, including a transcript of the court proceedings, see Henry Redhead Yorke, "A Stroke of Power in the Island of Jamaica," *Weekly Political Review* 2 (January–June 1807): 98–104. The breach was brought against several newspapers that published complaints by Kingston freeholders about the House's (mis)allocation of government funds (3,000 guineas) to purchase a "service of plate" as a reward for navy Admiral John T. Duckworth, who had defeated a French squadron off the coast of Jamaica in February 1806 (99).

15. As Cave observes, "there were, of course, plenty of examples of 'the literature of knowledge.' Manuals on tropical diseases, on the care of horses, on improved methods of distillation, on botany, and on methods of planting formed the backbone of local book production, while in the first third of the nineteenth century the controversy over the slave trade gave birth to many pamphlets" ("Early Printing and the Book Trade," 185).

16. *Jamaica Quarterly Journal, and Literary Gazette* 2, no. 2 (December 1818); the journal was "Printed and Published, for the Proprietors, at the Office of the Kingston Chronicle."

17. Anonymous, *Marly*, 250.

18. Ibid.

19. Ibid., 222.

20. Codell, *Imperial Co-histories*, 20.

21. As Cave points out, from the 1780s there were efforts across the anglophone Caribbean to establish literary magazines, but most were "doomed from the start." Although Cave sees most of these publications as inferior, he makes an exception of the *Jamaica Magazine*, which, along with the *Columbia Magazine or*

Monthly Miscellany published in Kingston from 1796 to 1800 by Andrew Lunan's one-time partner William Smart, was "competently produced and edited" ("Early Printing and the Book Trade," 181).

22. Cave identifies several prominent publishing families in Jamaica in the late eighteenth and early nineteenth centuries, e.g., the Aikmans, the Strupars, and the Lunans. For these families, he notes, "printing and bookselling were but part of their activities. All these families owned extensive lands: the Aikmans the properties of Wallenfield, Dunsinane, and Birnamwood, the Strupars the coffee plantation of Bellevue in the Port Royal Mountains. They had made it into the ranks of the plantocracy" ("Early Printing and the Book Trade," 172–73). Searches through the *Jamaica Almanac*s for the relevant period reveal that Andrew (active primarily in Kingston) and John Lunan (active in St. Jago de la Vega, or Spanish Town) were proprietors, though perhaps not on as an extensive scale as the Aikman family. However, both brothers were very involved in the political life of the island, each holding various political appointments throughout their lifetimes.

23. Ibid., 182.

24. See Benedict Anderson's descriptions of early North and South American newspapers: "They began essentially as appendages of the market. Early gazettes contained . . . commercial news (when ships would arrive and depart, what prices were current for what commodities in what ports), as well as colonial political appointments, marriages of the wealthy, and so forth. In other words, what brought together, on the same page, *this* marriage with *that* ship, *this* price with *that* bishop, was the very structure of the colonial administration and market-system itself. In this way, the newspaper of Caracas quite naturally, and even apolitically, created an imagined community among a specific assemblage of fellow-readers, to whom *these* ships, brides, bishops and prices belonged. In time, of course, it was only to be expected that political elements would enter in" (*Imagined Communities*, 61).

25. *Jamaica Quarterly Journal* (December 1818).

26. Rippingham, *Jamaica, Considered*, 31. Arguments against various trade restrictions, complaints about the burdens placed on planters by legislation like the 1816 Slave Registry Bill, and defenses against metropolitan criticism of the inadmissibility of slaves' testimony in trials against white people can be found scattered throughout the newspapers, periodicals, and novels produced by white creoles. See, for example, Letter I, "On the Admission of the Evidence of Slaves," prompted by recent moves in the British parliament to impose legislation to permit the testimony of the enslaved in cases involving whites. The letter writer lays out a very lengthy rationale for rendering such evidence inadmissible, and condemns Parliament's interference in the question (*Jamaica Quarterly Journal, and Literary Gazette* 2, no. 2 [June 1819]: 277–94).

27. Lambert, *White Creole Culture*, 5.

28. In *Mastery, Tyranny, and Desire,* Trevor Burnard traces a similar path taken by Thomas Thistlewood, whose (in)famous journal writings provide a

first-person account of the "creolization" process for white settlers. Thistlewood arrived in Jamaica in 1750 at the age of twenty-nine; he was employed first as a pen-keeper on Vineyard Pen and then as overseer on Egypt Estate. By 1767 he was the owner of a 160-acre property, Breadnut Island Pen, and thirty enslaved laborers. He died in Jamaica in 1786. His more than thirty-year relationship with an enslaved woman, Phibba, has been the subject of much scholarship, including Jenny Sharpe's reading (*Ghosts of Slavery*). Transcripts of journal extracts, the manuscript of which is housed in the National Library of Jamaica, have been printed in D. Hall, *In Miserable Slavery*. His story makes an interesting counter-narrative to Henry Montgomery's fictionalized adventures.

29. The letterpress for the engraving reads: "View of Harbour Street, Kingston, (looking eastward). Harbour Street and King Street, crossing each other at right angles, are the principal streets in Kingston. At the corner to the left is the store of Mr. Netlam Tory, and on the right that of Mr. John Mais, M.A. Further on, on the same side of the way, is Harty's Tavern, the flag indicating a public entertainment. Beyond is the Custom-House, marked by its high roof. The great tree stands in front of Wood's Tavern. The street is terminated, at the distance of about half a mile, by the residence of Edward Codd, Esq." (Hakewill, *Picturesque Tour*, n.p.).

30. The *Royal Gazette* advertisements were often reprinted by abolitionists to document the inhumanity of the buying and selling of enslaved people, particularly when such sales separated families. See *Second Report of the Committee of the Society for the Mitigation and Gradual Abolition of Slavery throughout the British Dominions* (London, 1825), 127; *Christian Observer* 24 (London, 1824), 480. See also Richard Madden's account of being assaulted on Harbour Street, outside the Commercial News-Rooms opposite Harty's Tavern. (*A Twelve-Month's Residence in the West Indies*, [London, 1825], 314).

31. E.g., the office of the *Jamaica Gleaner*, established in 1834 and still in circulation as one of Jamaica's largest daily newspapers, was located on Harbour Street from its inception until the 1960s.

32. *Jamaica Magazine* 1, no. 1 (February 1812): 1. These are the hallmarks of the best periodicals exemplified most clearly by *The Spectator* and later metropolitan publications like the *Monthly Magazine,* which—according to the self-deprecating language of the *Jamaica Magazine* editors—"cannot be supposed to be imitated or rivalled by a West India miscellany, for reasons which it would be wronging the reader's understanding to explain" (3).

33. *Jamaica Magazine* 1 (March 2, 1812): 3–4.

34. Anderson, *Imagined Communities;* Lunan, *Hortus Jamaicensis*, vi, vii.

35. Nair, *Pathologies of Paradise*, 48.

36. In many of the magazine's issues the Observer is identified as "N. T.," whose lengthy "Essay on the Good and Evil, Which Novels Are Likely to Produce on the Manners and Morals of Society" was published in one of the magazine's first numbers. There N. T. praises the works of Henry Fielding and Tobias Smollett

for "their diversity of striking and humorous characters and incidents" and for omitting from their pages "*monsters of perfection,*" "revolting improbabilities," and "unheard-of adventures" (*Jamaica Magazine* 1 [March 2, 1812]: 75), while cautioning that they do, at times, "overstep the strict line of decorum" (76). Samuel Richardson is criticized for the "unvaried sameness and voluminous prolixity" of works like *Sir Charles Grandison*. But, as N. T. points out, his works were "calculated to do much good" (76). As for later (Jacobin) novels that, according to N. T., promote "doctrines subversive of morality," like the "ravings of [William] Godwin and his beloved Mary [Wollstonecraft]!—that accomplished priestess of the goddess of reason" (75), such works clearly produce evil effects and should be condemned on both sides of the Atlantic.

To date, I have been unable to trace the identity of N. T., although one tantalizing possibility is Netlam Tory, a Kingston merchant who lived in Jamaica for many years before returning to Liverpool, where he died at the age of seventy-one. According to the *Gardener's Magazine and Register of Rural & Domestic Improvement* in July 1829, Tory became a member of the Jamaica Agricultural Society (also referred to as the Jamaica Society for the Encouragement of Arts and Agriculture) (*Gardener's Magazine* 6 [1830]: 330). Tory's store, as Hakewill's *Tour* illustrates, was located on Harbour Street; he was one of the subscribers to Watt's *New Theory of Optics* (1825), also published by Andrew Lunan's press.

37. Anonymous, *Montgomery*, 1.363.

38. According to William Beckford's *Remarks Upon the Situation of Negroes in Jamaica* (London, 1788), which is cited in the *Dictionary of Jamaican English* entry for "book-keeper," "Book-keepers are in subordinate command to the Overseers, they attend the still-houses in crop, and out of crop, the field. There are many so little deserving the name they bear, that so far from being able to calculate accounts they cannot many of them even read: and yet from this situation, from being frequently indented servants they become overseers, and have the conduct of a plantation" (Cassidy and Le Page, *Dictionary of Jamaican English,* 60, citing Beckford, *Remarks,* 89n).

39. "The Observer, No. V," *Jamaica Monthly* 2 (August 1, 1812): 6. Johnny Newcome was the generic name given to newly arrived white colonists (most typically, army officers) in the West Indies. This figure featured prominently in satires of West Indian life, like the prints *Johnny New-Come in the Island of Jamaica* (1800), *Johnny Newcome in Love in the West Indies* (1808), and *The Adventures of Johnny Newcome* (1812), and narratives like *The Adventures of Johnny Newcome in the Navy* (1818) by Alfred Burton [John Mitford], which was modeled on David Roberts's *The Military Adventures of Johnny Newcome* (1816).

40. "The Observer, No. V," 5–6.

41. Ibid., 8.

42. Ibid.

43. Anonymous, *Montgomery,* 1.viii–ix.

44. Moreton, *West India Customs,* 105.

45. Ibid.
46. Ibid., 28.
47. Ibid.
48. Ibid., 161, 128.
49. Ibid., 128–29.
50. Ibid., 129.
51. Ibid., 128.
52. Anonymous, *Montgomery*, 1.366.
53. S. Scott, *History of Sir George Ellison*, 10. For more on Scott, sentimental novels, and abolitionism, see Carey, *British Abolitionism*, esp. chap. 2. Matthew Lewis is another "accidental" slave owner, who, like the fictional Ellison, also attempts to control his identity as a metropolitan subject by distancing himself from the plantocratic community he becomes affiliated with. Lewis, better known as the author of *The Monk* (1796), traveled to Jamaica to inspect his properties in 1815–16 and again in 1817; he died on the return voyage to England in 1818. See *Journal of a West India Proprietor, Kept during a Residence in the Island of Jamaica* (London, 1834).
54. Anonymous, *Montgomery*, 2.103.
55. Ibid., 2.102.
56. S. Hartlib, *The Reformed Spiritual Husbandman with an Humble Memorandum Concerning Chelsy College* (London, 1652), qtd. in Drayton, *Nature's Government*, 52.
57. Qtd. in Drayton, *Nature's Government*, 52. As Drayton points up, Blith's second edition, *The English Improver Improved* (1652), also anticipated the benefits of husbandry: "Science joined to private property would make the Earth again abundant: England, he argued, might become the 'paradise of the World, if we can but bring ingenuity into fashion'. As Adam's heirs recovered his insight into Nature, they would reclaim Eden's plenty" (Drayton, *Nature's Government*, 52).
58. Mintz, *Sweetness and Power*, 51.
59. Ibid.
60. Ibid.
61. Anonymous, *Montgomery*, 2.124.
62. See, for example, Casid, *Sowing Empire*; and Bohls, *Slavery and the Politics of Place*.
63. Sandiford, *Cultural Politics*, 138.
64. Anonymous, *Montgomery*, 2.124.
65. Ibid., 2.122.
66. Ibid., 2.122, 2.125.
67. Ibid., 2.125.
68. Brathwaite, "Creative Literature," 158.
69. Sloane, *Voyage to the Islands,* lii. As Sloane explains, the enslaved "have *Saturdays* in the Afternoon, and *Sundays,* with *Christmas* Holidays, *Easter* call'd little or *Pigganinny, Christmas,* and some other great Feasts allow'd them for

the Culture of their own Plantations to feed themselves from Potatos, Yams, and Plantanes, &c. which they Plant in Ground allow'd them by their Masters, besides a small Plantain Walk they have by themselves" (lii). Nearly a hundred years after Sloane traveled to Jamaica, the Consolidated Slave Act of 1781 codified what was often described as customary practice: "all possessors of plantations are obliged, under the penalty of 50l.... to keep in proper cultivation one acre of land, at least, for every four negroes in plantain-walk and ground-provisions, exclusive of the negroes grounds; and in case the owners or possessors have not lands proper for that purpose, they are required to make some other ample provision for the support of their slaves" (Fuller, *Notes on the two reports,* 17–18).

70. Qtd. in Lunan, *Hortus Jamaicensis,* 2.73. Although Browne here refers to the plantain as an Amerindian food, neither the plantain nor the related banana is indigenous to the Americas. Portuguese Franciscan monks brought plantains from West Africa to Santo Domingo in the early sixteenth century. The African plantains, in turn, are believed to have been brought to the African highlands thousands of years ago from South Asia (see Edmund De Langhe, "Banana and Plantain: the Earliest Fruit Crops?" *INIBAP Annual Report,* Focus Paper 1 (Montpellier: International Network for the Improvement of Banana and Plantain, 1995), 6–8.

71. Turnbull, *Letters,* 34.

72. *Monthly Review,* 65.

73. Anonymous, *Montgomery,* 2.125. The horror Montgomery exhibits, aroused by the mutilated black body recalls Crevecoeur's famous Letter IX, in which the American Farmer encounters an emaciated slave, locked in a suspended iron cage where he has been left to die. Although not as graphic in detail as Crevecoeur's description, *Montgomery*'s depiction of the brutalized body of an enslaved man echoes that contained in *Letters from an American Farmer* (1782): both spectators are interrupted in their Rousseauesque contemplation of natural beauty, both men appear overcome by sympathetic horror, and both act to alleviate the enslaved man's physical pain by slaking his thirst; broadly speaking, both passages rely on sentimentalized antislavery discourse of the last half of the eighteenth century to convey their critique of American slavery. For more on the role of sentiment and sensibility in abolitionist writing, see Sypher, *Guinea's Captive Kings;* Amit Rai, *Rule of Sympathy: Sentiment, Rule, and Power, 1750–1850* (London: Palgrave Macmillan, 2002); Markman Ellis, *The Politics of Sensibility: Race, Gender and Commerce in the Sentimental Novel* (Cambridge: Cambridge University Press, 2004); and Carey, *British Abolitionism.*

74. R. Williams, *Marxism and Literature,* 13–14.

75. Anonymous, *Montgomery,* 2.125–26. The novelist's representation of the dying man's speech attests to a familiarity with spoken creole, including verb forms like "fum" (to flog or beat), "dead" ("to be dead, to die"), and "teef," i.e., "tief" ("to steal"). See Cassidy and Le Page, *Dictionary of Jamaican English* entries for these words.

76. Anonymous, *Montgomery,* 2.128; 2.126. As Douglas Hall points out, "Grass . . . was a profitable item in the eighteenth century. Before the steam and the internal combustion engines the grass seller was the equivalent of our present-day gasoline retailer. Bryan Edwards informed us that one acre of grass would maintain five horses for a year, allowing 56 lb of grass a day to each. Thistlewood reckoned that a horse would eat three bundles a day at 7 1/2d. a bundle. If they were on par, the common bundle must have weighed about 18 to 19 lb." (Hall, "Planters, Farmers and Gardeners," 110).

77. Anonymous, *Montgomery,* 2.128, 2.133.
78. Ibid., 2.130.
79. Lunan, *Hortus Jamaicensis,* viii.
80. Anonymous, *Montgomery,* 2.174.
81. Ibid., 2.297.
82. Ibid., 2.264, 2.265.
83. Ibid., 2.266.
84. B. Edwards, *History, Civil and Commercial,* 1.227.
85. Anonymous, *Montgomery,* 2.61.
86. Ibid., 2.62.
87. "N. T." in *Jamaica Magazine* describes at length the trials and sufferings of a woman much like Maria Woodford: Julia, a coffee planter's daughter, marries a young planter who ends up cheating on her. She endures, he repents, and the two live happily ever after, a resolution made possible only because of her long-suffering virtue.
88. Wyrick, "Madwoman in the Hut," 47.
89. Stoler, *Carnal Knowledge,* 2.
90. Anonymous, *Montgomery,* 2.163; Stoler, *Carnal Knowledge,* xxx.
91. Nair, *Pathologies,* 48.
92. Ibid.
93. Anonymous, *Montgomery,* 2.265.
94. Ibid., 3.499–500.
95. Ibid., 3.500.
96. Ibid., 2.266, 3.500.
97. Ibid., 3.500–501. Bracketed words are those that are nearly illegible in the edition of *Montgomery* that I consulted, housed in the National Library of Jamaica, Kingston.
98. Anonymous, *Montgomery,* 2.414.
99. See, e.g., O'Brien's discussion of James Thomson's influential celebration of Britain's colonial endeavors and military power ("These Nations," 296–97).
100. Anonymous, *Montgomery,* 2.426.
101. Ibid., 2.426–27, 2.429, 2.428–29.
102. Ibid., 2.429.
103. Ibid.

104. In his *History of the Maroons,* Robert C. Dallas provides a description (in the form of letters) of the First Maroon Wars and its conclusion in 1739/40. Before turning to the Second Maroon War, Dallas includes a lengthy description (Letter IV) of Maroon life and forms of governance, including their agricultural practices. See chapter 3 for a more in-depth reading of these practices.

2. "A Permanent Revolution"

1. B. Edwards, *History, Civil and Commercial,* 1.84.
2. Brathwaite, "Foreword," 6.
3. Ibid. Hamel was reissued by Macmillan Caribbean Classics in 2008 (intro. by Amon Saba Sakan, notes by John Gilmore), and by Broadview Press in 2010.
4. Brathwaite, "Creative Literature," 168–69.
5. Ward and Watson, Appendix A, 430. For more on Hamel's indebtedness to Walter Scott, see Watson, *Caribbean Culture,* 100–102. On the perceived changes among "present creole inhabitants," see the description of shifting musical taste among the enslaved: "[T]hose of the old school prefer[] the goombay and African dances, and those of the new, fiddles, reels, &. . . . The various African amusements, in which the negroes formerly took so much delight, are not now kept up with spirit, and Joncanoe himself is getting out of fashion" (De la Beche, *Notes,* 40–42). See also Isaac Belisario, *Sketches of Character, In Illustration of the Habits, Occupation, and Costume of the Negro Population in the Island of Jamaica, Kingston* (Kingston, 1837).
6. Ward and Watson, Appendix A, 436.
7. Watson, *Caribbean Culture,* 73.
8. Ibid.
9. Epple, "Global, the Transnational and the Subaltern," 158.
10. Ibid.
11. Rudwick, *Worlds before Adam,* 2.
12. Ibid.
13. Ibid.
14. Chakrabarty, *Provincializing Europe,* 8.
15. See, e.g., the fundamental contradiction observed by a contemporary reviewer in *The Scotsman*: despite the novel's explicit aim—"to exhibit the negroes as a race who cannot be made Christians, or entrusted with civil rights, and to give an exaggerated picture of the dangers arising to the white population of the West Indies, by any tampering with the condition or status of the slave population"—the novelist undercuts his own case, "since a race who can present such specimens of talent as we find here in the Obeah Man—who have moral feelings touched like those of Hamel . . . must have capacities for civilization and self-government" (Ward and Watson, Appendix A, 439–40).
16. As Chakrabarty describes its workings, "Historicism—and even the

modern, European idea of history—one might say, came to non-European peoples in the 19th century as somebody's way of saying 'not yet' to somebody else" (*Provincializing Europe*, 8).

17. Writers like Prince Saunders and Thomas Clarkson circulated the state papers of Henri Christophe to make the case for a "civilized" Hayti. See also republican historian Hérard Dumesle's *Le Voyage dans le Nord d'Hayti* (Aux Cayes, 1824).

18. C. Williams, *Tour,* 76.

19. Ibid.

20. De la Beche to Conybeare, 6 March 1824. I am enormously indebted to Tom Sharpe of the National Museum of Wales for sharing his typescript of De la Beche's correspondence and of his Jamaican journal.

21. De la Beche to Conybeare, 8 January 1824.

22. De la Beche's father, Thomas (1755–1801), was the eldest surviving son of Thomas Beach, who served as attorney general and chief justice of Jamaica; he inherited Halse Hall along with his sister Jannett, and John Hynes Beach in 1775. These siblings left Jamaica for England in 1777, when the family name was changed to De la Beche. Henry Thomas De la Beche was born in London in 1796 and inherited Halse Hall in 1801 on the death of his father. Another of De la Beche's ancestors was James Guthrie, who had helped negotiate the treaty that ended the First Maroon War of 1739. For more details of De la Beche's ancestry, see Chubb, "Sir Henry Thomas De la Beche," 9–28.

23. De la Beche to Conybeare, 8 January 1824.

24. As Tom Sharpe points out, De la Beche's appointment to the directorship of the national survey was made in response to his request: because Halse Hall no longer afforded him the financial resources to conduct his geological fieldwork independently, he needed government funding. "Were it not for the collapse of the Jamaican sugar market and the unrest associated with the abolition of slavery leading to the failure of De la Beche's private income, the history of the foundation of today's British Geological Survey could have been very different"; as it was, the "paid employment took De la Beche from the ranks of the gentlemen geologists with private means and turned him into a professional government scientist. Geology had taken a new direction" ("Slavery, Sugar, and the Survey," 93). In addition to his other scientific endeavors, De la Beche was instrumental in establishing the Royal School of Mines. In an ironic coincidence, Halse Hall, the title to which had passed to the holder of its mortgage, the Hibbert family, by 1835, is now owned by the Jamaican subsidiary of mining conglomerate ALCOA (Aluminum Company of America), with the Great House serving as its Jamaican headquarters.

25. De la Beche to Conybeare, 8 January 1824. Cf. Hegel's assessment of the emancipation debate: "Slavery is in and for itself injustice, for the essence of humanity is Freedom; but for this man must be matured. The gradual abolition of slavery is therefore wiser and more equitable than its sudden removal" (qtd. in

Susan Buck-Morss, *Hegel, Haiti, and Universal History* [Pittsburgh: University of Pittsburgh Press, 2009], 68). I am not suggesting that Williams or De la Beche was familiar with Hegel's gradualist stance. Rather, I cite Hegel in this context to emphasize the widespread acceptance throughout Europe of the gradualist position on slavery in the 1820s.

26. G. Allen, Rev. of *Idea of Race*, 175.

27. De la Beche, *Notes*, 1.

28. As P. J. McCartney points out, De la Beche's *Notes on the Present Condition in the Negroes of Jamaica* displays his attempt to validate through empirical evidence. "As a slave-owner living in England, and motivated by sentiments of what might be summed up as 'enlightened self interest,' he produced this descriptive account of the slave population, saying that it was not his intention 'to enter the field of controversy, but to state fairly and candidly' what he himself had witnessed. This introduction mirrored his recommended methodology in geological science" (*Henry De la Beche*, 22).

29. Heyrick, *Immediate*, 9.

30. Society for the Mitigation and Gradual Abolition of Slavery, *Substance of the Debate*, 11.

31. Ibid., 34. In a letter dated 13 May 1824, De la Beche told Conybeare that he "highly approv[ed]" Canning's recommendations. He went on to explain to Conybeare the "difficulty" that "attends the right of a slave to purchase his freedom, though it does seem but just that a ~~man~~ negro should be able to do, which is that the best people would be the only persons likely to do so, and the Proprietor would be saddled with the maintenance of the worthless with whom he would be unable to cultivate the property." Note the rhetorical significance of De la Beche's strikethrough, substituting "negro" for "man."

32. Qtd. in Stepan, *Idea of Race*, 30.

33. Ibid.

34. Ward, "What Time Has Proved," 49–74. An interesting point of comparison here is Charles Darwin's remark on Brazilian slavery, written during his voyage on the *Beagle:* "I was told before leaving England that after living in slave countries all my opinions would be altered; the only alteration I am aware of is forming a much higher estimate of the negro character. It is impossible to see a negro and not feel kindly towards him; such cheerful, open, honest expressions and such fine muscular bodies. I never saw any of the diminutive Portuguese, with their murderous countenances, without almost wishing for Brazil to follow the example of Haiti; and, considering the enormous healthy-looking black population, it will be wonderful if, at some future day, it does not take place" (Charles Darwin, letter to Catherine Darwin, 22 May–14 July 1833, Darwin Correspondence Project, Letter no. 206, http://www.darwinproject.ac.uk/DCP-LETT-206 [accessed 1 January 2017]).

35. Heringman, *Romantic Rocks*.

36. C. Williams, *Hamel*, 266.

37. Ibid., 60–61.

38. Ibid., 62.

39. Ibid., 63. As Noah Heringman argues, sublime gothic rhetoric like the language of this description was part of the shared literary and geological lexica of the Romantic period; more specifically, the "Romantic recognition of the earth's unpredictability and difference from human interests . . . permit progressive analogies to human nature. As [James] Hutton [*Theory of the Earth*] and [George] Lyell [*Principles of Geology*] begin to read evidence of 'remote convulsions' in terms of renovative and naturally recurring violence, rather than in terms of divinely ordained catastrophe, poems such as "Mont Blanc" are increasingly able to mobilize the analogy between geology and political revolution" (*Romantic Rocks*, 13–14). Useful as Heringman's reading is, I would argue that for white creoles, a different mobilization was being attempted. That is, white creoles like Williams engaged the same metaphor, but attempted to retain its suggestion of catastrophic violence as opposed to renovative.

40. C. Williams, *Tour*, 140. The tale is relayed by Diana, the beautiful quadroon slave woman who nurses the narrator through a bout of yellow fever. She is, as the narrator describes her, "another Scherezade," an allusion that recalls another cave, the cave of the forty thieves plundered by Ali Babba in *A Thousand and One Nights*.

41. For an overview of the different versions of the history of Three-Fingered Jack circulating at the turn of the nineteenth century, see Srinivas Aravamudan's introduction to William Earle's 1800 novel, *Obi; or, The History of Three-Fingered Jack* (Peterborough, ON: Broadview Press, 2005). See also Fran Botkin's work on the performance history of the theatrical versions of the Mansong story: "Revising the Colonial Caribbean: 'Three-Fingered Jack' and the Jamaican Pantomime," *Callaloo* 35, no. 2 (2012): 494–508.

42. C. Williams, *Tour*, 142.

43. Ibid., 148.

44. In terms of its print history, the story of Cato and Plato was reprinted several times: It appeared with no attribution under the title "The West Indian Free-booter" in *The Portfolio of Entertaining and Instructive Varieties in History, Science, Literature, the Fine Arts, &, &*, (London, 1826), 6.338–40; it appeared as "Cato and Plato, A Story of Jamaica" in *Chambers' Edinburgh Journal,* with a footnote identifying its source as Williams's *Tour* (London, 1835), 3.365–66; and again unattributed under the title "Superstition: A Tale by a West Indian Quadroon" in *North American Magazine* (Philadelphia, 1835), 5.42–45.

45. De la Beche to Conybeare, 29 July 1824.

46. Ibid.

47. De la Beche read his paper to the society over the course of two meetings, 2 December 1825 and 6 January 1826.

48. De la Beche, "Remarks," 185.

49. Buckland qtd. in Rudwick, *Bursting the Limits*, 626.

50. De la Beche, "Remarks," 144.
51. Rudwick, *Bursting the Limits,* 638.
52. Ibid., 631.
53. Ibid., 636.
54. Ibid.
55. Rev. of *How To Observe Morals and Manners* by Harriet Martineau, 34. De la Beche had written the first of the "How To Observe" series in 1835, with *How To Observe Geology.* The reviewer suggests that despite its mission to address the "uninformed," De la Beche's book is too perplexing. "But even in this work"—as opposed to Martineau's, which is ridiculed by the reviewer—"though much of it is above ordinary capacities, there are some things not uninteresting even to very young tastes—such as the precept that every body should be constantly furnished with a cup half full of treacle to ascertain the direction of earthquakes" (34).
56. C. Williams, *Hamel,* 67.
57. Ibid., 67–68.
58. Ibid., 68.
59. Ibid., 71.
60. Ibid., 77.
61. Ibid., 82.
62. Greenhouse, *Moment's Notice,* 99. Greenhouse draws from the work of Johannes Fabian (*Time and the Other*). Laura Brown's reading of Oroonoko provides a more pointed use of Fabian for literary historians, which is, in turn, useful for a reading of Hamel: "Temporalizations placing the native in the 'primitive' past or in a 'passage from savagery to civilization, from peasant to industrial society' [*Time and the Other,* 95] have constituted the discipline [anthropology] from its inception, and Fabian argues that this systematic 'denial of coevalness' [Fabian, *Time and the Other,* 31] has operated in the ideological service of colonialism and neocolonialism" (Brown, *Ends of Empire,* 33). Brown proposes instead that literary historians follow Fabian's advice to anthropologists and "read from the perspective of radical contemporaneity [Fabian xi]" in order to "seek in the texts of colonialism signs of the dialectical confrontations embodied in the historical formations of this [our own] colonial period" (34).
63. C. Williams, *Hamel,* 129. As Richard Price points out, what enslaved African religious leaders were "not able to bring with them on the ships seems clear enough: in addition to 'óbia pots and stools' (and other material objects), what couldn't cross the ocean were most of the traditional African institutions themselves. . . . Priests and priestesses arrived, but priesthoods and temples had to be left behind. Princes and princesses crossed the ocean, but courts and monarchies could not. Commanders and foot soldiers came, but armies could not. . . . Yet . . . immense quantities of knowledge, information, and belief were transported in the hearts and minds of the captive Africans. Moreover, even though they came from many different ethnic and linguistic groups and were rarely in a position to

carry on specific cultural traditions from their home societies, these people shared a number of cultural orientations that … characterized most West and Central African societies," including religious practices like Hamel's obeah (Price, *Travels with Tooy,* 289).

64. Greenhouse, *Moment's Notice,* 95; Fabian, *Time and the Other,* 31; xi.
65. Beckles, "Caribbean Antislavery," 869.
66. C. Williams, *Hamel,* 133.
67. Spivak, "Can the Subaltern Speak," 281.
68. De La Beche, "Remarks," 186.
69. C. Williams, *Hamel,* 162; 163.
70. Long, *History of Jamaica,* 2.97. Long's description of the caverns, like De la Beche's description of Portland Cave, expresses fascination and regret: "We were anxious to investigate further: but, upon examining our stock of torch-wood, we found scarcely sufficient left for conducting us back to the entrance, and we were obliged to use dispatch in regaining it, for fear of rambling into some one of the numerous passages opening to the right and left, where, puzzled with mazes or perplexed with errors, we might have rambled on without the probability of ever finding our way out again: and in such a distressful event we could not reasonably have expected any human assistance.… These are the most remarkable curiosities as yet discovered in this parish; but it may probably contain others, the grotto not having been found out, or at least generally known, till within these few years. We are uncertain whether it was known to the Spaniards; but it is supposed that run-away Negroes were not unacquainted with so convenient a hiding-place" (2.99–100).
71. One of the first "improvements" De la Beche instituted on Halse Hall was to replace the whip as chronometer with a bell; drivers in the field were also required to use a naval boatswain's whistle rather than crack a whip.
72. C. Williams, *Hamel,* 71.
73. Ibid., 82.
74. Ward and Watson, Appendix A, 438. The ties between Methodism (and other forms of non-Anglican sectarianism) and antislavery activity were well established according to proplanter affiliates, from the dominance of the Clapham sect in metropolitan abolitionist circles to agitation in the colonies associated with Methodist missionaries like John Smith in Demerara. For more on antimissionary sentiment in Jamaica, see Mary Turner, *Slaves and Missionaries: The Disintegration of Jamaican Slave Society, 1787–1834* (Kingston: University of the West Indies Press, 1998), esp. 1–37. Unlike many resident planters, De la Beche supported missionary instruction on Halse Hall. As he wrote to a Methodist missionary active on his estate, "I hope to hear a favourable report … as to the progress your labours make among my people, feeling as I do, perfectly satisfied, that you will do everything to improve their moral character" (De la Beche to Crofts, 13 Dec. 1824).
75. Elsewhere I argue that Hamel's abilities in this respect are akin to an

application of theories of geohistory laid out most famously in James Hutton's *Theory of the Earth* (1788; 1795): "In examining things present, we have data from which to reason with regard to what has been; and, from what has actually been, we have data for concluding with regard to that which is to happen hereafter.... In what follows, therefore, we are to examine the construction of the present earth, in order to understand the natural operations of time past; to acquire principles, by which we may conclude with regard to the future course of things, or judge of those operations, by which a world, so wisely ordered, goes into decay; and to learn, by what means such a decayed world may be renovated, or the waste of habitable land upon the globe repaired" (*Theory of the Earth, In Four Parts*, vol. 1 [Edinburgh, 1795], n.p. http://www.gutenberg.org/files/12861/12861-h/12861-h.htm [accessed 25 April 2014]). See Ward, "What Time Has Proved," esp. 64.

76. C. Williams, *Hamel*, 425.
77. Ibid.
78. Ibid.
79. "[L]ook at Hayti. . . . Look still at Hayti," from C. Williams, *Hamel*, 351.
80. Trouillot, "Unthinkable History," 73.
81. Dash. Rev. of *Haitian Revolutionary Studies*, 198.
82. Dubois and Garrigus, *Slave Revolution*, 90.
83. Ibid.
84. De la Beche, unpublished journal entry, 7 April 1824.
85. C. Williams, *Hamel*, 121.
86. Ward and Watson, Appendix C, 444. Aravamudan, in his excellent edition of William Earle's 1800 novel *Obi*, includes excerpts from Moseley's *Treatise on Sugar*, the *Report*, and relevant selections from Long's *History*.
87. Paton, "Obeah Acts," 2.
88. C. Williams, 130, 128.
89. Ibid., 128.
90. Greenhouse, *Moment's Notice*, 99.
91. Dubois, *Avengers*, 101.
92. Greenhouse, *Moment's Notice*, 99; C. Williams, *Hamel*, 129.
93. C. Williams, *Hamel*, 427.
94. Ibid.
95. Ibid.
96. Ibid.
97. Ibid.
98. Brathwaite, "Creative Literature," 168–69.

3. "Lost Subjects"

1. P. L. Simmonds to Serena Simmonds. "Busher," more commonly spelled "Busha," is defined in the *Dictionary of Jamaican English* (Cassidy and Le Page) as "an overseer on any kind of estate; in general charge. Also as a term of address."

2. According to the 1830 returns, Fort Stewart was owned by Francis Smith; there were 472 enslaved people on the property (*Jamaica Almanac* 1831).

3. P. L. Simmonds to Serena Simmonds. Cf. Marly's experience in the boiling house and the novel's description of enslaved people's attitude toward the theft of sugar: "all their endeavours" in the boiling house, Marly learns, were spent in "contriving how to steal it, for they had no allowance of that article. They might naturally enough think, therefore, that as they performed the whole work in making it, they had some right to a part, and as this seemingly equitable claim was refused to them, it was only justice on their part to steal as much as they could, and in that manner receive their share. If they did not argue in this way, it was in this way they acted, and actions are a better proof of opinion than words" (Anonymous, *Marly*, 38). The morning after Marly's first spell in the boiling house, the overseer explains the workings of Calibash Estate—the name given facetiously to the "estate" from which "the great part of the white people in the towns and the free browns and blacks supply themselves with the essential article of sugar." It derives its name, the overseer explains, "chiefly owing to no coopered casks being used, the substitute for which are calibashes, procured from the calibash tree, . . . and in which the sugar is not only carried out of the estate, but conveyed to market and sold, according to the apparent size of the calibash, no weights or measures being used by the proprietors of this large estate" (38–39). Unlike Marly's assumption that the enslaved take sugar for their own consumption, the overseer sees it as part of the "supply" chain for Calibash Estate and its "nefarious traffic" (39).

4. Anonymous, *Marly*, 93–94.
5. Anonymous, "Preface," 326.
6. P. L. Simmonds to Serena Simmonds.
7. Cundall, "Press and Printers of Jamaica," 343; Williamson, "Introduction," xi.
8. Watson, *Caribbean Culture*, 20.
9. Anonymous, *Marly*, 324.
10. Ibid., 17.
11. Ibid., 326.
12. Ibid. The missionary's discussion of the "distinction of colour" that forms "an impassable boundary between these two races of mankind," appears on page 190; Wogan's scheme is laid out on pages 191–92; and the lengthy speech of Marly's schoolfellow appears on pages 161–79. For a discussion of the opinions expressed by the "brown gentleman" and the novel's representation of mixed-race characters, see Sara Salih, *Representing Mixed Race in Jamaica and England from the Abolition Era to the Present* (London: Routledge, 2011), 56–70.

Williamson points out that of the attitudes expressed through set speeches, Broadcote's relatively enlightened position appears privileged; the plan he advocates is the one Marly ultimately plans to follow according to the last paragraphs of the novel.

13. Lalla, *Defining Jamaican Fiction*, 31. Although *Marly*'s author prefaces his novel with a typical assertion about his objective delineation of life in Jamaica—the default position of ultimately proslavery writers of the 1820s, like Henry De la Beche—Lalla points out that the text "cannot effect what a debate is intended to effect, which is a logical analysis and argument leading to a conclusion" (31). Persuasive or not, abolitionist James Stephen identified *Marly*'s author as a "serious and zealous apologist of slavery, and champion of the colonial cause." Stephen's comment appears in a footnote to the 1830 edition of his two-volume *Slavery of the British West India Colonies Delineated* (2.106). His brief denunciation, also quoted in Williamson's introduction to the novel, is the only contemporary critical comment I have found. Whereas *Montgomery, Hamel*, and *Warner Arundell* generated reviews in a number of literary magazines, none seem to have been written about *Marly*.

14. Lalla, *Defining Jamaican Fiction*, 32.

15. Joseph, *Warner Arundell*, 1.46; Anonymous, "Preface," 327.

16. Williamson, "Introduction," xi.

17. As Williamson explains, there were two editions and two reissues of *Marly*. The text of the novel remained unchanged in all, although the front matter was altered: the first edition's note "To the Public" was replaced with a "Preface to the Second Edition," dated from Glasgow, 2 October 1828; the title of the first issues of the first and second editions, *Marly; or, a Planter's Life in Jamaica* was changed for the reissues to *Marly; or, The Life of a Planter in Jamaica; comprehending characteristic sketches of the present society and manners in the British West Indies. And an impartial review of the leading questions relative to colonial policy* (1828) and *Marly; or, The Life of a Planter in Jamaica; comprehending characteristic sketches of the present society and manners in the British West Indies* (1831). For more details, see Williamson, "Note on the Text," in Anonymous, *Marly*, xxxiii.

18. Anonymous, "Preface," 326.

19. Stephen, *Slavery*, 2.145n.

20. Anonymous, "Preface," 326.

21. For Kamau Brathwaite, *Marly*'s primary interest for postcolonial readers is the "picture of white society below the level of plantocracy" that the novel presents. But even those descriptions, Brathwaite notes, become merely the occasion "for comment and debate on slavery and the wrongs of the poorer social ladder," as a number of the set speeches demonstrates. ("Creative Literature," 153). For some of the class tensions in Jamaican society, see the complaints of the overseer Mr. Fitzhughes, who despises the "mighty Dons and the proud Bushas . . . who look down upon a poor book-keeper, when they ought to remember they were once such themselves" (Anonymous, *Marly*, 106–7). Similarly, one of the anonymous commentators who holds forth in *Marly* describes an unintended consequence of the 1807 Act to Abolish the Slave Trade: "It has destroyed that portion of the people, who are denominated in England, the middle classes of society, and

with the slight exception of the professional and mercantile interest, the inhabitants of this country are now divided, only into rich and poor. The middle classes, whether white or brown, have gradually verged towards poverty. They have been compelled to part with their negroes to enable them to pay their debts and colonial taxes—debts contracted in consequence of their being possessed of too few servants, to carry on any profitable concern to advantage. These servants have been eagerly purchased by the great landed proprietors; and one of the consequences of the abolition act has been, to put into the hands of the wealthy planters, nearly the whole of the slaves, to the impoverishment and destruction of a numerous and valuable portion of the community. . . . [T]he time is not very far distant, when these landed proprietors will be the only slave owners in the island" (53).

22. Anonymous, *Marly,* 323.
23. Ibid., 318–19.
24. Ibid., 80, 81. A litany of murdered white people appears in chapter 13, esp. 199–208; although one or two cases are provoked by white cruelty, most of the murders are described as the work of ungrateful slaves (208).
25. Ibid., 318.
26. Lewis, *Journal,* 61.
27. Ibid., 62.
28. Anonymous, *Marly,* 37.
29. Ibid., 37, 35–36.
30. Ibid., 318.
31. Ibid., 324.
32. Lalla, *Defining Jamaican Fiction,* 32.
33. For an in-depth study of idleness in the long eighteenth century, see Sarah Jordan, *The Anxieties of Idleness: Idleness in Eighteenth-Century British Literature and Culture* (Lewisburg, PA: Bucknell University Press, 2003).
34. Grainger, *Sugar-Cane,* 4.168–70, 4.167, 4.187.
35. Anonymous, *Marly,* 318.
36. Ibid., 82.
37. Ibid., 82, 220.
38. Ibid., 82.
39. Ibid.
40. Ibid., 82, 220.
41. Ibid., 18. For the different chronologies operating in the novel—fictional, textual, and compositional—see Williamson, "Introduction," xvi–xvii.
42. Anonymous, *Marly,* 18.
43. Ibid. Although no details are given about the elder Marly's jobbing gang, later in the novel the younger Marly will observe the poor treatment of members of jobbing gangs; this conforms to the observations of many commentators that enslaved people who were hired out in such gangs were subject to much harsher conditions than estate slaves.
44. Ibid.

45. See, e.g., the story of Good Montano, in James Grainger's *Sugar-Cane* (1.580–647).

46. Burnard, *Mastery, Tyranny and Desire*, 54.

47. Qtd. in ibid.

48. Ibid., 55.

49. Ibid., 58. There was, as Burnard points out, an added benefit derived from this demand for labor: unlike land, work forces comprised of enslaved people "were inherently dividable," enabling a slaveholder short of cash to easily "sell one or two slaves without having to liquidate all of his holdings" (58).

50. Anonymous, *Marly*, 18.

51. Ibid., 19.

52. From the image of the wealthy West Indian in Richard Cumberland's *The West Indian* (1770), to Tobias Smollett's complaints about tasteless and extravagant planters and "negro-drivers" in *Humphrey Clinker* (1771), to the oft-cited apocryphal story of George III's comments to William Pitt about West Indian wealth, provoked by the sight of a planter's splendid equipage ("Sugar, sugar, hey? All *that* sugar! How are the duties, hey Pitt, how are the duties?"), such perceptions gave rise to the every-day expression, "As rich as a West Indian." See Fryer, *Staying Power*, 18.

53. Tomich, *Through the Prism of Slavery*, 61.

54. Playfair, *Inquiry*, 156–57.

55. Tomich, *Through the Prism of Slavery*, 80.

56. Ibid., 79.

57. Anonymous, *Marly*, 224.

58. Ibid., 224–25.

59. Drayton, "Collaboration of Labour," 110.

60. Ibid. As Drayton continues, "Slave-powered globalization reached its climax in the early decades of the nineteenth century, when it was the partner of industrialization and urbanization within Europe, and a principal direct and indirect cause of the settlement of European populations on new continents. It shared a world with newer regimes of taste and technology, religious and economic ambition, which it had helped to bring into being, and which in time would destroy it. In a few generations, emancipations would remove the whip and chain from the plantations, and crystals and syrups extracted from beet and maize would drive down the price of sugar. But the plantations remained, and spread their discipline into Africa, south Asia and the Pacific. Their legacies continue in the destructive ways we price labour and human life and share the resources of the planet, all the world of darkness which surrounded our self-congratulatory millennium fireworks" (110–11).

61. Anonymous, *Marly*, 227.

62. Ibid., 355n.

63. Ibid., 225.

64. Ibid., 240.

65. Ibid., 112; 57.
66. Ibid., 144–45.
67. Ibid., 147.
68. Ibid.
69. Ibid.
70. Ibid., 145.
71. Ibid.
72. Ibid.
73. Ibid., 236.
74. Ibid., 324.
75. See, e.g., Zachary Macauley, *East and West India Sugar; or, a Refutation of the Claims of the West India Colonists to a Protecting Duty on East India Sugar* (London, 1823): "It must be admitted, indeed, that the agricultural machinery of the peasant of Bengal is of a very rude and simple kind: his little plough, drawn by a horse or a cow . . . may excite the ridicule of our British agriculturalists; but it is an engine of great power in turning up the soil, when compared with the manual labour which, aided only by the hoe, is employed, with few exceptions, to turn up the soil in the West Indies" (51). James Cropper, *Vindication of a Loan of £15,000,000 to the West India Planters Shewing that It Might Not Only Be Lent with Perfect Safety, But with Immense Advantage Both to the West Indians and to the People of England* (London, 1833): "The plough ought to be generally introduced; but, as is natural, the Planters do not admit that any further improvement could be made in their practice; . . . It may be said that we are meddling with things we do not understand; our reply to this is, the planters want our money to compensate for their own neglect; and that it is strictly our business to look to that. Slavery, the source of all these evils, is the great hindrance to the use of the plough" (13). James Stephen, *England Enslaved by Her Own Slave Colonies* (London, 1826): "They [the planters] find fault in short with every thing, except their own wretched inferior system, the true source of all their evils. It is in vain pointed out to them that the exhaustion of their lands is the natural effect of the substitution of human labour for that of cattle, and the consequent want of manure; that the expenses of their culture are enormously enhanced by the same cause, and by the want of such machinery and implements as all other farmers employ; . . . We should laugh at the complaints of a farmer, that he could not obtain adequate returns, even from the best lands, raising the richest produce, if, rejecting ploughs and harrows and wains, he employed a hundred labourers on as many acres, maintaining them to boot, and had paid besides for removing them from a distant country at the rate of eighty or a hundred pounds per man" (19). Anon., *East India Sugar; or an Inquiry respecting the Means of Improving the Quality and Reducing the Cost of Sugar Raised by Free Labour in the East Indies* (London, 1824): "[T]he use of the plough has such obvious advantages, that to a cursory observer it is wonderful that it has not been more generally adopted in West Indian cultivation. . . . If the plough were brought into general use, and

cattle were therefore more generally employed, the fertility of the soil, by means of a change of crops, of manuring, and good management, would be gradually improved instead of being, as now, continually deteriorated" (18).

76. "The first record to be found of any agricultural society"—The Agricultural Society—"in Jamaica occurs in 1807," later known as the Cornwall Agricultural Society for the parish in which it was located. "In 1825 was founded a Jamaica Horticultural Society, at Kingston, with Dr. E. N. Bancroft as president, two vice-presidents, a treasurer, a secretary, a foreign secretary, and a large and influential committee of management (afterwards called the Council). In 1827 this had become the 'Jamaica Society for the cultivation of Agriculture and other Arts and Sciences,' the objects of which were to afford assistance to such as are desirous of enquiring into various branches of art or science, as well as to encourage all improvements in Agriculture and Horticulture" (*Journal of the Institute of Jamaica*, 202). By 1842, four years after the end of the Apprenticeship period, there were agricultural societies in numerous parishes, and by 1843, "about which time interest in agricultural matters in Jamaica appears to have reached its zenith, the Governor . . . offered two prizes of £100, the one for the best essay upon the cultivation of the sugar cane and the other on the 'Best Mode of establishing and conducting Industrial Schools, adapted to the wants and circumstances of an agricultural population'" (202).

77. According to Hicks, "The industrial nature of [sugar] plantations, involving the processing of sugar cane as well as its cultivation, made constant experimentation possible. These experiments, in the fields and the sugar works were fuelled by fast-developing new concerns with productivity and the application of scientific techniques of agriculture" ("Material Improvements," 214). These innovations included everything from new varieties of cane introduced in the 1780s, improvements in water management, the increasing use of dung fertilization, and the plough, which in the case of Antigua at least, "developed . . . from the 1750s . . . and was 'almost universal' there by 1820" (214). There were also innovations in the machinery involved in sugar processing, such as the increasing use of horizontal rollers for crushing cane, the use of solid iron rollers, use of cane trash for fuel as well as the importation of coal to increase efficiency of the boilers. "[T]he use of clarifiers . . . and the mixture of juice with lime to promote crystallisation, became far more common from the mid 18th century. . . . And use was made of the vacuum pan, which increased the efficiency of evaporation by allowing it to take place under vacuum, after its patenting in 1813. In 1808, microscopes were sent from London to one group of planters for the examination of the effects of different procedures on sugar crystallisation. Centrifuges were introduced during the early 19th century, separating molasses from the sugar granules in order to speed up the curing process" (214–15).

78. In response to Cornwall's suggestion to employ the plow, the resident manager of La Taste expressed skepticism that it would increase production, citing the topography of the estate, "the immense Expense of importing Ploughs,

Ploughmen & Ploughing Stocks," and the efficiency of La Taste's enslaved workers wielding hand hoes and performing the necessary labor "cheerfully" and "with ease" (Seymour, Daniels, and Watkins, "Estate and Empire").

79. For Thistlewood's engagement with gardening, see Burnard, *Mastery, Tyranny, and Desire,* esp. 241–71. "Agricola" was the pen name of W. F. Whitehouse, whose *Agricola's Letters and Essays on Sugar Farming in Jamaica,* comprised mainly earlier letters written to various Jamaican newspapers, was published in Kingston in 1845. The first three of these letters advocate plow tillage, detailing the cost–benefit ratios of its adoption; in a separate letter to the Jamaican governor, Agricola suggests that plowing matches be promoted by Jamaica's agricultural societies to encourage it [n.p.].

80. Anonymous, *Marly,* 82.
81. Ibid., 80–81.
82. Ibid., 81.
83. Ibid.
84. Ibid.
85. Ibid., 82.
86. Doyle, *Freedom's Empire,* 3.
87. Ibid.
88. Anonymous, *Marly,* 82.
89. Doyle, *Freedom's Empire,* 5.
90. Doyle alludes to Toni Morrison in *Playing in the Dark:* "That is, Anglo-Atlantic novels from the beginning practice what Morrison calls Africanism, unwittingly manifesting how the production of white identity, articulated as free and modern, depends on an African-Atlantic presence and labor" (*Freedom's Empire,* 5–6).
91. Anonymous, *Marly,* 60, 59.
92. Ibid., 60.
93. Ibid., 61.
94. For contemporary descriptions of mountain grounds and provision growing in Caribbean fiction, see Michael Thelwell's *The Harder They Come:* "A stranger might see [in the Jamaican mountainside] only an undifferentiated mass of lush tropical jungle. But to Miss 'Mando it was nothing of the kind—it was home and history, community and human industry, sweat, toil, and joy." This assertion is followed by a rich description of the agrodiversity of the mountain grounds and the produce cultivated as signifiers of autonomous (agri)culture (Thelwell, *Harder They Come,* 15). The entirety of Erna Brodber's *The Rainmaker's Mistake* is a celebration of provision ground over plantation. See DeLoughrey, "Yams, Roots, and Rot," 58–75.
95. Anonymous, *Marly,* 61.
96. Ibid.
97. Ibid.
98. Marhsall, "Provision Ground and Plantation Labour," 51.

99. Ibid., 51–52.
100. Anonymous, *Marly*, 233.
101. Ibid.
102. Ibid., 219.
103. See, for example, N. Edwards, "Talking about a Little Culture"; Dalleo, *Caribbean Literature*, 199–205; and DeLoughrey, "Yams, Roots, and Rot," for recent engagements with Wynter's cultural analyses. See Erna Brodber's *The Rainmaker's Mistake* (2007) for a dramatic novelization of the plot/plantation relationship.
104. Wynter, "Novel and History," 99.
105. Ibid., 100.
106. Ibid.
107. Anonymous, *Marly*, 222–23.
108. Ibid., 76.
109. Lalla, *Defining Jamaican Fiction*, 34, 1.
110. Dallas, *History of the Maroons*, 1.104.
111. Ibid., 1.104–6.
112. Price, "Introduction," 5.
113. Qtd. in "A Black Companion of the Bath," *Anti-Slavery Reporter* 9 (January 1, 1861): 19–22.

4. Recentering the Caribbean

1. Baucom, *Specters of the Atlantic*, 333. Portions of my reading of *Warner Arundell* have been adapted from an earlier essay, "In the Free: The Work of Emancipation in the Anglo-Caribbean Historical Novel," *Journal of American Studies* 49, no. 2 (2015): 359–81.
2. Brathwaite, "Foreword," 6.
3. Arundell's Christian name Warner refers to his matrilineal descent from Sir Thomas Warner, who was among the first English colonists of St. Kitts, arriving there in 1623.
4. C. Hall, "Reconfiguring Race," 163.
5. Brereton et al., "Introduction," xxx.
6. Noting the influence of Laurence Sterne's *Tristram Shandy*, Brereton et al. remind us that, according to the fictional editor's preface, Arundell's manuscript (from which the "adventures" are culled) is titled "The Life, Adventures, and Opinions, of Warner Arundell, Esquire."
7. Joseph, *Warner Arundell* (1838), 1.44.
8. Aravamudan, *Tropicopolitans*, 4.
9. Addison, Essay No. 69.
10. Ibid. Although commodities are important to Addison's cosmopolitanism, his essay suggests that it's the place/space/activity of commercial exchange represented by the place of the London Exchange that is fetishized.
11. According to Christopher Rollason, the first of the Paris Arcades, Passage

des Panoramas, opened in 1800 when Napoleon Bonaparte was First Consul. Most of its successors were constructed between 1800 and 1830—i.e., through the Napoleonic period and under the post-1815 Bourbon monarchy, as restored after Napoleon's defeat at Waterloo; the last was built in 1860 (Rollason, "Passageways of Paris"). John Nash's Royal Opera Arcade followed a similar model of the Paris *Passages;* it was completed in 1818.

12. Roach, *Cities of the Dead,* 16.
13. Joseph, *Warner Arundell* (1838), 1.146–47.
14. Brereton et al., "Introduction," xxxii.
15. Noyes, "Goethe on Cosmopolitanism," 448. On the other side of this exchange, Christopher P. Iannini suggests that "[t]hroughout much of the eighteenth century, the [metropolitan] demand for factual eyewitness reports on New World nature provided one of the primary channels—in many cases, one of the only reliable channels—through which learned provincials could take part in the broader intellectual culture of the Atlantic world, refashioning themselves as enlightened authors and subjects" (*Fatal Revolutions,* 4). Iannini's observations, useful as they are, do not cover the role of the colonial reader. As discussed in chapter 1, a figure like John Lunan, whose *Hortus Jamaicensis* was published in Jamaica, circulated among fellow Jamaicans or recently arrived colonists wishing to familiarize themselves with their New World.
16. Joseph, *Warner Arundell,* 105.
17. Cudjoe, *Beyond Boundaries,* 77.
18. Ibid.
19. Joseph, *Warner Arundell* (1838), 2.2.
20. Ibid., 2.13.
21. Ibid.
22. Ibid., 2.17.
23. Ibid., 2.18.
24. Petley, "Gluttony," 91.
25. Ibid., 92. West Indian hospitality, of course, also had its practical purposes. As Trevor Burnard puts it, the "all-embracing cult of hospitality" served as a mechanism by which white colonists across social classes bonded and maintained white unity, a necessity given the demographic realities of the sugar colonies and the ever-present threat of insurrection. (*Mastery, Tyranny, and Desire,* 249; also cited in Petley, "Gluttony," 87).
26. Cudjoe, *Beyond Borders,* 79.
27. This is somewhat different but still related to "the romantic pro-planter view of the slave system as a benevolent organization where the estate owner knows and cares for 'his' slaves," and that suggests there is a "social network already existing that joins black and white Jamaicans in mutual recognition, from which 'strangers' are a kind of deviation precisely in their non-Jamaicanness" (Ward and Watson, "Introduction," 17).
28. S. Hall, "Negotiating Caribbean Identity," 26.

29. Petley, "Gluttony," 99.
30. Qtd. in Sennett, "Cosmopolitanism," 43.
31. Ibid.
32. Ibid., 43.
33. Brereton et al., "Introduction," xxx.
34. Ibid., xxxi.
35. Joseph, *Warner Arundell* (1838), 2.30.
36. Ibid., 1.141.
37. Ibid., 1.142.
38. Ibid.
39. Ibid.
40. Iannini, *Fatal Revolutions,* 12.
41. Joseph, *Warner Arundell* (1838), 1.100.
42. Ibid., 1.76–77.
43. Ibid., 1.147–48.
44. Brereton et al. point to a slightly different formal consideration of Joseph's emphasis on acts of translation. Referring to the novel's framing device—an anonymous editor's preface and occasional intrusions into the main body of the novel allow Joseph to incorporate and annotate numerous creole words and expressions—Brereton et al. argue that movements between "proper" English and creolisms generate a degree of ambivalence. On the one hand, the editor apologizes for "unwittingly" retaining creolisms that "will scarcely be understood on the other side of the Atlantic." "It is difficult to live many years in a country," he explains, "without contracting some of the peculiarities of its dialect or idiom" (Joseph, *Warner Arundell* [1838], 1.6), while on the other hand he revels in the insider's knowledge that allows for easy translation on behalf of uninitiated, monolingual English readers (Brereton et al., "Introduction," xxxvii). "By inserting the self-deprecating editor between the reader and the text, Joseph is able to eat his cake and have it too: he pays lip service to his readers' sensibilities, while establishing himself as their equal [superior?] in terms of mastery of language and his erudition. At the same time, the frame allows him to define a space within which he can experiment with language registers that challenge the boundaries of what in his age would have been considered cultivated speech" (xxxvii).
45. Joseph, *Warner Arundell* (1838), 2.2; S. Hall, "Negotiating Caribbean Identities," 27. Hall continues: "The melting-pot of the British islands produced a different combination of genetic features and factors everywhere, and in each island elements of other ethnic cultures—Chinese, Syrian, Lebanese, Portuguese, Jewish—are present. I know because I have a small proportion of practically all of them in my own inheritance." The difference between Arundell's case and Hall's is that the fictional construct of 1838 insists on his status as an "unmixed" white man—though one who appreciates the inheritance of people who share Hall's inheritance.
46. Joseph, *Warner Arundell* (1838), 1.46.

47. Ibid., 1.235.
48. Ibid., 1.237–38.
49. Ibid., 1.238, 1.234.
50. *Literary Gazette*, 71.
51. Roach, *Cities of the Dead*, 4.
52. Ibid., 5, 4.
53. Joseph, *Warner Arundell* (1838), 1.12.
54. Forstescue, "West Indian Rebellion," 456.
55. For more on the history of Grenada's French and French-creole inhabitants see John Angus Martin, *Island Caribs and French Settlers in Grenada, 1498–1763* (St. Georges: CreateSpace Independent Publishing, 2013).
56. Joseph, *History of Trinidad*, 186.
57. Ibid., 186n.
58. Gordon Turnbull's *Narrative* provides a contrast: "Before proceeding to the narrative of particular events, it may not be improper to inquire into the more remote, as well as immediate causes which produced them. In endeavouring to trace this horrid rebellion to its source, the mind is lost in astonishment and doubt. We contemplate, with equal indignation and surprise, the conduct of such of the *new subjects* [as the French inhabitants of Grenada were denominated] who possessed valuable property in the island, and, compared with their deluded countrymen under the new-modelled government of France, might be said to enjoy ease and perfect freedom;—yet joined, or abetted, a band of the vilest miscreants, in the perpetration of the blackest crimes! thereby forfeiting all the blessings which they had experienced for a length of time under a mild and well-poised constitution, in common with his Majesty's British-born subjects.

But we can more readily account for the defection of those of desperate fortunes, or of turbulent and malignant dispositions, differing only in colour from the *banditti* with whom they enlist themselves, under the banner of rapine, treason and murder" (8–9).
59. Ibid., 36–37. The "we" of Fédon's declaration is intriguing. Kit Candlin persuasively argues that Fédon's Rebellion was propelled by a sense of aggrievement shared by a very large and increasingly disenfranchised community of people of color living in Grenada and in the neighboring Grenadines, in Trinidad, Martinique, and throughout the larger Caribbean. Their grievances as French-descended planters were exacerbated by racial discrimination. Candlin's study of this group—in particular his discussion of the Fédon and Philip families—also points out the alliances of kinship, property, and race that shaped this community, along with varied responses to their disenfranchisement and the fluidity of their movements, not only as transcolonial subjects but as transnational subjects as well. Kit Candlin, *Last Caribbean Frontier*, esp. Chapter 1, "What Became of the Fédon Rebellion?" (1–23).
60. Cary, personal correspondence.
61. Jenkins, "Colonial Robespierre," 326–27.

62. Joseph, *History of Trinidad*, 186.
63. Joseph, *Warner Arundell* (1838), 1.14.
64. Cudjoe, *Beyond Boundaries,* 70. In identifying Hugues as a man of color, Cudjoe is passing along an error: Hugues came from a middle-class French family that, although they emigrated to Haiti in the 1780s and returned to France from that colony at the outbreak of the Revolution, was not of African descent. According to David Geggus, when C. L. R. James described Hugues as "a wealthy Mulatto," he was drawing from erroneous sources. [personal email correspondence, August 2, 2014].
65. Cudjoe, *Beyond Boundaries,* 74–75.
66. Joseph, *Warner Arundell* (1838), 1.26.
67. Ibid., 1.38–40.
68. In some respects, Joseph's depiction of Fédon anticipates twentieth- and twenty-first-century historians, who look back to Fédon as a man who was not seeking independence for Grenada, but one who "wanted to rid Grenada of British Colonial rule and then make her part of the New French Republic created by the French Revolution in 1792. In this, Fédon could have been deluded, being so distant from the main current of political affairs in France; for by 1795 France was in a state of political chaos and the existing leadership had indeed abandoned most of the lofty aims of 1789. . . . The fact that Fédon took orders from Victor Hugues, an agent of the Republican Government in Guadalupe, and received arms and ammunition and other forms of assistance from him showed that he was not politically autonomous, but was controlled, albeit partially, by external forces" (Brizan, "Fédon Rebellion").
69. Joseph, *Warner Arundell* (1838), 1.40.
70. Everson, "Redeeming the Specter," 440.
71. Joseph, *Warner Arundell* (1838), 3.118. According to Joseph's Old Julie, she was the wise woman who predicted Toussaint's death in France, Napoleon's subsequent downfall, and the fate of the Martinican creole Marie Josèphe Tascher, who would become Napoleon Bonaparte's Empress Josephine. See Joseph, *Warner Arundell* (1838), 3.117–18.
72. Ibid., 3.42.
73. Ibid., 3.43.
74. According to Arundell's (or perhaps the fictitious editor's) footnote, this was "A term of reproach applied by negroes to white people" (Joseph, *Warner Arundell* [1838], 3.116n.)
75. Trinidad's La Brea Pitch Lake is one of the world's largest deposits of natural emulsified asphalt in the world. Sir Walter Raleigh was introduced to the surrounding area in 1595 by Amerindian guides and began to export "piche" (Carib and Arawak translated to the English "pitch") to England on his second return voyage from Trinidad.
76. Joseph, *Warner Arundell* (1838), 3.123.
77. Ibid., 3.122.

78. Ibid., 3.125–126.
79. Ibid.
80. Gilmore, "Too Oft Allur'd," 75–94.
81. Ibid., 85; John Singleton, *A General Description of the West-Indian Islands, As far as relates to the British, Dutch and Danish Governments, from Barbados to Saint Croix. Attempted in Blank Verse.* (Barbados: Esmand and Walker, for the Author, 1767), 4.413–19. Qtd. in Gilmore, "Too Oft Allur'd," 86.
82. Joseph, *Warner Arundell* (1838), 3.125.
83. Elsewhere I argue that Fédon's return to Grenada before his (second) death is central to Arundell's white creole identity, an event that secures his place in the post-Emancipation plantocratic order; see Ward, "In the Free," 359–381.

Conclusion

1. Philip, *Emmanuel Appadocca*, 6.
2. Donnell, *Twentieth-Century Caribbean Literature*, 2.
3. See Cudjoe, "Preface," xiii–xiv.
4. Piérola. "At the Edge," 152.
5. Ibid., 156. Defining the historical novel in this way, argues Piérola, paves the way for a theoretical frame that "does not define a 'form' with fixed and predictable effects on reality, but rather one that allows us to understand what the historical novel is, how it works, and how it relates to reality" (155).
6. Questioning the "why" and "how," insists Piérola, is necessary if readings of historical fiction are to move beyond historicizing the work by revealing the underlying ideologies of its moment of production, important as that is ("Edge of History," 157).
7. Gray, *Old Port-Royal*, 5.
8. Ward and Watson, Appendix A, 436–37.
9. Gray, *Old Port-Royal*, 7.
10. Ibid., 8.
11. Ibid., 11. Ellen's mother dies while she is an infant; Mansvelt names his daughter Ellen, the narrator confides, "no doubt after some fair girl who, in early years, had imprinted her image on his heart" (11).
12. Ibid., 271.
13. Ibid., 272.
14. Ibid., 250.
15. Frohock, *Buccaneers and Privateers*.
16. Gray, *Old Port-Royal*, 54.
17. Ibid., 58.
18. Rev. William May to the Bishop of London, c. 1720, qtd. in Oliver, *Caribbeana*, 3.5.
19. Gray, *Old Port-Royal*, 270.
20. Ibid., 82.
21. Ibid., 83.

22. Ibid., 122–23.
23. See Ward, *Desire and Disorder*, 201–16.
24. See Gilmore, "Introduction," 16.
25. Ashcroft et al., *Empire Writes Back*, 153.
26. Philip, *Emmanuel Appadocca*, 6.
27. Joseph, *Warner Arundell* (1838), 1.235.
28. Philip, *Emmanuel Appadocca*, 6.
29. Cain, "Introduction." *Emmanuel Appadocca,* xxxvii.

30. Piérola, "Edge of History," 156. Defining the historical novel in this way, argues Piérola, paves the way for a theoretical frame that "does not define a 'form' with fixed and predictable effects on reality, but rather one that allows us to understand what the historical novel is, how it works, and how it relates to reality" (155).

31. C. Williams, *Hamel*, 427.

32. For a testimony to Philip's political activism in Trinidad, see the obituary reprinted in the University of Massachusetts Press edition of the novel (*Emmanuel Appadocca*, 7–10).

33. Celeste appears only briefly, to tell the fortune of the young South American woman Feliciana. Feliciana falls in love with Appadocca when she nurses him to health after his escape from the British naval ship where he has been imprisoned. Appadocca, though sympathetic to her feelings, leaves her to continue his pursuit of his father. After the pirate's death, Feliciana suffers a brief spell of madness, then joins a convent; she makes an annual pilgrimage to Trinidad to tend the graves of Appadocca and his mother.

34. Philip, *Emmanuel Appadocca*, 99.
35. Ibid.
36. Candlin, *Last Caribbean Frontier*, 20.
37. Philip, *Emmanuel Appadocca*, 100.
38. Ibid.
39. Candlin, *Last Caribbean Frontier*, 28–29.
40. Philip, *Emmanuel Appadocca*, 106.
41. Ganser, "Pirate Ship," 65.
42. Philip, *Emmanuel Appadocca*, 50–51.
43. See Ficke, "Pirates and Patriots," esp. 126–28.
44. Philip, *Emmanuel Appadocca*, 245.
45. Ibid., 248.
46. Brodber, *Rainmaker's Mistake*, 150.
47. Brodber, *Myal*, 66.

Bibliography

Addison, Joseph. Essay No. 69. *The Spectator* (1722).
Advertisement for *Montgomery* in *Morning Chronicle* (11 July 1817 and 16 July 1818).
Allen, Carolyn. "Creole Then and Now: The Problem of Definition." In *Questioning Creole: Creolisation Discourses in Caribbean Culture. In Honour of Kamau Brathwaite,* edited by Verene A. Shepherd and Glen L. Richards, 47–63. Kingston: Ian Randle, 2002.
Allen, Garland E. Rev. of *The Idea of Race in Science: Great Britain, 1800–1960.* By Nancy Stepan. London: Macmillan, 1982. In *Victorian Studies* 29, no.1 (1985): 173–75.
Anderson, Benedict. *Imagined Communities: Reflections on the Origin and Spread of Nationalism.* 2nd ed. London: Verso Press, 1991.
Anonymous. *Marly; or, A Planter's Life in Jamaica.* 1828. Rpt. Edited by Karina Williamson. Oxford: Macmillan Caribbean, 2005.
Anonymous. *Montgomery; or the West Indian Adventurer.* 3 vols. Kingston: Offices of the Kingston Chronicle, 1812–13.
Anonymous. "Preface to the Second Edition." In *Marly; or, A Planter's Life in Jamaica,* by Anonymous, 326–27. 1828. Rpt. Edited by Karina Williamson. Oxford: Macmillan Caribbean, 2005.
Aravamudan, Srinivas. *Tropicopolitans: Colonialism and Agency, 1688–1804.* Durham, NC: Duke University Press, 1999.
Ashcroft, Bill, Gareth Griffith, and Helen Tiffin. *The Empire Writes Back: Theory and Practice in Post-colonial Literatures.* London: Routledge, 1989.
Baucom, Ian. *Specters of the Atlantic: Finance Capital, Slavery, and the Philosophy of History.* Durham, NC: Duke University Press, 2005.
Bauer, Ralph, and Jose Antonio Mazzotti. "Introduction." In *Creole Subjects in the Colonial Americas: Empires, Texts, Identities,* edited by Bauer and Mazzotti, 1–57. Chapel Hill: University of North Carolina Press, 2009.
Beckles, Hilary McD. "Caribbean Antislavery: The Self-Liberation Ethos of Enslaved Blacks." *Journal of Caribbean History* 22, nos 1–2 (1988): 1–19.

Rpt. in *Caribbean Slavery in the Atlantic World: A Student Reader,* edited by Verene A. Shepherd and Hilary McD. Beckles, 869–78. Kingston: Ian Randle, 2000.

Behrendt, Stephen D., David Eltis, and David Richardson. "The Costs of Coercion: African Agency in the Pre-Modern Atlantic World." *Economic History Review* 54, no. 3 (2001): 454–76.

Benítez-Rojo, Antonio. *The Repeating Island: The Caribbean and the Postmodern Perspective.* Translated by James E. Maraniss. 2nd ed. Durham, NC: Duke University Press, 1996.

Berry, Stephen R. *A Path in the Mighty Waters: Shipboard Life and Atlantic Crossings to the New World.* New Haven, CT: Yale University Press, 2015.

Bohls, Elizabeth A. *Slavery and the Politics of Place: Representing the Colonial Caribbean, 1770–1830.* Cambridge: Cambridge University Press, 2014.

Bolland, O. Nigel. "Creolisation and Creole Socieities: A Cultural Nationalist View of Caribbean Social History." In *Questioning Creole: Creolisation Discourses in Caribbean Culture. In Honour of Kamau Brathwaite,* edited by Verene A. Shepherd and Glen L. Richards, 15–46. Kingston: Ian Randle, 2002.

Brathwaite, Edward [Kamau]. "Creative Literature in the British West Indies during the Period of Slavery." *Savacou* 1, no. 1 (June 1970): 46–74. Rpt. in *Roots,* 127–70. Havana: Casa de las Americas, 1986.

Brathwaite, Edward [Kamau]. *The Development of Creole Society in Jamaica, 1770–1820.* 1971. Rpt. Kingston: Ian Randle, 2005.

Brathwaite, Kamau. "Foreword." In *Hamel, the Obeah Man,* edited by Candace Ward and Tim Watson, 6. Peterborough, ON: Broadview, 2010.

Brereton, Bridget, Rhonda Cobham, Mary Rimmer, and Lise Winer. "Introduction." In *Warner Arundell, The Adventures of a Creole,* by E. L. Joseph, edited by Lise Winer, xi–xliii. Kingston: University of of the West Indies Press, 2001.

Brizan, George I. "The Fédon Rebellion, 1795–96: Anti-Colonial or Anti-British?" Unpublished paper, n.d.

Brodber, Erna. *Myal.* 1988. Long Grove, IL: Waveland, 2014.

Brodber, Erna. *The Rainmaker's Mistake.* London: New Beacon, 2007.

Brown, Laura. *Ends of Empire: Women and Ideology in Early Eighteenth-Century English Literature.* Ithaca, NY: Cornell University Press, 1993.

Buckley, Roger Norman. *The British Army in the West Indies: Society and the Military in the Revolutionary Age.* Gainesville: University Press of Florida, 1998.

Buckley, Roger Norman. "The Frontier in the Jamaican Caricatures of Abraham James." *Yale University of Library Gazette* 58, nos. 3–4 (April 1984): 152–62.

Burnard, Trevor. *Mastery, Tyranny, and Desire: Thomas Thistlewood and His Slaves in the Anglo-Jamaican World.* Kingston: University of the West Indies Press, 2004.

Cain, William E. "Introduction." In *Emmanuel Appadocca; or, Blighted Life. A Tale of the Boucaneers,* by Maxwell Philip, edited by Selwyn R. Cudjoe, xv–lv. Amherst: University of Massachusetts Press, 1997.

Candlin, Kit. *The Last Caribbean Frontier, 1795–1815*. London: Palgrave Macmillan, 2012.
Carey, Brycchan. *British Abolitionism and the Rhetoric of Sensibility: Writing, Sentiment, and Slavery, 1760–1807*. London: Palgrave Macmillan, 2005.
Cary, Samuel, Jr. Personal correspondence to his father, Samuel Cary of Massachusetts. May 1795. Xerox collection. National Library of Grenada.
Casid, Jill H. *Sowing Empire: Landscape and Colonization*. Minneapolis: University of Minnesota Press, 1999.
Cassidy, F. G., and F. B. Le Page. *Dictionary of Jamaican English*. Kingston: University of the West Indies Press, 2002.
Cave, Roderick. "Early Printing and the Book Trade in the West Indies." *Library Quarterly* 48, no. 2 (1978): 163–92.
Cave, Roderick. *Printing and the Book Trade in the West Indies*. London: Pindar, 1987.
Chakrabarty, Dipesh. *Provincializing Europe: Postcolonial Thought and Historical Difference*. Princeton: Princeton University Press, 2000.
Christopher, Emma. *Slave Ship Sailors and Their Captive Cargoes, 1730–1807*. Cambridge: Cambridge University Press, 2006.
Chubb, Lawrence J. "Sir Henry Thomas De la Beche." In *Jamaican Rock Stars, 1823–1971: The Geologists Who Explored Jamaica*, edited by S. K. Donovan, 9–28. Boulder, CO: Geological Society of America, 2010. Rpt. of article published by Geological Society of Jamaica, 1958.
Codell, Julie F., ed. *Imperial Co-histories: National Identities and the British and Colonial Press* Rutherford, NJ: Farliegh Dickinson University Press, 2003.
Cudjoe, Selwyn R. *Beyond Boundaries: The Intellectual Tradition of Trinidad and Tobago in the Nineteenth Century*. Wellesley, MA: Calaloux Press, 2003.
Cudjoe, Selwyn R. "Preface." *Emmanuel Appadocca; or, Blighted Life. A Tale of the Boucaneers*. by Maxwell Philip, edited by Selwyn R. Cudjoe, ix–xiv. Amherst: University of Massachusetts Press, 1997.
Cundall, Frank. *A History of Printing in Jamaica from 1717 to 1834*. Kingston: Institute of Jamaica, 1935.
Cundall, Frank. "The Press and Printers of Jamaica Prior to 1820." *Proceedings of the American Antiquarian Society*, n.s., 26 (1916): 290–412.
Dallas, R[obert] C. *History of the Maroons, in Two Volumes*. London, 1803.
Dalleo, Raphael. *Caribbean Literature and the Public Sphere: From the Plantation to the Postcolonial*. Charlottesville: University of Virginia Press, 2011.
Darwin, Charles. *Charles Darwin's* Beagle *Diary*. Edited by Richard Darwin Keynes. Cambridge: Cambridge University Press, 1988.
Dash, J. Michael. Rev. of *Haitian Revolutionary Studies*. By David Patrick Geggus. In *Research in African Literatures* 35, no. 2 (2004): 197–98.
De la Beche, Henry. *Notes on the Present Condition of the Negroes in Jamaica*. London, 1825.

De la Beche, H[enry] T[homas]. Personal correspondence to Rev. I. Crofts, 13 December 1824. MS733. National Library of Jamaica.
De la Beche, H[enry] T[homas]. Personal correspondence to Rev. W[illiam] D[aniel] Conybeare, 8 January 1824. Henry De la Beche Papers. National Museum of Wales.
De la Beche, H[enry] T[homas]. Personal correspondence to Rev. W[illiam] D[aniel] Conybeare, 6 March 1824. Henry De la Beche Papers. National Museum of Wales.
De la Beche, H[enry] T[homas]. Personal correspondence to Rev. W[illiam] D[aniel] Conybeare, 29 July 1824. Henry De la Beche Papers. National Museum of Wales.
De la Beche, Henry. "Remarks on the Geology of Jamaica." *Transactions of the Geological Society* 2, pt. 2 (1827): 143–94.
De la Beche, Henry Thomas. Unpublished journal entry, 7 April 1824. Henry De la Beche Papers. National Museum of Wales.
DeLoughrey, Elizabeth. "Yams, Roots, and Rot: Allegories of the Provision Grounds." *Small Axe* 34 (2011): 58–75.
Dillon, Elizabeth Maddock. "The Original American Novel, or, The American Origin of the Novel." In *A Companion to the Eighteenth-Century English Novel and Culture,* edited by Paula Backsheider and Catherine Ingrassia, 235–60. Oxford: Blackwell, 2005.
Donnell, Alison. *Twentieth-Century Caribbean Literature: Critical Moments in Anglophone Literary History.* London: Routledge, 2005.
Doyle, Laura. *Freedom's Empire: Race and the Rise of the Novel in Atlantic Modernity, 1640–1940.* Durham, NC: Duke University Press, 2008.
Draper, Nicholas. "Helping To Make Britain Great: The Commercial Legacies of Slave-Ownership in Britain." In *Legacies of British Slave-ownership: Colonial Slavery and the Formation of Victorian Britain,* edited by Catherine Hall, Nicholas Draper, Keith McClelland, Katie Donington, Rachel Lang, 78–126. Cambridge: Cambridge University Press, 2014.
Draper, Nicholas. "The Rise of a New Planter Class? Some Countercurrents from British Guiana and Trinidad, 1807–33." *Atlantic Studies: Global Currents* 9, no. 1 (2012): 65–83.
Drayton, Richard. "The Collaboration of Labour: Slaves, Empires, and Globalizations in the Atlantic World, c. 1600–1850." In *Globalization in World History,* edited by A.G. Hopkins, 98–114. London: Pimlico, 2002.
Drayton, Richard. *Nature's Government: Science, Imperial Britain and the "Improvement" of the World.* New Haven, CT: Yale University Press, 2000.
Dubois, Laurent. *Avengers of the New World: The Story of the Haitian Revolution.* Cambridge, MA: Harvard University Press, 2004.
Dubois, Laurent, and David Garrigus, eds. *Slave Revolution in the Caribbean, 1789–1804: A Brief History with Documents.* New York: Bedford/St. Martins, 2006.

Edwards, Bryan. *The History, Civil and Commercial, of the British Colonies in the West Indies: In Two Volumes.* London, 1793.
Edwards, Nadi. "'Talking about a Little Culture': Sylvia Wynter's Early Essays." *Journal of West Indian Literature* 10, nos. 1–2 (2001): 12–38.
Epple, Angelika. "The Global, the Transnational and the Subaltern: The Limits of History beyond the National Paradigm." In *Beyond Methodological Nationalism: Research Methodologies for Cross-Border Studies,* edited by Anna Amelina, Devrimsel D. Nergiz, Thomas Faist, and Nina Glick Schiller, 155–75. New York: Routledge, 2012.
Equiano, Olaudah. *The Interesting Narrative of the Life of Olaudah Equiano.* 1789. Rpt. Edited by Robert J. Allison. Boston: Bedford/St. Martin's, 1995.
Everson, Sally. "Redeeming the Specter of Slave Revolt: *Warner Arundell,* Colonial Modernity and the Woodford Era." *La Torre* 11, nos. 41–42 (2006): 433–48.
Fabian, Johanes. *Time and the Other: How Anthropology Makes Its Object.* New York: Columbia University Press, 1983.
Ficke, Sarah H. "Pirates and Patriots: Citizenship, Race, and the Transatlantic Adventure Novel." In *Transatlantic Literary Exchanges, 1790–1870: Gender, Race, and Nation,* edited by Kevin Hutchings and Julia M. Wright, 115–29. Farnham: Ashgate, 2011.
FitzRoy, Robert. *Narrative of the Surveying Voyages of His Majesty's Ships* Adventure *and* Beagle, *Between the Years 1826 and 1836. . . . Proceedings of the Second Expedition.* 3 vols. London, 1839.
Forstescue, J. W. "The West Indian Rebellion. I. Grenada." *Macmillan's Magazine* 70 (May 1894–October 1894): 456–63.
Frohock, Richard. *Buchaneers and Privateers: The Story of the English Sea Rover (1675–1725).* Newark: University of Delaware Press, 2012.
Fryer, Peter. *Staying Power: The History of Black People in Britain.* London: Pluto Press, 1984.
Fuller, Stephen. *Notes on the two reports from the Committee of the Honourable House of Assembly of Jamaica, appointed to examine into, and to report to the House, the Allegations and Charges contained in the several Petitions which have been presented to the British House of Commons, on the subject of the slave trade, and the Treatment of the Negroes, &c. &c. &c. By a Jamaica Planter.* London, 1789.
Ganser, Alexandra. "The Pirate Ship as a Black Atlantic Heterotopia: Michel Maxwell Philip's *Emmanuel Appadocca.*" In *Contact Spaces of American Culture: Globalizing Local Phenomena,* edited by Petra Eckhard, Klaus Rieser, and Silvia Schultermandle, 51–75. Vienna: LitVerlag, 2012.
Gilmore, John. "Introduction." *Creoleana,* edited by Gilmore, 1–18. London: Macmillan Caribbean Classics, 2002.
Gilmore, John. "'Too oft allur'd by Ethiopic charms'? Sex, Slaves and Society in

John Singleton's *A General Description of the West-Indian Islands* (1767)." *ARIEL: A Review of International English Literature* 38, no. 1 (2007): 75–94.

Goudie, Sean X. *Creole America: The West Indies and the Formation of Literature and Culture in the Early Republic.* Philadelphia: University of Pennsylvania Press, 2006.

Grainger, James. *The Sugar-Cane: A Poem in Four Books.* London, 1764.

Gray, Samuel. *Old Port-Royal, or, The Buccaneer's Home. An Historical Novel.* Kingston, 1841.

Greenhouse, Carole J. *A Moment's Notice: Time Politics across Cultures.* Ithaca, NY: Cornell University Press, 1996.

Hakewill, James. *Picturesque Tour of the Island of Jamaica.* London, 1825.

Hall, Catherine. *Civilising Subjects: Metropole and Colony in the English Imagination 1830–1867.* Chicago: University of Chicago Press, 2002.

Hall, Catherine. "Reconfiguring Race: The Stories the Slave-Owners Told." In *Legacies of British Slave-ownership: Colonial Slavery and the Formation of Victorian Britain,* edited by Catherine Hall, Nicholas Draper, Keith McClelland, Katie Donington, Rachel Lang, 163–202. Cambridge: Cambridge University Press, 2014.

Hall, Douglas. *In Miserable Slavery: Thomas Thistlewood in Jamaica, 1750–86.* Kingston: University of the West Indies Press, 1999.

Hall, Douglas. "Planters, Farmers and Gardeners in Eighteenth-Century Jamaica." In *Slavery, Freedom and Gender: The Dynamics of Caribbean Society,* edited by Brian L. Moore, B. W. Higman, Carl Campbell, and Patrick Bryan, 97–114. Kingston: University of the West Indies Press, 2001.

Hall, Stuart. "Cultural Identity and Diaspora." In *Identity: Community, Culture, Difference,* edited by Jonathan Rutherford, 222–37. London: Lawrence & Wishart, 1990.

Hall, S. "Negotiating Caribbean Identity." In *New Caribbean Thought: A Reader,* edited by Brian Meeks and Folke Lindahl, 24–39. Kingston: University of the West Indies Press 2001.

Heringman, Noah. *Romantic Rocks, Aesthetic Geology.* Ithaca, NY: Cornell University Press, 2004.

Heyrick, Elizabeth. *Immediate, Not Gradual Emancipation.* London, 1824.

Hicks, Dan. "'Material Improvements': The Archaeology of Estate Landscapes in the British Leeward Islands, 1713–1838." In *Estate Landscapes: Design, Improvement and Power in the Post-Medieval Landscape,* edited by Jonathan Finch and Kate Giles, 205–28. Woodbridge: Boydell, 2007.

Holt, Thomas C. *The Problem of Freedom: Race, Labor, and Politics in Jamaica and Britain, 1832–1938.* Baltimore: Johns Hopkins University Press, 1992.

Iannini, Christopher P. *Fatal Revolutions: Natural History, West Indian Slavery, and the Routes of American Literature.* Chapel Hill: University of North Carolina Press, 2012.

The Jamaica Quarterly Journal, and Literary Gazette 2, no. 2 (December 1818): title page.
Jenkins, H. J. K. "The Colonial Robespierre: Victor Hugues." *History Today* 27, no. 11 (1977): 734–40.
Joseph, Edward Lanza. *History of Trinidad*. Port of Spain, Trinidad, 1838.
Joseph, E[dward] L[anza]. *Warner Arundell: The Adventures of a Creole*. 3 vols. London: Saunders and Otley, 1838.
Joseph, E[dward] L[anza]. *Warner Arundell: The Adventures of a Creole*. 1838. Rpt. Edited by Lise Winer. Kingston: University of the West Indies Press, 2001.
Journal of the Institute of Jamaica. For the Encouragement of Literature, Science and Art, 1 (November 1891–December 1893). Kingston: Institute of Jamaica, 1894.
Lalla, Barbara. *Defining Jamaican Fiction: Marronage and the Discourse of Survival*. Tuscaloosa: University of Alabama Press, 1996.
Lambert, David. *White Creole Culture, Politics and Identity during the Age of Abolition*. Cambridge: Cambridge University Press, 2005.
Lamming, George. *The Pleasures of Exile*. Ann Arbor: University of Michigan Press, 1992.
Lears, Jackson. "We Came, We Saw, He Died." Rev. of *Hard Choices* by Hillary Clinton, and *HRC: State Secrets and the Rebirth of Hillary Clinton*. By Jonathan Allen and Amie Parnes. In *London Review of Books* 37, no. 3 (2015): http://www.lrb.co.uk/v37/n03/jackson-lears/we-came-we-saw-he-died (accessed 7 December 2016).
Lewis, Matthew. *Journal of a West India Proprietor, Kept during a Residence in the Island of Jamaica*. London, 1834.
Literary Gazette; and Journal of Belles Lettres, Arts, Sciences, &c. for the Year 1838: 71.
Long, Edward. *History of Jamaica*. 3 vols. London, 1772.
Lunan, John. *Hortus Jamaicensis*. 2 vols. St. Jago de la Vega: Offices of the St. Jago de le Vega Gazette, 1814.
Marshall, Woodville K. "Provision Ground and Plantation Labour in Four Windward Islands: Competition for Resources during Slavery." In *The Slaves' Economy: Independent Production by Slaves in the Americas,* edited by Ira Berlin, 48–67. London: Frank Cass, 1991.
McCartney, P. J. *Henry De la Beche: Observations on an Observer*. Cardiff: Friends of the National Museum of Wales, 1977.
McClelland, Keith. "Redefining the West India Interest: Politics and the Legacies of Slave-Ownership." In *Legacies of British Slave-ownership: Colonial Slavery and the Formation of Victorian Britain,* edited by Catherine Hall, Nicholas Draper, Keith McClelland, Katie Donington, Rachel Lang, 127–62. Cambridge: Cambridge University Press, 2014.
Mintz, Sidney. *Sweetness and Power: The Place of Sugar in Modern History*. New York: Penguin, 1985.

Mintz, Sidney W. *Three Ancient Colonies: Caribbean Themes and Variations.* Cambridge, MA: Harvard University Press, 2010.
Monthly Review; or, Literary Journal: From January to June, inclusive, M, DCC, LXXXVI (1786): 65.
Moreton, J. B. *West India Customs and Manners.* London, 1793.
Morrison, Toni. "The Site of Memory." In *Inventing the Truth: The Art and Craft of Memoir,* edited by William Zinsser, 183-200. New York: Mariner, 1998.
Nair, Supriya. *Pathologies of Paradise: Caribbean Detours.* Charlottesville: University of Virginia Press, 2013.
Noyes, John K. "Goethe on Cosmopolitanism and Colonialism: Bildung and the Dialectic of Critical Mobility." *Eighteenth-Century Studies* 39, no. 4 (2006): 443-62.
O'Brien, Karen. "'These Nations Newton Made His Own': Poetry, Knowledge, and Imperial Globalization." In *The Postcolonial Enlightenment: Eighteenth-Century Colonialism and Postcolonial Theory,* edited by Daniel Carey and Lynn Festa, 281-304. Oxford: Oxford University Press, 2009.
O'Callaghan, Evelyn. "'The Unhomely Moment': Frieda Cassin's Nineteenth-Century Antiguan Novel and the Construction of the White Creole." *Small Axe* 29 (June 2009): 95-105.
Oliver, Vere Langford, ed. *Caribbeana being miscellaneous papers relating to the history, genealogy, topography, and antiquities of the British West Indies.* London: Mitchell, Hughes, and Clarke, 1914.
Orderson, J. W. *Creoleana; or, Social and Domestic Scenes and Incidents in Barbados in Days of Yore.* London: Saunders and Otley, 1842.
Paton, Diana. *No Bond but the Law: Punishment, Race, and Gender in Jamaican State Formation, 1780-1870.* Durham, NC: Duke University Press, 2004.
Paton, Diana. "Obeah Acts: Producing and Policing the Boundaries of Religion in the Caribbean." *Small Axe* 28 (2009): 1-18.
Petley, Christopher. "Gluttony, Excess, and the Fall of the Planter Class in the British Caribbean." *Atlantic Studies* 9, no. 1 (2012): 85-106.
Philip, Maxwell. *Emmanuel Appadocca; or, Blighted Life. A Tale of the Boucaneers.* 1854. Rpt. Edited by Selwyn R. Cudjoe. Amherst: University of Massachusetts Press, 1997.
Piérola, José de. "At the Edge of History: Notes for a Theory for the Historical Novel in Latin America." *Romance Studies* 26, no. 2 (2008): 151-62.
Playfair, William. *Inquiry into the Permanent Causes of the Decline and Fall of Powerful and Wealthy Nations.* London, 1805.
Pratt, Mary Louise Pratt. *Imperial Eyes: Travel Writing and Transculturation.* London: Routledge, 1992.
Price, Richard. "Introduction: Maroons and Their Communities." In *Maroon Societies: Rebel Slave Communities in the Americas,* edited by Price, 1-30. 3rd ed. Baltimore: Johns Hopkins University Press, 1996.

Price, Richard. *Travels with Tooy: History, Memory, and the African American Imagination.* Chicago: University of Chicago Press, 2008.
Rajan, Tilottama. "Wollstonecraft and Godwin: Reading the Secrets of the Political Novel." *Studies in Romanticism* 27, no. 2 (1988): 221–51.
Rediker, Marcus. *The Slave Ship: A Human History.* London: Penguin, 2007.
Reeve, Clara. *The Progress of Romance, through Times, Countries, and Manners; with Remarks on the Good and Bad Effects of It, on Them Respectively in a Course of Evening Conversations.* 2 vols. London, 1784.
Rev. of *Creoleana.* In *Tait's Edinburgh* 9 (1842): 405.
Rev. of *How to Observe Morals and Manners.* By Harriet Martineau. In *London Quarterly Review* 64 (January–April 1839): 34.
Rev. of *Montgomery; or the West Indian Adventurer.* In *Monthly Review,* 2nd ser. 76 (January 1815): 101–2.
Rippingham, John. *Jamaica, Considered in Its Present State, Political, Financial, and Philosophical.* Kingston: Office of the *Kingston Chronicle,* 1817.
Roach, Joseph. *Cities of the Dead: Circum-Atlantic Performance.* New York: Columbia University Press, 1996.
Rollason, Christopher. "The Passageways of Paris: Walter Benjamin's *Arcades Project* and Contemporary Cultural Debate in the West." In *Modern Criticism,* edited by Christopher Rollason and Rajeshwar Mittapalli, 262–96. New Delhi: Atlantic Publishers, 2002.
Rosenberg, Leah R. *Nationalism and the Formation of Caribbean Literature.* London: Palgrave Macmillan, 2007.
Rudwick, Martin J. S. *Bursting the Limits of Time: The Reconstruction of Geohistory in the Age of Revolution.* Chicago: University of Chicago Press, 2007.
Rudwick, Martin J. S. *Worlds before Adam: The Reconstruction of Geohistory in the Age of Reform.* Chicago: University of Chicago Press, 2008.
Sandiford, Keith. *The Cultural Politics of Sugar: Caribbean Slavery and Narratives of Colonialism.* Cambridge: Cambridge University Press, 2000.
Schaw, Janet. *Journal of a Lady of Quality; Being the Narrative of a Journey from Scotland to the West Indies, North Carolina, and Portugal, in the Years 1774 to 1776.* Edited by Evangeline Walker Andrews. New Haven, CT: Yale University Press, 1927.
Scott, David. *Conscripts of Modernity: The Tragedy of Colonial Enlightenment.* Durham, NC: Duke University Press, 2004.
Scott, Sarah. *The History of Sir George Ellison.* Edited by Betty Rizzo. Lexington: University Press of Kentucky, 1996.
Sennett, Richard. "Cosmopolitanism and the Experience of Cities." In *Conceiving Cosmopolitanism: Theory, Context, and Practice,* edited by Steven Vertovec and Robin Cohen, 42–47. New York: Oxford University Press, 2002.
Seymour, Susanne, Stephen Daniels, and Charles Watkins. "Estate and Empire: Sir George Cornewall's Management of Moccas, Herefordshire and La Taste, Grenada, 1771–1819." *Journal of Historical Geography* 24 (1998): 313–51.

Sharpe, Jenny. *Ghosts of Slavery: A Literary Archaeology and Black Women's Lives*. Minneapolis: University of Minnesota Press, 2003.

Sharpe, Tom. "Slavery, Sugar, and the Survey." *OUGS Journal* 29, no. 2 (2008): 88–95.

Simmonds, P. L. Personal correspondence to Serena Simmonds, January 1832. National Library of Jamaica.

Sloane, Hans. *A Voyage to the Islands Madera, Barbados, Nieves, S. Christophers and Jamaica, With the Natural History of the Herbs and Trees . . . Of the last of those Islands; to which is prefix'd an Introduction, wherein is an Account of the Inhabitants, Air, Waters, Diseases, Trade &c*. London, 1707.

Smallwood, Stephanie E. *Saltwater Slavery: A Middle Passage from Afirca to American Diaspora*. Cambridge, MA: Harvard University Press, 2007.

Society for the Mitigation and Gradual Abolition of Slavery throughout the British Dominions, *Substance of the Debate in the House of Commons, on the 15th May, 1823, on a Motion for the Mitigation and Gradual Abolition of Slavery throughout the British Dominions*. London, 1823.

Spivak, Gayatri. "Can the Subaltern Speak." In *Marxism and the Interpretation of Culture*, edited by Cary Nelson and Lawrence Grossberg, 271–313. London: Macmillan, 1988.

Stepan, Nancy. *The Idea of Race in Science: Great Britain, 1800–1960*. London: Macmillan, 1982.

Stephen, James. *Slavery of the British West India Colonies Delineated*. London, 1830.

Stoler, Ann. *Carnal Knowledge and Imperial Power: Race and the Intimate in Colonial Rule*. Berkeley: University of California Press, 2002.

Sypher, Wylie. *Guinea's Captive Kings: British Anti-Slavery Literature of the XVIIIth Century*. Chapel Hill: University of North Carolina Press, 1942.

Sypher, Wylie. "The West Indian as a 'Character' in the Eighteenth Century." *Studies in Philology* 36, no. 3 (1939): 503–20.

Thelwell, Michael. *The Harder They Come*. New York: Grove Press, 1980.

Tomich, Dale W. *Through the Prism of Slavery: Labor, Capital, and World Economy*. Lanham, MD: Rowman and Littlefield, 2004.

Trouillot, Michel-Rolph. "An Unthinkable History: The Haitian Revolution as a Non-event." In *Silencing the Past: Power and the Production of History*. 70–107. Boston: Beacon, 1995.

[Turnbull, Gordon]. *Letters to a young planter; or, observations on the management of a sugar-plantation. To which is added, The planter's kalendar. Written on the island of Grenada, by an old planter*. London, 1785.

[Turnbull, Gordon]. *Narrative of the Revolt and Insurrection of the French Inhabitants in Grenada. By an Eye-Witness*. Edinburgh, 1795.

Ward, Candace. *Desire and Disorder: Fevers, Fictions, and Feelings in Georgian England*. Lewisburg, PA: Bucknell University Press, 2007.

Ward, Candace. "In the Free: The Work of Emancipation in the Anglo-Caribbean Historical Novel." *Journal of American Studies* 49, no. 2 (2015): 359–81.

Ward, Candace. "'What Time Has Proved': History, Rebellion, and Revolution in *Hamel, the Obeah Man*." *ARIEL: A Review of International English Literature* 38, no. 1 (2007): 49–74.

Ward, Candace, and Tim Watson. "Appendix A, 'Contemporary Reviews.'" In *Hamel, the Obeah Man,* by Cynric R. Williams, edited by Ward and Watson, 429–40. Peterborough, ON: Broadview, 2010.

Ward, Candace, and Tim Watson. "Introduction." In *Hamel, the Obeah Man,* by Cynric R. Williams, edited by Ward and Watson, 9–46. Peterborough, ON: Broadview, 2010.

Watson, Tim. *Caribbean Culture and British Fiction in the Atlantic World, 1780–1870.* Cambridge: Cambridge University Press, 2008.

Williams, Cynric R. *Hamel, the Obeah Man.* 1827. Rpt. Edited by Candace Ward and Tim Watson. Peterborough, ON: Broadview, 2010.

Williams, Cynric R. *A Tour through the Island of Jamaica, from the Western to the Eastern End, in the Year 1823.* London, 1826.

Williams, Raymond. *Marxism and Literature.* Oxford: Oxford University Press, 1977.

Williamson, Karina. "Introduction." In *Marly; or, A Planter's Life in Jamaica,* by Anonymous, edited by Williamson, xi–xviii. Oxford: Macmillan Caribbean, 2005.

Wynter, Sylvia. "Novel and History, Plot and Plantation." *Savacou* 5 (1971): 95–102.

Wyrick, Deborah. "Madwoman in the Hut: Scandals of Hybrid Domesticity in Early Victorian Literature from the West Indies." *Pacific Coast Philology* 33, no.1 (1998): 44–57.

Index

Italicized page numbers refer to illustrations.

abolition and abolitionists: Act to Abolish the Slave Trade (1807), 187–88n21; advertisements for slave sales as examples used by, 174n30; effect on British Caribbean sugar trade, 94; effect on plantation owners' views of their roles, 87; generous nature of planters as counter to, 120; gradualism in antislavery writings, 63, 180–81n25; likelihood of success of, 14; in same "problem-space" as supporters of West Indian slavery, 170n72; sentiment and sensibility in writing of, 177n73; volume of literature devoted to, 168n39
Addison, Joseph: *Spectator* essay No. 69, 116–18, 122, 193n10
Africanness, 57–59, 71, 136–37
"Agricola" essays, 100, 192n79
agricultural societies, 100, 191n76
Aikman family, 173n22
ALCOA mining conglomerate, 180n24
Ali Babba: *A Thousand and One Nights*, 182n40
Allen, Carolyn, 8, 167n20
Alvarez, Julia, 162
ambivalence: in *Emmanuel Appadocca* on creole's place in past and present, 155; in *Warner Arundell* toward racial tolerance, 132–33; Wynter on ambivalence between plantation and plot for slaves, 105–6
ameliorism, 27, 39, 46, 63, 82–84, 90, 96. *See also* gradualism
Ananci (African Caribbean trickster), 151

Anderson, Benedict, 173n24
anthropology, 71, 183n62
anti-missionary sentiments, 65, 73, 78, 184n74
Antislavery Society, 63
anxieties. *See* tensions and anxieties
apocalyptic language, 145
Apprenticeship period, 110, 112, 141, 144, 191n76
Aravamudan, Srinivas, 116, 182n41, 185n86
Atlantic modernity, 21
Austen, Jane, 1

Baptist War (Jamaica 1831–32), 15, 110
Barbados, 141–42; William Henry's (British prince's) visits to, 151–53
Baucom, Ian: *Specters of the Atlantic*, 21, 112, 170n72
Bauer, Ralph, 8, 11
Beach, Thomas, 180n22
Beckford, George, 23, 170n74
Beckford, Peter, 148
Beckford, William, 147, 148; *Picturesque Tour of . . . Jamaica*, 28; *Remarks Upon the Situation of Negroes in Jamaica*, 175n38
Behn, Aphra: *Oroonoko*, 22, 46, 183n62
Benítez-Rojo, Antonio, 29, 171n9
Benjamin, Walter, 21, 117
Berryman, William: "Plantain Walk—Bookkeeper—Watchman and Hut—man with casks of water/greattoe in stirrup" (watercolor), 44, *45*

Besson, Jean, 104
Bibliografia Jamaicensis, 143
black West Indians: disdain for African and black creole cultures in West Indian colonies, 12; in early creole novels, 24; effaced from fictional texts, 11; in *Warner Arundell,* 133. See also Africanness; free blacks; Maroons; racial difference
Blake, William, 46
Blith, Walter: *The English Improver,* 43; *The English Improver Improved,* 176n57
Bois-Caïman ceremony (Haiti 1791), 75–79
Bolas, Juan de, 149
Bolívar, Simón, 138
Bolívarian wars, 138–39
Bolland, O. Nigel, 9
Botkin, Fran, 182n41
Boyer, Jean Pierre, 60
Brathwaite, Kamau, 8, 9, 24, 25, 27, 58, 165n1, 187n21
Brereton, Bridget, 115, 117, 122, 193n6, 195n44
Britain: ability to overlook West Indian practices prior to abolition movement, 120; Granada rebellion as part of French war against, 130–31; as homeland, described in *Warner Arundell,* 118–22; ignorance of world beyond confines of, 122–23; Londoners' lack of compassion, 119–20; superiority to colonial subjects, 12, 113, 122. See also white superiority
British ships, journeys of, 3–4. See also trade routes
Brizan, Sir George, 129, 197n68
Brodber, Erna, 122; *Myal,* 162–63; *The Rainmaker's Mistake,* 162, 192n94, 193n103
Brooks diagram of slave ship's hold, 5
Brown, Laura, 183n62
Brown, William Hill: *The Power of Sympathy: or, The Triumph of Nature,* 172n13
Buckland, William, 67–70, 69
Burnard, Trevor, 92, 121, 189n49; *Mastery, Tyranny, and Desire,* 173–74n28, 192n79, 194n25
busher, terminology of, 80, 185n1
Bussa's Rebellion (Barbados 1816), 15
Buxton, Thomas Fowell, 63

Cain, William, 154, 159
Campbell, Alexander: *Sermon Preached in the Parish Church of St. Catherine's, Jamaica,* 31
Candlin, Kit, 157, 196n59
Canning, George, 63, 181n31
capitalism, 116–17
Cary, Samuel, 131
"Cato and Plato, A Story of Jamaica," 182n44
Cave, Roderick, 171n10, 172n15, 172–73nn21–22
cave systems, 66–67, 69–70, 72–74, 182n40, 184n70
ceremony upon crossing Tropic of Cancer or Equator, 6, 7, 166nn14–15
Césaire, Aimé, 155
Chakrabarty, Dipesh, 179–80n16
charity and hospitality, 119–20, 194n25
Charles II (English king), 147
Cheshire, James, 165n6
Christophe, Henri, 180n17
Christopher, Emma, 166n9
civilization: as crucial measurement of racial difference, 64; improvement discourse to engender, 39–41, 46–47, 54, 96, 144; plantocracy's civilization as beneficial model for slaves, 25, 46, 63, 120; threat posed by emancipation to, 61, 100, 105. See also white superiority
Clapham sect, 184n74
Clark, William: *Ten Views of the Island of Antigua,* 97
Clarkson, Thomas, 180n17
Climatological Database for the World's Oceans, 1750–1850 (CLIWOC) project, 165n6
Codell, Julie, 30
Collingwood, Luke, 21
colonial culture: early creole novels reproducing, 2, 14, 23, 26; fiction's role in (re)shaping colonial identity, 144; *Marly*'s illustrating, as its main goal, 84; obeah practices and, 77–78. See also plantocracy and plantation system
Columbia Magazine, 172n21
Condé, Maryse, 163
contact zone of two cultures, 10, 167n29. See also crossing the line
contemporary Caribbean writers, connecting to early creole novels, 162–63

Conybeare, William Daniel, 61–62, 67–68, *68*, 69, 181n31
Cornewall, George, 100, 190–92nn78
Cornwall Agricultural Society, 191n76
Cornwall Estate (Jamaica), 86
cosmopolitanism, 95, 115–26, 131, 139, 193n10
creole, use of term, 7–13; Americans rejecting, 167n27; in anglophone and European writings of eighteenth century, 8; from earliest days of colonial activity, 8, 167n20; instability of terminology, 8; as result of Atlantic crossing and colonization, 8
Creoleana; or, Social and Domestic Scenes and Incidents in Barbados in Days of Yore (Orderson), 141, 150–53; destructive imperialism in, 153; interracial romance in, 24, 150–51; Lucy as mixed-race antiheroine, 25, 150, 153, 156, 158; madness and irrationality depicted in, 153; reconstruction of creole subjectivity in, 26; sexual agency of the enslaved in, 25; trickster outwitting white master in, 25, 150–53; William Henry (British prince) in, 151–53
creole cosmopolitanism, 116–26, 131. *See also* cosmopolitanism
creole dialect, 16–17, 80–81, 124–25, 169n49, 177n75
creole identity and culture: Britain not true "home" of the creole, 118–22; British moral superiority to, 12; countering stereotypes of creole identity in *Emmanuel Appadocca*, 158; fluidity of, 4–6, 10, 124–26, 167n34; metropolitan culture vs. global experience, 122; promotion of, 120–21. *See also* eyewitness insiderism; white creoles; *specific novels*
"creole realism," 18, 20
creolization/creolisation, 8–10, 24, 25, 71, 91, 174n28
Crevecoeur, J. Hector St. John de: Letter IX in *Letters from an American Farmer*, 46, 177n73
criadillo as origin of word "creole," 8
critical race theory, 1
Cropper, James: *Vindication of a Loan of £15,000,000 to the West India Planters*, 190n75

crossing the line: ceremony as ships crossed over Tropic of Cancer or Equator, 6, 7, 166nn14–15; coloniality/modernity border, 102; colonists' experience, 6, 42; cross-racial hospitality, 120–21; nautical origins of term, 3; slave trade as crossing of ethnicity, race, language, and religion, 5; violence associated with, 4–5
Cruikshank, George: "Crossing the Line," 6, 7
Cudjoe, Selwyn, 119, 121, 132, 160, 197n64
culture, evolution in meaning of, 29. *See also* civilization; creole identity and culture; plantocracy and plantation system
Cumberland, Richard: *The West Indian*, 11, 189n52
Cundall, Frank, 27, 143, 170n2, 171n10, 172n14

Dallas, Robert C., 167n62; *History of the Maroons*, 107–9, 179n104
Dalleo, Raphael, 21
Dalmas, Antoine: *Histoire de la revolution de Saint-Domingue*, 75–77
Danticat, Edwidge, 163
Darwin, Charles, 166n14, 180n34
Dash, J. Michael, 8, 75
Davy, Humphrey, 68–69
decolonization, 9
Defoe, Daniel, 1
degeneracy: of colonial subjects, 11; mixed-race characters depicted as regenerative in contradiction to, 127; West Indian, 26, 28, 34, 37–38, 41–42; of white men, 52–53
De la Beche, Henry Thomas: correspondence with William Daniel Conybeare, 61–62, 67–68, *68*, 180n20, 181n31; family background of, 180n22; geologist career of, 62, 72, 180n24, 184n70; Halse Hall and, 62, 67, 86, 184n71, 184n74; Hegel and, 181n25; *How to Observe Geology*, 183n55; *Notes on the Present Condition of the Negroes in Jamaica*, 62–63, 180n28; on Obeah Jack conspiracy, 76, 78; as proslavery writer, 187n13; "Remarks on the Geology of Jamaica," 67
De la Beche, Thomas, 180n22
de las Casas, Bartolomé, 83

de la Vega, Garcilaso, 167n20
De Lisser, H. G.: *Morgan's Daughter*, 149; *White Witch of Rosehall*, 149
DeLoughrey, Elizabeth: "Yams, Roots, and Rot," 193n103
Demarara Revolt (1823), 15
destructive imperialism, 153
Díaz, Junot, 162
Dillon, Elizabeth Maddock, 22
diversity: of Grenada forces fighting against the British, 131; of present-day Caribbean islands, 125–26; of slave trade crews as well as of slaves, 5; of West Indian colonies, 6–7. *See also* racial difference
Dominique, Lyndon, 169n62
Doyle, Laura, 102, 192n90
Draper, Nicholas, 23, 114
Drayton, Richard, 43, 95, 176n57, 189n60
Dryden, John: *Annus Mirabilis*, 116
Duckworth, John T., 172n14

Earle, William: *Obi; or, The History of Three-Fingered Jack*, 182n41, 185n86
early creole novels: creating a new kind of novel, 19, 22–23; "creole realism" of, 18, 20; cross-genre mix of, 18–19; cultural role of, 2, 9–10, 112; as defense of white creole position, 18, 25, 28, 89–90, 112, 169n53; dismissed as being on "wrong side of history," 23; future research topics on, 162; goal of gaining legitimacy for Creole civilization, 14–16; narrative authority on subject matter, 16–17, 28, 47, 122, 168n43; place of publication, 17–18, 169n51; reception in Britain, 17–18; revisionist history of, 15, 26, 143, 154; romance genre and, 18; separating fact from fiction in, 18, 20, 32–33; short lifespan of, 15; soothing anxiety about race in, 151, 153; terminology to refer to, 7–8; traces of, in subsequent periods, 26, 141, 144, 147, 150; and West Indian literary history, 2, 25–26. *See also* historiography; quest narrative; *specific titles of* Hamel, Marly, Montgomery, *and* Warner Arundell
earthquakes, 65, 146, 182n39
East India Sugar (Anon.), 190n75
East Indies' sugar growers as threat to West Indies, 95–96, 99, 167n33

Edgeworth, Maria: *Belinda*, 11–12, 169n62
Edwards, Bryan, 50, 169n62, 178n76; *The History, Civil and Commercial, of the British Colonies in the West Indies*, 108
Edwards, Norval (Nadi), 165n3; "Talking about a Little Culture," 193n103
Emancipation: colonial press in fight against, 32; compensation from British government paid to slave owners, 23; and early creole novels, 19, 23; Hegel's assessment on debate over, 180–81n25; ill-preparedness of enslaved people for, 32, 90, 101–2; insurrections during, 17; planters' anxieties in light of coming Emancipation period, 61, 94, 100, 105; between publication of *Marly* and *Warner Arundell*, 113. *See also* abolition and abolitionists; gradualism, arguments for; post-Emancipation novels
Emmanuel Appadocca; or, Blighted Life. A Tale of the Boucaneers (Philip), 9, 153–62; African ancestry's presence in, 154, 159–61; background of main character in, 156; *The Black Schooner* ship as extranational site, 159–60; *The Black Schooner* ship's sinking, 161; Feliciana's fate as unconsummated love, 161–62, 199n33; first anglophone Caribbean novel written by a person of color, 153–54; mulatto rights in, 24, 25; outwitting white masters in, 25; reconstruction of creole subjectivity in, 26, 161; slavery's presence in, 154–55, 158, 160–61; social injustice as trigger for revenge in, 154, 157; stereotypes of women of color and, 158; suicides in, 159, 161; white character contrasted with mixed-race character to counter stereotypes, 158–59
Enlightenment, 8, 154, 157
environmental determinism, 8
Epple, Angelika, 59
equality, 131–34
Equiano, Olaudah, 11; *Interesting Narrative*, 4–5, 165n7
European attitudes: creating sense of exile in postcolonial Caribbean writers, 122; in epoch of exclusive Eurocentrism, 59, 60, 63, 179–80n16; racial attitudes, 134; toward Afro-Caribbean subjects, 11–12; toward colonial subjects, 11–12;

Index

toward sexual relations between women of color and white men, 40–41
exotic, the, 17, 20, 54, 65, 71, 79, 118
Exquemelin's *History of the Bucaniers*, 146
"eyewitness insiderism" (Watson), 2, 15, 16–17, 82, 169n49, 194n15. *See also* narrative authority

Fabian, Johannes, 71, 183n62
fact vs. fiction, 18, 20, 32–33, 157. *See also* historical novels
Fédon, Julien, 127–31, 132–38, 155, 156, 196n59, 197n68, 198n83
feminist writers, 157
Ficke, Sarah H., 159, 160
Fielding, Henry, 174n36
Fielding, Sarah, 28, 41
First Maroon War of 1739, 106, 179n104, 180n22
fluid identities, 4–6, 10, 124–26, 162, 167n34, 196n59
Fortescue, J. W., 128
Fort Stewart Estate (Jamaica), 80–81, 186n2
Foucault, Michel, 72
free blacks: as emerging class of consumers, 95, 101; enlightened view of, 87–88; inability to understand responsibilities of freedom, 32, 90, 101–2; *Marly*'s view of future for, 83, 87–88, 90, 113; white fear of destruction in British West Indies from, 61, 100, 105, 106–7. *See also* Emancipation; gradualism, arguments for; Maroons
French colonies and creoles, 93–94, 129, 130, 133, 196n58
French Revolution, 128, 134, 197n68
French war against Britain, 130–31; Napoleonic Wars, 94, 197n71
Frohock, Richard, 147

Ganser, Alexandra, 159, 161
Garvey, Marcus, 155
Geggus, David, 197n64
geographical ignorance of Britons, 123
geology: cave systems of Jamaica, 66–67, 69, 73, 184n70; emergence of science of, 59, 62, 65–66, 180n24; Kirkdale caves (North Yorkshire), 67–68; shared lexicon with language of romantic revolution, 64, 184–85n75

George III, 130, 189n52
ghostly aftereffects, 21, 134, 136
Gilmore, John, 137, 151
Gilroy, Paul, 124
Glissant, Edouard, 8
globalization of slavery, 189n60
Godwin, William, 14, 175n36; *Caleb Williams*, 154
Gomez de Avellaneda, Gertrudis: *Sab*, 163
Goudie, Sean, 8, 167n27
gradualism, arguments for, 63, 66, 83–84, 88, 101, 113, 180–81n25; necessary to teach West Indian laborers the desire for goods, 90, 103, 105, 109–10
Grainger, James: *The Sugar-Cane*, 12, 92, 167n34
Gray, Samuel, 26, 141. *See also* Old Port-Royal
Greenhouse, Carol, 78, 183n62
Grenada: British vs. French in 1795 battles over, 130–31; French history in, 196n55; Philip's family connection with, 156; in *Warner Arundell* as birthplace of main character, 129–30
Grenadian rebellion (1795–96), 127–31, 133, 135, 138, 156, 196nn58–59, 197n68
Guthrie, James, 180n22

Haitian Revolution, 32, 60, 75–79, 93–94, 100, 112, 128, 132, 135
Hakewill, James: *Picturesque Tour of the Island of Jamaica*, 35, 175n36; *View of Harbour Street*, 35
Hall, Catherine, 10, 24
Hall, Douglas, 178n76; *In Miserable Slavery*, 174n28
Hall, Stuart, 8, 10, 11, 125, 195n45
Halse Hall, 180n22, 180n24, 184n71, 184n74
Hamel, the Obeah Man, 2, 57–79; African superstition in, 57; *The Atlas* review on, 19–20, 58; cave systems in, 66–67, 69–70, 72–74; chronology in terms of geological strata, 72; *Emmanuel Appadocca* recalling, 155; Eurocentrism and, 59, 60; eyewitness insiderism of translating creole dialect and, 16–17, 169n49; Haitian Revolution and, 60, 75–79, 100; marriage and creole domesticity in, 24, 150; narrative authority of,

218 Index

Hamel, the Obeah Man (*continued*)
16, 17, 20, 168n40; natural phenomena, imagery of, 64–65; order of plantation system forcing temporal structure on operations, 73; outwitting white masters in, 25; passage of time and history in, 61–75, 79; rebellion plot in, 67, 73–79; as repudiation of British view of West Indies, 15, 20, 57, 61; romance with white creole Joanna Guthrie, 72, 74; sales in Britain of, 169n52; sales in Jamaica and West Indies of, 169n52; *The Scotsman* review on, 179n15; sexual agency of the enslaved in, 25; *Westminster Review* on, 1, 58, 168n40; white creole women of virtue and civilized tastes in, 51, 178n87; white labor depicted in, 25; white vs. black knowledge in, 72–73
Harbour Street (Kingston, Jamaica), 35–36, *36*, 56, 174nn29–31
Harris, Wilson, 153
Hays, Mary, 157; *Victim of Prejudice,* 154
Hegel, Georg Wilhelm Friedrich, 180–81n25
Heringman, Noah, 64, 182n39
Herzfeld, Michael, 78
Heumann, Gad, 132
Heyrick, Elizabeth, 63
Hicks, Dan, 191n77
historical novels: *Emmanuel Appadocca* and, 142–43; *Hamel* and, 58–59; later Caribbean historical fiction, 150; mixed-race mother's place in, 156; *Old Port-Royal* and, 146; Piérola on, 142–43, 199n30; tension between history and fiction, 155; *Warner Arundell* and, 127
historiography, 59, 75, 76, 112, 127, 141, 143, 155
Hogarth, William, 89
"Holeing a Cane-Piece" (illustration), *97,* 97–98
Holland, William, *151,* 168n35
Holt, Thomas C., 2, 10
Home, Ninian, 130–31
Hugues, Victor, 128, 130–31, 132–33, 197n64, 197n68
hurricanes, 65
husbandry, conceptions of, 42–44, 49, 176n57
Hutton, James, 182n39; *Theory of the Earth,* 185n75

Iannini, Christopher, 124, 194n15
imperialism of the division of labor, 95
improvement: discourse of model white creole civilization on, 39–41, 46–47, 54; of the enslaved, 89–90; moral improvement instruction for white creoles, 37–39

Jacobin ideals of liberty and equality, 14, 131–32, 138, 154, 175n36
Jamaica: as crown jewel among British colonies, 148–49; development of creole society in, 9; Harbour Street (Kingston), 35–36, *36,* 56, 174nn29–31; publisher and printers in, 30, 32–40, *33,* 56; Royalists living side by side with Cromwellians in, 147
Jamaica Free Press, 110
Jamaica Magazine, 32–37, *33;* on agricultural innovations, 99; moral improvement instruction for readers, 37–39; "N.T." as the Observer in, 174–75n36, 178n87; "Observer" column and Juvenis correspondence, 37–40; quality of, 172–73n21, 174n32
Jamaica Quarterly Journal, and Literary Gazette, 34, 119, 127, 172n16
Jamaica Royal Gazette (newspaper), 35
Jamaica Society for the cultivation of Agriculture and other Arts and Sciences, 191n76
James, C. L. R., 26, 197n64
James, Marlon: *Book of Night Women,* 150, 163
Jameson, Frederic, 21
Jenkins, H. J. K., 131
Jewish author, marginalized social position of, 113
"Johnny Newcome" prints, 12, *13,* 34, 167–68n35, 175n39
Jordan, Edward, 110
Joseph, E. L.: *History of Trinidad,* 129–30, 131, 133, 135; life of, 112–13, 129. See also *Warner Arundell*
Josephine, Empress, 197n71
Juvenis (correspondent in "Observer" column of *Jamaica Magazine*), 38–40, 43

Kikoongo language and origins of word "creole," 8

Index

Kingston Chronicle, 27, 30–36, 39, 172n14
Kingston publishers/printers, 30, 32–40, 33, 56
Kirkdale caves (North Yorkshire), 67–69, 69
Kupperman, Karen Ordahl, 11

labor and laborers: comparison of British laboring classes to West Indian slaves, 89; division-of-labor imperialism, 95; industry vs. idleness, 82, 85, 88–89, 100–105, 188n33; planting season as most laborious work, 96–98, 101; reforms in future, 88; taxonomy of, 90–100; wage laborers, 95, 114; white labor and its comparison to slave's work, 25, 44, 49, 52, 80–82, 146. *See also* free blacks; plantocracy and plantation system; slavery
La Brea Pitch Lake (Trinidad), 197n75
Lalla, Barbara, 84, 107, 187n13
Lambert, David, 10, 11, 12, 34, 167n32
Lamming, George, 26, 122
language: Afro-Trinidadian speech in *Emmanuel Appadocca*, 160; creole dialect, 16–17, 80–81, 169n49, 177n75, 195n44; creole French, 124–25; Kikoongo language and origins of word "creole," 8; multilingual exchanges as symbol of liberation from nationalist boundaries, 125; polyglot as threat to national hegemony, 124; slave trade as crossing of, 5; Warner Arundell's ability to master multiple languages, 124
Leslie, Charles: *New History of Jamaica*, 34
Levitt, Kari, 170n74
Lewis, Matthew, 62, 76, 77, 86, 176n53; *Journal of a West India Proprietor, Kept during a Residence in the Island of Jamaica*, 98, 176n53
Ligon, Richard: *True and Exact History of the Island of Barbadoes*, 15, 28, 158
Linebaugh, Peter, 147
literary magazines, 172–73n21, 187n13
literature of knowledge, 171n15
Long, Edward, 13, 37, 73, 168n35, 168n37, 169n62, 184n70; *History of Jamaica*, 137, 159
Lunan, Andrew, 30, 31, 32, 39, 171n10, 172n14, 173n22, 174n36

Lunan, John, 100, 170n10, 173n22; *Hortus Jamaicensis*, 30, 37, 49, 92, 194n15
Lunan, John, Sr., 170n10
Lunan family, 170n10, 173n22
Lyell, George, 182n39

Macauley, Zachary: *East and West India Sugar; or, a Refutation of the Claims of the West India Colonists to a Protecting Duty on East India Sugar*, 190n75
MacDermot, Thomas, 26
machinery of novel and mechanization of industrialization, 85, 88
Mackenzie, Henry, 28, 41
Madden, Richard, 174n30
Makandal's plot (Haiti), 76
Mansfield, Lord Chief Justice, 167n32
Mansong, Three-Fingered Jack, 66, 76, 182n41
marginalization of the Caribbean and Creole subjects in British empire, 123
Marly; or, A Planter's Life in Jamaica, 2, 80–111; agricultural plots and plantation culture, 105–11; benefits of plantation system ensuring transition to post-Emancipation future, 83, 87–88, 90, 113; book-keepers' role, 80–82; on coloniality/modernity border, 102; editions and reissues of, 187n17; as failed text, 84; industry vs. idleness in, 82, 85, 88–89, 100–105, 188n33; Lalla's criticism of, 84, 187n13; Maroons' depiction in, 109–10; marriage and creole domesticity in, 83, 85, 93, 150; mulatto rights in, 24; novel's ability to draw from life and validate colonial position, 14, 18; prefatory note explaining choice of fictional mode, 84–85; prefatory note to assure readers of author's qualifications, 17, 187n13; quoting from Tobias Smollett's *The Adventures of Roderick Random*, 166n16; sales in Britain of, 169n52; slavery depiction in, 86–87; Stephen's reaction to proslavery apologetics in, 18, 187n13; taxonomy of labor in, 90–100; theft by slaves in, 81, 186n3; title change of, 187n17; white creole women of virtue and civilized tastes in, 51; white labor depicted in, 25, 147; Williamson's introduction to, 82

Maroons, 89, 106–10, *108*, 149, 179n104. *See also* First Maroon War; Second Maroon War
Marshall, Woodville, 103–4, 109
Martineau, Harriet, 183n55
May, William, 148
Mazzotti, José Antonio, 8, 11
McCartney, P. J., 180n28
McKay, Claude, 26
McKeon, Michael, 22
metropole: cosmopolitanism and, 116–17; as distinct from creole sense of identity, 119
metropolitan fiction: antislavery activist tone of, 14; authors removed from "true" Britons, 2; black characters in, 11–12; race and social constructs missing in, 24
metropolitan reviewers of early creole novels, 19
middle class in West Indies, 187–88n21
Middle Passage, 5–6
Mignolo, Walter, 102
Mintz, Sidney, 8, 43, 104, 166n18
mixed-race persons, 13, 186n12; *Creoleana*'s Lucy as antiheroine, 25, 150, 153, 156, 158; in early creole novels, 13, 24; in *Emmanuel Appadocca*, 142, 156; in *Hamel*, 156; illegitimacy of, 13; *Old Port-Royal*'s Ellen Mansvelt, 25, 145, 146, 150, 153, 156, 198n11; in *Warner Arundell*, 125, 126–28, 132–38, 194n45; whites' superiority over, 126–27. *See also* mulatto and mulatto rights
Montgomery; or, the West-Indian Adventurer, 2, 27–56; advertising of, 169n53; author's identity, 27; "bad" white women in, 51; Brathwaite's assessment of, 27; brutalized slave encounter, meaning attributed to, 46–49, 55; Cundall's assessment of, 27; garden depiction in, 49–53; improvement discourse of model white creole civilization in, 39–41, 46–47, 54, 96, 144; marriage and creole domesticity in, 49, 51; *Monthly Review* on slave-trade defense in, 169n53; plantain walk in, 44–47, *45*, 50, 55; plantation system and husbandry in, 42–44, 49; planter picturesque and, 43–44, 48, 54, 64, 85; publication date, 172n13; publication in Kingston (first novel composed and printed in anglophone Caribbean), 17, 27, 30, 31–40, 169n52; racial differences, reenforcement of, 53; romance and domesticity in, 49–53, 150; Second Maroon War described in, 16, 54–56; sense of dislocation in, 44; sentimental novel conventions and, 28, 37, 39, 41–42, 51; simultaneously dealing with agriculture and culture-building, 29, 56; slaves depicted in, 24, 27; transformative cultivation attempts in, 56; violence in, 29, 31, 43, 56; white creole women of virtue and civilized tastes in, 51; white labor and its comparison to slave's work, 25, 44, 49, 52, 80–82, 147
Monthly Magazine, 174n32
Monthly Miscellany, 173n21
Monthly Review on Turnbull's *Letters to a Young Planter*, 46
moral laxitude. *See* degeneracy
Moreton, J. B., 12, 42, 168n35; *West India Customs and Manners*, 34, 37, 40–41, 159
Morgan, Henry, 142, 145–48, 154
Morrison, Toni, 10, 145, 192n90
mulatto and mulatto rights, 13, 24, 25, 41, 83, 117, 120, 121, 132–38, 161, 168n37, 186n12. *See also* mixed-race persons
musical taste of slaves, 179n5

Naipaul, V. S., 122
Napoleonic Wars, 94, 197n71
narrative authority, 16–17, 20, 28, 47, 122, 168n40, 168n43, 187n13. *See also* "eyewitness insiderism"
narrative genealogies, 2, 113, 114–15, 147
Nash, John, 194n11
nationalism, 2, 9, 29, 120, 124, 131
nature: in *Hamel* natural phenomenon imagery, 64; intertwined with culture, 36–37; in *Montgomery* garden imagery, 49–53, 64
newspapers, history of, 110, 173n24
novels: American version of, 22; instrumental in "imagining cosmopolitan identities," 118; more research needed to connect with early creole novels, 162–63; theory of knowledge attached to, 22. *See also* early creole novels; historical

novels; post-Emancipation novels; quest narrative
Noyes, John K., 118, 121
Nugent, Lady Maria, 12, 34, 168n35

oath-taking ceremonies, 6, 76, 77–78
obeah: caves and deep time of, 70–71, 74; commonalities with various African societies, 183–84n63; linked to rebellion, 76–79; secret work of, 73–74; writings on, 57, 169n62
O'Callaghan, Evelyn, 10
Old Port-Royal; or, The Buccaneer's Home (Gray), 141, 143–50; background of main character, 148; compared to *Montgomery*, 144; Ellen Mansvelt's mixed-race character in, 25, 145, 146, 150, 153, 156, 198n11; instructional purpose of, 144–45; intended audience of, 144; interracial romance in, 24; Kingston printing of, 17; missing volume two, 143–44; narrative authority described in, 17; reconstruction of creole subjectivity in, 26; slavery discussions in, 25, 149–50; white creole women of virtue and civilized tastes in, 51
Orderson, J. W., 26, 142. See also *Creoleana*
Osborn, Robert, 110
"other," identity of, 10, 71, 78, 113–14, 122

Paris Arcades, 192–94n11
Paton, Diana, 23, 77
Patterson, Orlando, 8
Petley, Christopher, 120, 121
Phibba (slave), 13, 168n36, 174n28
Philip, Honore and Jeanette, 156
Philip, Judith, 156
Philip, Michel Maxwell, 26, 142, 156, 199n32. See also *Emmanuel Appadocca*
picturesque, 155. See also planter picturesque
Piérola, José de, 142–43, 155, 198nn5–6, 199n30
piracy, 142, 145, 148, 154
plantains: cultivation on plantain walk, 44–47, 45, 50, 55; origins of, 177n70
planter picturesque, 43–44, 48, 54, 64, 85
plantocracy and plantation system: Act to Abolish the Slave Trade (1807), effect on, 187–88n21; benevolence and, 24, 120, 194n27; book-keepers' role, 80–82, 175n38; civilization and nobility of, considered as benefit to slaves, 25, 46, 63, 120; in early nineteenth century, 144; and Emancipation, 23, 110, 114, 126, 135; European attitudes toward, 11–12; fear of freed slaves refusing to continue working, 25, 105, 110; globalization of, 189n60; in *Hamel*, 59, 60, 74; homecoming scenes of plantation owners, 86–87; *Jamaica Magazine* and, 36; in late eighteenth-century Barbados, 142; maintaining legitimacy of in post-Emancipation world, 126; in *Marly*, 17, 85–86, 91, 94, 110; origins of, 170n9; resistant to change, 98–100, 105; theories of plantation economics, 94, 170n74; in *Warner Arundell*, 114, 126; wealth of, 93, 189n52; and white rule, 17, 171n9. See also slavery
Playfair, William: *Inquiry into the Permanent Causes of the Decline and Fall of Powerful and Wealthy Nations*, 94
political theory in novel form, 14
Port Royal earthquake (1692), 145
Portuguese in Cape Verde Islands, 170n9
post-Emancipation novels, 9, 24, 26, 141; blurred lines between fiction and history in, 127; revisionist history of, 154. See also *Creoleana; Emmanuel Appadocca; Old Port-Royal; Warner Arundell*
post-independence societies, 9
Price, Richard, 109, 183n63
Prince, Mary: *History*, 46, 110
Pringle, Rachel, 151–53, *152*
printing/publishing business in Jamaica, 30, 56, 170n2, 171–72n10, 173n22
"problem-space," 31, 170n72, 172n12
progress. See time and progress
proslavery arguments, 18, 24, 25, 28, 86, 89–90, 112, 148, 169n53, 187n13. See also De la Beche, Henry Thomas; *specific early creole novels of Hamel, Marly, and Montgomery*
provisions, 99, 101, 102–3, 177n69, 192n94

quest narrative, 83, 154; romance-quest narrative, 88, 91

racial difference: categories of, 9–10; civilization as crucial measurement of, 64; colonialist theories of, 8; creolization and racialized identities in the Caribbean, 9, 150–53; generosity that crosses lines of, 120–21; indolence of blacks vs. industry of whites, 89–90, 100, 106–7; *Montgomery* and, 53; between mulatto and black Africanness, 136; religion vs. superstition and, 77–78, 179n15; *Warner Arundell* depicting, 117–18, 126–28, 132–33; white creole writers upholding, 9, 24; white women employing black wet nurses, 137. *See also* mixed-race persons; white creoles
Rajan, Tilottama, 14
Raleigh, Sir Walter, 197n75
Rediker, Marcus, 147; *The Slave Ship*, 4, 5
Reeve, Clara, 15
religion: African religions surviving crossing of ocean, 183–84n63; antimissionary sentiments, 65, 73, 78, 184n74; in *Hamel*, 65, 70–71, 73; methodism and antislavery activity, 184n74; as race-making term, 77; superstition vs., 57, 70–71, 77–78, 179n15. *See also* obeah
revisionist history, 15, 26, 143, 154
revolutionary history of Caribbean, 127–35
Rhys, Jean, 122
Richardson, Samuel, 28, 175n36
Rippingham, John: *Jamaica Considered in Its Present State, Political, Financial, and Philosophical*, 31
Roach, Joseph, 117, 128
Rollason, Christopher, 193–94n11
Romanticism, 18, 85, 88, 182n39. *See also* historical novels
Rowlandson, Thomas (after "E.D."): "Rachel Pringle of Barbadoes" (portrait), *152*
Royal Exchange in Addison's *Spectator* essay, 116–18, 122, 193n10
Royal Gazette advertisements for slave sales, 174n30
Royal School of Mines, 180n24
Rudwick, Martin, 69; *Worlds before Adam*, 59

St. Domingue uprising. *See* Haitian Revolution

Salih, Sara, 132
Sancho, Ignatius, 11
Sandiford, Keith, 28; *The Cultural Politics of Sugar*, 15–16, 167n34
Sanois, Old Julie, 135–38, 197n71
Saunders, Prince, 180n17
Schaw, Janet, 13
Scott, David, 23, 170n72, 172n12
Scott, Sarah, 11, 28, 42
Scott, Sir Walter, 58, 142, 179n5; *Waverley*, 58–59
searching as mandatory act for contemporary Caribbean novelists, 162
Second Maroon War of 1795–96, 16, 54–56, 128, 179n104
Sennett, Richard, 121
sentimental novel conventions, 28, 37, 39, 41–42, 51
Seven Years' War, 129
Sevilla Nueva (Spanish Jamaican city), 149–50
sexual relations: sexual agency of the enslaved, 25; between white men and female slaves, 12–13, 40–41, 51, 168n36
Sharpe, Jenny: *Ghosts of Slavery*, 10, 168n36, 174n28
Sharpe, Sam, 15, 110
Sharpe, Tom, 180n24
Sheller, Mimi, 104
Sheridan, Frances: *Sidney Bidulph*, 11
silenced voices in early creole fiction, 10
Simmonds, P. L., 80, *81*, 185n1
Simmonds, Serena, *81*
Singleton, John: *A General Description of the West-Indian Islands*, 137
slave rebellions: 1795 as "most terrible" year of, 128; fears of, 73, 131; in Grenada, 127–28; linked to obeah, 76; resulting from weight of interculture performance, 128; in West Indies, 15. *See also* Haitian Revolution; *specific events by name*
Slave Registry Bill (1816), 173n26
slavery: Brazilian, 181n34; colony vs. metropolitan view of, 34; community formation of slaves in the diaspora, 5; "creole," origins of term tied to, 8; effect on white masters, 11, 87; food cultivation for enslaved laborers and a plantain walk, 44–45, *45*; inefficiency

of, compared to "free" labor, 88, 95–96; jobbing gangs of slaves, 91–92, 98, 188n43, 189n49; mutilated bodies of slaves, encounters in eighteenth-century writing, 46; nineteenth-century views on, 32; outwitting white masters, 25; planters' nineteenth-century views on, 32; romanticized (re)production of, 58; scientific argument for, 62; sexual relations between white men and female slaves, 12–13, 40–41, 51, 168n36; testimony of slaves, admissibility of, 173n26; theft by slaves, 48, 81, 186n3; U.S. slavery debate prior to American Civil War, 154; West Indian defense of, 18, 89–90, 169n53; and West Indian planters' role in British minds, 12; white prosperity predicated on, 91–92, 189n52, 189n60; Wynter on ambivalence between plantation and plot for slaves, 105–6. *See also* plantocracy and plantation system; slave rebellions; slave trade; "West India Question"

slave trade: diversity of crews as well as of slaves, 5; enriching British empire, 12; mutinies and rebellions aboard ships, 5, 166n9; New World origins of African trade, 83; plantations' reliance on, 89; violence and dehumanizing effects of, 4–5, 43, 165n7; *Zong* massacre (1781), 21, 23. *See also* trade routes

Sloane, Hans: *Voyage to the Islands*, 176–77n69

Smallwood, Stephanie, 5

Smart, William, 172n21

Smith, Francis, 186n2

Smith, John, 184n74

Smollett, Tobias, 174n36; *The Adventures of Roderick Random*, 166n16; *Humphrey Clinker*, 189n52

Society for the Mitigation and Gradual Abolition of Slavery (Antislavery Society), 63

sociopolitical fictions in anglophone Atlantic life, 2

South America: "creole," origins of term tied to children of African slaves in, 8; opportunities presented by independent countries of, 114, 138–39

Spectator, The, 174n32

Spivak, Gayatri, 72

Stedman, John: *Narrative of a Five Years' Expedition, Against the Revolted Negroes of Surinam*, 46, 158

Stephen, James, 18, 187n13; *England Enslaved by Her Own Slave Colonies*, 190n75; *Slavery of the British West India Colonies Delineated*, 187n13

Sterne, Laurence, 28; *Tristram Shandy*, 193n6

Stoler, Ann, 51

Storer, James Sargant: "Trelawney Town, the Chief Residence of the Maroons" (engraving), *108*

strangeness and the "stranger," 121–22. *See also* "other," identity of

Strupar family, 173n22

subversive possibilities, 5, 25, 70, 73, 153, 174

sugar industry: daily routine on, 80–82, 87; difference from European agriculture and husbandry, 42–44; East Indies as threat to West Indies, 95–96, 99, 167n33; era of peak British Caribbean wealth from, 91–92, 94, 191n76; Haitian Revolution's effect on French sugar production, 93–94; modernizing agricultural production methods in West Indies, 98–99, 104, 170n9, 190–92nn75–78; planting season as most laborious work, 96–98; theft by slaves, 48, 81, 186n3. *See also* East India; plantocracy and plantation system

superstition, 57, 77–78, 179n15

"Superstition: A Tale by a West Indian Quadroon," 182n44

Sypher, Wylie, 11, 168n39

Tacky's Revolt of 1760 (Jamaica), 76, 77

Taino Indians, 66

Tascher, Marie Josèphe (Empress Josephine), 197n71

Taylor, Simon, 12

temporalizations, 183n62

tensions and anxieties: in British West Indies, 15, 29, 56, 131; class tensions in Jamaica, 187–88n21; in contact zone of two cultures, 10, 167n29; Maroons as cause for, 55, 89, 106; from Montgomery's crossing the line, 42; over cultural dilution, 167n34; of planters in light

tensions and anxieties (*continued*)
of coming Emancipation period, 94, 105. *See also* European attitudes; white creoles; white superiority
Thelwell, Michael: *The Harder They Come*, 192n94
Thistlewood, Thomas, 12–13, 92, 100, 168n36, 173–74n28, 192n79
Thomson, James, 178n99; "Summer," 54–55
time and progress, 58–59, 61–75; forward-looking perspective in *Warner Arundell*, 112–13; historical novel's role, 141–42; measure of progress based on productive labor, 82, 89–90; metropolitan cosmopolitanism and, 116–17; present time in 1820s Jamaica, 71–72; primordial and deep time, 65–66, 69, 74. *See also* geology
Tomich, Dale, 93
Tory, Netlam, 175n36
Toussaint L'Ouverture, 136, 137, 199n71
trade routes between Africa and British West Indies, 3–4, 165n6; map of, 4
Transactions of the Institute of Jamaica, 144
transatlantic frame of reference, 10, 22, 34
transnational identities, 9
Treadway, Frank, 169n52
Trelawney Town, 107, *108*
trickster figure in *Creoleana*, 151
Trinidad, 123, 129, 136, 154–57, 196n59
tropicopolitans vs. cosmopolitans, 116
Trouillot, Michel Rolphe, 75
Turnbull, Gordon: *Letters to a Young Planter*, 46; *Narrative of the Revolt and Insurrection of the French Inhabitants in Grenada*, 130, 133, 196n58
Turner, Mary, 104

unseen made visible, 23

violence: in contact zone of two cultures, 10; *Marly*, murdered white people in, 188n24; *Montgomery*, essential element in, 29, 31, 43, 56; nature's violence matched to man's, 65, 182n39; in post-Emancipation novels, 141; of slavery and slave trade, 4–5, 24–25, 47–48, 165n7
vodou, 76

Walcott, Derek, 122
Ward, Candace, 166n17
Warner Arundell: The Adventures of a Creole (Joseph), 2, 6, 112–39; background of main character, 113, 114–15, 117, 128–29, 134, 148; Bolívarian wars in, 138–39; British homeland described in, 118–22; condemnation of British ignorance of geography, 123–24; condemnation of Londoners for lack of compassion, 119–20; creole cosmopolitanism in, 116–26, 131; *Emmanuel Appadocca* compared to, 155; Fédon depiction in, 132–37, 197n68, 198n83; fictional preface in, 193n6; fixity and localized knowledge of main character, 115, 118, 124; forward-looking perspective in, 112–13; intended audience of, 118; marriage and creole domesticity in, 139, 150; mulatto rights in, 24, 132–38; narrative authority described in, 17, 122; New World loyalties of, 115; origins of first name of, 193n3; in post-Emancipation period, 110, 112–13, 131; racialized differences in, 117–18, 126–28, 132–33; vibrancy of New World in, 117, 194n15; white creole version of the past in, 114–15; white creole women of virtue and civilized tastes in, 51
Warner-Lewis, Maureen, 8
Watchman (newspaper), 110–11
Watson, Tim: on construct of Caribbean region, 166n17; on "creole realism," 20; on "eyewitness insiderism," 16; on fiction dealing with facts, 18; on *Hamel*, 59, 112, 169n52, 179n5; on post-Emancipation plantocracy, 23; on romance and realism, 169n60
Watt, Alexander: *New Theory of Optics and New Theory of Physical Astronomy*, 31, 175n36; *Proceedings of the Society for the Encouragement of Horticulture and Agriculture, and the Arts Connected with Them in Jamaica*, 31
Wedderburn, Robert: *Horrors of Slavery*, 46
West Indian colonies, 3; cultural elements of, 7–8; disdain for African and black creole cultures in, 12; diversity of images of, 6–7; as drain on British national wealth, 167n33; Emancipation equated with destruction of, 61. *See also* plan-

tocracy and plantation system; *specific islands and locations*
"West Indian Free-booter, The" (story), 182n44
"West India Question," 14, 18, 61
white creoles: anxiety about race in early creole novels, 151; and categories of racial difference, 9–10; consciousness of "in-between," 10, 12; defense of white creole position in early creole novels, 18, 25, 28, 89–90, 112, 169n53; dependent on Britishness for self-definition, 10; early creole novels' depiction of, 2; entitlement claims of privilege, 17, 32, 111, 155; European attitudes toward, 11–12; heterogeneity of white creole society, 83–84; knowledge of agricultural arts of, 100; on Maroons as threat to, 107; moral improvement instruction for, 37–39; Moreton's description of, 40; "negrofied" character of, 12, 13, 41; slaveholding foundations of, 12; strangeness of British homeland for, 121–22; war of representation with British homeland, 121–22; white endogamy and, 51, 53, 150. *See also* early creole novels; proslavery arguments
Whitehouse, W. F., 192n79
whites: in colonial order in post-Emancipation Caribbean, 135; enlightened whites vs. superstitious slaves, 57; hospitality and bonding among white colonists, 194n25; identity's dependence on African-Atlantic presence and labor, 192n90; white women employing black wet nurses, 137. *See also* racial difference
white superiority, 25, 46, 59, 63, 89–90, 120, 126–27, 133, 159. *See also* European attitudes
William Henry (British prince), 151–53
Williams, Cynric, 179n25; *A Tour through the Island of Jamaica*, 61, 66–67, 182n40, 182n44. See also *Hamel, the Obeah Man*
Williams, Raymond, 29
Williamson, Karina, 82, 96, 100, 186n12, 187n17
Wollstonecraft, Mary, 14, 156, 175n36; *Maria; or, the Wrongs of Woman*, 154
women and gender: abandoned women of color in West Indian writings, 158; black creole women as stock characters, 150; *Emmanuel Appadocca*'s views on, 156–58; matriarchy of Philip family in Eastern Caribbean, 156; sexual relations between white men and female slaves, 12–13, 40–41, 51, 168n36; stereotypes of women of color, 158; white creole women of virtue and civilized tastes, 51, 178n87; white women employing black wet nurses, 137
Wynter, Sylvia, 8, 23, 193n103; "Novel and History, Plot and Plantation," 105–6
Wyrick, Deborah, 51

Zong massacre (1781), 21, 23

www.ingramcontent.com/pod-product-compliance
Lightning Source LLC
Chambersburg PA
CBHW030825230426
43667CB00008B/1377